Democrats and Republicans

TEN YEARS OF THE REPUBLIC

Edited by LOUIS FILLER

FROM HARRY THURSTON PECK'S
"Twenty Years of the Republic"

CAPRICORN BOOKS, New York

Manufactured in the United States of America

TEN YEARS OF THE REPUBLIC

A Classic Era in American Politics

Louis Filler

I

POLITICS are a will-o'-the-wisp of our lives as citizens.
Sometimes we feel sure we are getting somewhere by following particular political hopefuls, though just where depends
on whether we are Democrats or Republicans.   At other
times we became more conscious of the heavy presence of the
wheelhorses of our national and local politics—those who
plod on in good times and bad, dragging their political machines along.   It then seems to us, unless we are among the
devout, to be less momentous just who has won a political
plum.   Some students of our politics even think that most
Americans, whatever they may claim in exalted moments, approach an election as a kind of sporting event and are less
absorbed by issues than by winners and losers.   Many of us,
undoubtedly, are not overly serious about public affairs.   In
some cases, one could wish that certain foolish countrymen
might be persuaded to be less earnest about public affairs and
divert their attention to their private concerns, whatever they
might be, leaving social concerns to those who can handle
them with greater competence.   But, however inadequate
may be the political responses of some elements of our society,

iii

they do represent *interests* which must be served, and which can be better served, or worse, through our political decisions.

In such circumstances, there is always the need for a degree of political independence and simple individualism.   The role of the independent needs more probing than it has received. Much of the attention he attracts has been purely pragmatic —political aspirants attempt to gage his preferences so they may better appeal to his desires.   But the independent can serve more significant purposes.   Election Day propaganda, that one should vote the party of his choice, but vote, does not tell the whole story.   For the vote, *or the threat of not voting,* are both powerful weapons, and neither should be lightly disowned.   Each vote is really *two* votes: the one we give to a candidate, and the one we have withheld from his competitor.   Both votes should be judiciously administered.

But however serious or frivolous we may be in our politics, it is clear that some eras have been more significant politically than others.   Politics furnished day-in day-out excitement during New Deal times; it was less conspicuous in the war period that followed.   And so it has been from our very beginnings as a nation.   The Jefferson administrations are famous for the national political crises they posed, the Monroe administrations less so.   It seems fair to say that, recently, the times of Grover Cleveland have not seemed to us suggestive of great deeds and crucial events.   Men in Cleveland's time whose names and faces were followed closely in the press for years have been forgotten.   How often do we find occasion to mention Governor David B. Hill of New York, William C. Whitney, "Fireworks" Joseph B. Foraker, Thomas F. Bayard, Roscoe Conkling, and even Presidents Chester A. Arthur and Benjamin Harrison?   How many of us are aware of Admiral George Dewey's could-be presidential moment?   I think there has been an obvious loss to our understanding because we have forgotten how to deal with these historical figures.

The wiseacres like to say that we are right about something, but for the wrong reasons. I hope it will not sound like an attempt at cleverness if I say that, in the present case, the forgetful public has been wrong, but for the right reasons. The time of Cleveland, of James G. Blaine, of "Czar" Tom Reed of the House of Representatives, is a classic period of politics, when political machines seemed more potent than public issues, personalities more notable than programs. This was the era of giant torchlight parades, of brass-knuckled bullies who terrorized citizens at the polls, of violent and flamboyant newspaper and soapbox haranguers. It was a time of city politics made turbulent by the organization of Irish, Italian, and other picturesque Old and New Immigrations, so-called. Its rural politics featured farmers fearful of railroads, Wall Street, and the big city political bosses. All this made for excitement and eventfulness. Yet we rightly ask ourselves how ultimately significant it all was. Would it have made a difference if Winfield Scott Hancock had defeated James A. Garfield in the election of 1880—the closest election, so far as popular votes went, in American political history?* Cleveland was doubtless a more upright public

---

* Garfield polled 4,454,433 votes to Hancock's 4,444,976, a difference of 9,457 votes. Garfield, however, had 214 *electoral* votes to Hancock's 155. It would have taken a shift of 10,517 votes in New York State to have added its 35 electoral votes to Hancock's total, giving him 190, and to have thus *deprived* Garfield of these 35 votes, leaving him with a defeated total of 179. It is perpetually amazing to realize how little it has taken to turn political defeat into victory and vice versa. Four years later, in the even more extraordinary election of 1884, a switch of no more than 575 votes— five hundred and seventy-five—in New York State would have given its electoral votes and the Presidency to James G. Blaine and defeated Cleveland. (See Svend Petersen, *A Statistical History of the American Presidential Elections* [New York, 1963], for this and numerous other thought-

servant than Blaine, in 1884, and a more decisive executive than Harrison, in 1892.   But what did Cleveland actually *do* that was momentous?   What policy did he establish by which we live?   To be sure, he was personally honest in an age that frequently forgot what political integrity implied, an age that made a principle of party loyalty without inquiring into the meaning of party principles.   But there are limits to what one can make of honesty shorn of program.   Thus, the sainted Grover sent troops in 1894 to Pullman, Illinois, and helped to break the great strike there on which rested the hopes for better living of thousands of railroad workers. Even his greatest admirers no longer consider this a memorable achievement.

As we survey the politics of the period which Harry Thurston Peck vividly treats, it might occur to us to wonder just what large significance it had, and why we need to better know the politics of the era.   Who were the vital figures of the time?   Cleveland and Blaine—or John D. Rockefeller, Andrew Carnegie, J. Pierpont Morgan, and others among the entrepreneurs who made this pre-eminently an Age of Big Business?   Did Cleveland control Rockefeller, or did Rockefeller's minions in a real sense control Cleveland?   The President was, without doubt, a free man who acted according to his own best understanding.   Fortunately for the industrial statesmen of his time, he believed in free enterprise in its copybook sense.   Let the best man win.   From rags to riches.   Don't interfere with natural economic law.   Cleveland never faced up to the fact that through skulduggery,

provoking analyses which often reveal how inaccurate are reports and rumors of "landslides."   Incidentally, Peck quotes a source on the Garfield-Hancock returns for 1880 which differs from the above, without harming the point; "official" reports are often controversial.   Peck and Petersen agree on the Cleveland-Blaine shadow finish.)

abyssmal force, the use of strikebreakers, the injunction, and the infamous blacklist, and with the help of outmoded law, the *worst* man might win, unless society through its agents interposed its veto upon their plots and stratagems.

As each succeeding national election year rolls around, certain principles deserve to be dusted off and reviewed. In our skepticism, we often look disdainfully at political platforms as so much conversation intended to befuddle voters. We listen ironically to partisan promises and denunciations intended to nominate this man or that. We remember old honeymoon periods of national political unity under one successful candidate or another that broke down on bread-and-butter, sectional, or bluntly opportunistic issues.

Our skepticism sometimes causes us to miss important points. Take political platforms: *Are* they futile? They do represent the final formulations of a convened political party, and they do nail down promises which may indeed be broken but nevertheless linger on to affect newspaper debates, Congressional maneuvers, new political candidacies—in short, our entire process of democratic politics. No, political platforms are not futile, unless we are impatient to welcome the millennium and are uninterested in the details of our real political and civic lives.

But, more specifically, the 1880's and 1890's—what have we to learn from them? In a sense, it is unfair to put the question this way. Knowledge is indivisible. A person who will not learn from one era will not understand another; for the experiences of our several eras provide necessary contrasts and comparisons to make sense. Some years ago, it was à la mode to profess an interest in Andrew Jackson's administration. The present writer used to ask people about it, and was always surprised at how little they had to report out of their reading. Andy Jackson fought the Second Bank of the United States.   Did one have to read *anything* to have heard of this?   What else had Jackson done?   Were his policies as directed against the Cherokee Indians progressive or reactionary?   Were his Maysville veto and his Specie Circular landmarks of political achievement?   The person who will be interested in the answers to these questions will also be interested in the problems of the age of Cleveland. For the issues of his time, as of Jackson's, or any other President's, reveal the character, the contour of the American mind, the kind of ground Americans chose to quarrel over. Such issues tell us the way Americans thought, and the means they chose for dealing with what they saw as the problems of their generation.   We see ourselves in better perspective when we understand our forebears.

But, more important, whether the politicos of Cleveland's time did or did not cope with consequential problems is a serious question.   We can't afford to mistake its significance. Misjudging the past, we might misjudge our own present. As a matter of fact, something of great importance *was* happening in the Cleveland period which the casual eye could misconstrue.   It deserves to be comprehended.

II

In the first place, we often forget how dangerous were our political circumstances in the post-Civil War years.   The Radical Republicans had been the leading group in the defense of the Union.   In smashing the Confederate South, they had smashed much of the power of the Democratic Party.   Thad Stevens, Ben Wade, Ben Butler, and the other Republican chieftains triumphed with the triumph of the Union forces. They undertook a political campaign that equated Democrats with treason, even though Northern Democrats had died by the tens of thousands in defense of the Union.   They disenfranchised the Southern whites almost en masse, and they leveled an attack on President Andrew Johnson which, had it succeeded, could have harmed the effectiveness of the executive office.   In essence, the Radical Republicans sought to destroy the two-party system; and, having Congress in their hands, having the suffrage of the Grand Army of the Republic, and of the new Negro voters, they stood a good chance of achieving their goal.   There were earnest and splendid men among the Republicans, statesmen like Lyman Trumbull and William Pitt Fessenden, but the net effect of their party's drive to power could have been to wound the American political system as we have known it, perhaps irreparably.

What saved our two-party system, and the office of the presidency?   In the final analysis: dissension in Republican ranks.   They quarreled over customhouse appointments and patronage in general.   They quarreled over the plot to annex Santo Domingo, as it then was.   They quarreled over the tariff, over the maintenance of federal troops in the South, over tolerance of government scandals that discredited their party to increasing numbers of dissatisfied voters.   They quarreled over matters of personality (and continued to do so through the era chronicled by Peck).   When the differences between the Stalwart and Mugwump* factions, as they came to be called, grew sufficiently wide, the Republicans split, and Grover Cleveland, the first Democratic President since James Buchanan, took office.   Thus our political system survived.   This is the story behind the story told by Harry Thurston Peck.

---

* Stalwarts accepted official Republican Party leadership and policies without question; Mugwumps were Republicans disturbed of conscience, and ready to take a walk to the opposition, if their party appeared to them disgraced. They straddled the fence, in the satiric phrase of their antagonists, with their mugs on one side and their wumps on the other.

By reading Peck's book carefully we can become familiar with the dynamics of freedom that give meaning to his political discussions, evaluations of individuals, and witticisms. His account emphasizes politics-as-usual and the professional political leaders who directed those politics. It treats social issues as the politicians perceived them, rather than in the broader, analytical terms that certain types of historians, psychologists, and economists prefer. But Peck gains a peculiar strength through his method. It enables him to show us his times as they appeared to his contemporaries. We, having more perspective, can see through the self-serving attitudes of Peck's day; but, by studying those attitudes, can help gain insight into some of our own.

Given the particular emotional atmosphere of the time— the Civil War psychology, the sentimentalization of Negro "emancipation," the inordinate concern for Free Trade and Protection, and other issues—it is good to be able to feel that the way in which our forebears met their rapidly changing conditions spoke well for them, and for our rude, careless democracy. We can take heart in discouraging days, and believe that our people are, on the whole, committed to an open-ended society and will defend it if it should again be threatened. Demagogues often seem inordinately powerful; and we have our own demagogues as they had theirs. They are cynical in their plottings, and confident of success. They scorn our thoughtless, spendthrift communities. But there are always more of us than there are of them, and we can reduce them to piddling frustration, if we will.

So, we can learn much in these pages about the relationship of politics to politicians. But we can learn as much about the relationship of politicians to businessmen, possibly even more easily, more clearly, because politics and business were not then so complexly entwined as they are now. In the

1880's and the 1890's laws governing business were few and public relations more individual and direct. What does this tell us about the progress of government-business relations? *Were* the Rockefellers more potent that the Clevelands in steering society? *Did* the businessmen buy legislatures and, indeed, defy law and public opinion? There was a time when Rockefeller and Morgan were names to inspire fear and apprehension. But now the name of Rockefeller does not call to mind the old trust master and philanthropist, and the name of Morgan is likely to remind us spontaneously of—whom?

If Rockefeller and Morgan once wielded power greater than that of the President of the United States, is this not a fact we ought to know and understand? Can sophistication evade the challenge in so remarkable an assertion? How, if this was the case, did we escape the trap of private domination of public-controlled agencies? As one ponders Peck's story of big business in the late nineteenth century, he is bound to compare it with our own. Not too long ago, there was a flurry of concern over the so-called Dixon-Yates contract which, it was claimed, threatened the future of the great Tennessee Valley Authority. I do not here say that it did or it didn't; the subject is too important for peremptory judgment. I do say that not to inquire into the proper role of government in private concerns, whether in the time of Grover Cleveland and Benjamin Harrison, or in the time of President Lyndon B. Johnson, is to evade one of the major challenges of American political life. Several years ago, the late President Kennedy forced the steel companies to rescind a price increase. Recently, steel executives have been charged with price fixing of a most serious kind. Between price fixing and price raising lie problems of government responsibility that will require informed public opinion, if we are to adopt positions that do not leave us mere pawns of quarreling bureaucrats, whether in business, unions, or government.

In the end, there is always the problem of achievement. But, as I have suggested, we deceive ourselves in thinking that one President was important and another was not— that Kennedy's steel crisis was more significant than Cleveland's tariff crisis, for example. *All Presidents are important,* for they reflect the state of public opinion, public responsibility, public decisions. Political fashions change, but political responsibility never sleeps. Policies are instituted that affect future policies, whether we know of them or not. Like the stars, what we see is not what is actually there. Our bureaucrats make commitments all the time, in quiet conferences, for which we will ultimately stand responsible. Until we master this fact, the results of our routine operations of government, at home and abroad, will continue to surprise us as they unfold in the daily press.

III

One does not have to conjure up reasons for enjoying the following account of our American political thousand-and-one-nights. Harry Thurston Peck wrote so well, so knowledgeably, and with such easy familiarity that his work provides its own justification. It also provides particular challenges to understanding. Peck's curious combination of liberalism and conservatism probably ultimately contributed to his undoing. He reproved the great Governor John P. Altgeld for having freed the surviving victims of the trial that followed the historic Haymarket Riot, though posterity honors Altgeld for this courageous act. But Peck also expressed concern over the antisocial acts of the mushrooming monopolies, wrote of Jay Gould with the utmost contempt, and expressed attitudes showing compassion for the poor and

TEN YEARS OF THE REPUBLIC 3irespect for some forms of bold and unconventional social thought. Peck and his era were more complicated than some modern students have imagined. His account of his times has unique features, and includes a host of details that are nowhere else available. Peck lived his pages as a citizen of his times, and as a uniquely talented student of the events that evolved about him. There is more to his tale than we have provided in this volume. *Twenty Years of the Republic* brought Peck's chronicle of our nation up through the early years of Theodore Roosevelt's administrations. It is, all of it, a marvelous combination of social history, personalities, elections and political crises—and it is all as rich, entertaining and illuminating as the portion included in this volume.

Antioch College

THE AUTHOR

THE phenomenon of Harry Thurston Peck (1856-1914) is yet to be assimilated into American life and letters. He was a prodigy of universal interest and close to universal grasp: a combination of scholar and popularizer, of humanist and technician. The son of a Connecticut schoolmaster, he read voraciously in his youth, had a brilliant undergraduate career at Columbia College, and studied classical philology in Paris, Berlin, and Rome. By 1890, he was Professor of Latin at Columbia University. In 1896, at the dedication of the new site of the University on Morningside Heights, his Dedication Ode in Latin was sung to the air *"Integer vitae."*

Peck was esteemed one of Columbia's most distinguished pillars of scholarship and instruction. He was also conspicuous for his cream-colored derby hat, spats and carnation, and other signs of concern for the punctilios of good living as well as good Latin pronunciation. He was, indeed, the wonder of all who met him. A former student noted: "If you took Latin from him, you got a full measure of Latin— and a little of everything else, besides." Apparently, nothing escaped him. He compared classical drama with the latest Broadway productions, analyzed the Battle of Waterloo, and wrote articles for popular publications on such topics as "The Morality of Perfume," always with a circumstantiality that left his hearers and readers with a sense of awe. He produced a series of books in the Latin field, and in 1897 edited the 1700-page *Harper's Dictionary of Classical Literature*

xiv

and Antiquities. But his exploits as a Latinist no more than touched his exploits as an editor, writer, and critic. He edited the *International Encyclopedia.* He was literary editor of the *Commercial Advertiser* (1897-1901) and served on the staff of *Munsey's Magazine* (1907-1911). He was editor of *Bookman* (1895-1902) and then contributing editor (1902-1907), turning out commentary, book reviews, and articles at an unbelievable rate on every subject. His books reflected some of his interests, but meagerly: *The Personal Equation* (1897); *What Is Good English? and Other Essays* (1899); *William Hickley Prescott* (1905); *Studies in Several Literatures* (1909); and *The New Baedeker* (1910), this last a tour de force comparing travel in the United States with travel in Europe, which he visited often. He was a conscientious professor, and he discoursed to friends at social gatherings on subjects from cooking to politics, in all ages and everywhere.

His fall rang through the popular press. In 1908 his wife divorced him. The following year he married a New York schoolteacher. In June 1910, a former stenographer of his sued him for breach of promise, producing letters which, reproduced in the newspapers, excited shock and ridicule, revealing him as a naive and inept philanderer. Columbia University dropped him, as did all his friends. He lost his editorships. His first wife took him in after he had suffered a collapse, but he tired of her company after he had somewhat recovered. He moved into a lodging house and tried to earn a living by writing hack articles for his old *Encyclopedia.* He tired of this, too, and on March 23, 1914, he committed suicide. His old President at Columbia, Nicholas Murray Butler, thought he had suffered from inherited mental disease. A perhaps more perceptive comment was that he got lost somewhere between the Appian Way and Herald Square.

Contents

TEN YEARS OF THE REPUBLIC, iii
By Louis Filler

I

THE RETURN OF THE DEMOCRACY, 1

II

TWO YEARS OF PRESIDENT CLEVELAND, 49

III

THE REPUBLICAN RALLY, 97

IV

THE PRESIDENCY OF BENJAMIN HARRISON, 136

V

THE ELECTION OF 1892, 222

VI

PRESIDENT CLEVELAND ONCE MORE, 261

TWENTY YEARS OF THE REPUBLIC

I

ON the fourth day of March, 1885, Grover Cleveland of
New York took the oath prescribed by the Constitution
and became, in doing so, the twenty-second President of
the United States. As he paused for a moment, after
pronouncing the solemn words, and looked out over the
multitude which filled the vast expanse before the Capitol, he must have felt, unimaginative though he was, a
thrill of irrepressible emotion. Three years before, his
name had been unknown beyond the limits of the provincial
city where he lived. Now, the tumultuous cheers that
drowned even the thunder of saluting cannon, acclaimed
him as the elected ruler of the mightiest republic upon
earth. He had accomplished the impossible. He had succeeded where men of large experience and wide renown
had ignominiously failed. He had led to victory a political
party which seemed to have incurred the fate of perpetual
banishment from power. And, in achieving this, he, a country lawyer with no especial knowledge of statecraft or of
national policies, had defeated the most brilliant, the
most resourceful, and the most passionately loved of all
American party leaders.

Washington had never before seen so great a concourse assembled to witness the inauguration of a President. More than half a million people had poured into the city during the preceding week. They came from every State and Territory of the Union, eager to share in celebrating the return of the Democratic party, at last again triumphant. The military display was in itself a splendid spectacle. Not since the great reviews which marked the end of the Civil War had so many marching regiments swung down the noble boulevard which leads from the White House to the Capitol. Every arm of the regular establishment was represented,—cavalry, infantry, artillery, and engineers,—with detachments of blue-jackets and marines. A whole division of the National Guard of Pennsylvania was in line. A body of Southern soldiers, headed by General Fitzhugh Lee, and with the famous Fifth Maryland in the van, was there. Contingents from New York and Rhode Island in the East, and from Missouri in the West, marched close behind the regulars. There was also a battalion of coloured troops, whose fine appearance called forth hearty and prolonged applause. The civic organisations were still more numerous; and political clubs, with picturesque regalia and often in striking costume, completed the long line which later passed in review before the President to the music of a hundred military bands. The day was redolent of spring; and as the stream of bayonets flashed in the sunshine and the flags unfurled their folds in the soft west wind, the sight was inspiring in its animation and movement and vivid colour.

Yet the throng which lined the avenue was no less interesting in the variety of types which it exhibited. It was a different gathering from that which Washington had been wont to see at the inauguration of Republican presidents. The men of the South were far more numerous, and there were many present who had long been strangers to the capital city. For them it was the dawning of a new era; and their mingled faith and triumph were almost touching to behold. There were, besides, not a few gaunt figures of an old-time quaintness, intense and half fanatical partisans from remote localities, displaying with a sort of pride the long white beards which, years before, they had vowed never to shave until a Democratic president should be inaugurated. A feeling of eager expectancy, of pleasurable excitement and frank exultation swayed the entire multitude; and even those who owed allegiance to the defeated party could not wholly resist the spell. It was, for the moment, an apotheosis of the Democracy.

When the new President entered the carriage which was to convey him to his official home, few gave any thought to a gentleman who had stood quietly beside him throughout the simple ceremonial, and who presently took friendly leave of him with a cordial clasp of the hand and a word or two of congratulation and good will. It was the familiar little scene that has been so frequently enacted in our country—when one who, for a few short years, has been the ruler of a nation and the peer of monarchs, goes back, at the stroke of the clock, into the obscurity of private citizenship, unheeded and unheralded amid the strident din that welcomes his successor. There is always something half pathetic in this sudden transformation, yet it is impressive too; for it symbolises American reverence for law. Ex-President Arthur, though unnoticed at the moment when he quietly slipped away from Washington, carried with him into private life the respect and confidence of all his countrymen, for he had governed well and wisely.

Yet no President had ever entered into office under circumstances of such perplexity and personal embarrassment.
Mr. Arthur had been nominated for the Vice-Presidency
on the ticket with General Garfield, in the hasty, almost
reckless, fashion of our national conventions. He was
chosen not because he was thought to be peculiarly fitted
for the honour, but simply, as the politicians' slang expresses it, to " placate " the Stalwart or Conkling wing
of the Republican Party, which had fought bitterly to
secure the selection of General Grant, and which resented
fiercely the nomination of General Garfield.

At that time the country knew very little of Mr. Arthur,
and what it did know was not wholly favourable. He was
regarded as a typical New York politician, an active member of the so-called " Custom-House gang," which par-
celled out the local Federal appointments and dickered for
the petty spoils of office. This estimate was not entirely
unjust. Mr. Arthur had been by no means too fastidious
in his political associations. He had kept some rather
dubious company while acting as the lieutenant of the aggressive Conkling, whose intimate friend he was. But
Mr. Arthur had another side of which the country was not
then aware. He was one who drew a very sharp line
between his public and his private life. Personally he was
a gentleman of cultivated tastes, a university graduate, familiar with the usages of polite society, and having an easy
adaptability which made him equally at home in a lady's
drawing-room, in the *fumoir* of a club, or in the noisome
atmosphere of a riotous ward primary. Intellectually he
was well trained and disciplined. In the years preceding
the Civil War he had attained to eminence in the practice
of law. He conducted to a successful issue a case which
affected the validity of the Fugitive Slave Law, and he

secured a decision which is still a classic in American po-
litico-legal history.[1] Nor was he without experience of
administrative responsibility. During the war he had at
different times been Inspector-General and Quartermaster-
General of the State of New York, and had won high
commendation for his efficiency in organising and equip-
ping the six hundred thousand troops with which that State
met the requisitions of President Lincoln. Later, he had
been Collector of the Port of New York under President
Grant. But when he became Vice-President in 1881, the
country at large knew him only as a local politician of
no very high repute. He sided with Senator Conkling
when that arrogant leader soon after declared open war
on President Garfield for refusing to let the New York
Senator dictate the Federal appointments in his State;
and Mr. Arthur was loyal to Conkling throughout the
bitter strife that followed. Then in the midst of it, the
President was shot down by a crazed fanatic, Charles
Guiteau, and lay for months fighting against death with
splendid courage.

---

[1] This was the once famous Lemmon case. In 1852, a Virginian named
Jonathan Lemmon had brought eight slaves from Norfolk to New York intending to re-ship them thence to a Texan port. On petition, a writ of
habeas corpus was issued by the Superior Court of New York, requiring
the persons in charge of the slaves to bring them before the court. After
hearing argument, Mr. Justice Paine ordered the release of the slaves on
the ground that the Fugitive Slave Law did not apply to them, inasmuch as
they had been brought voluntarily by their owner to free soil and were
therefore not fugitives. This decision practically freed all slaves sent or
brought by their masters within the boundaries of a free State. An appeal
was taken from Justice Paine's decision at the instance of the Legislature
of Virginia. The New York Legislature authorised the Governor to appoint counsel, and Mr. Arthur with Mr. W. M. Evarts conducted the case.
Justice Paine's decision was sustained by the Supreme Court and by the
Court of Appeals.—See Smalley, *Life of Chester A. Arthur*, pp. 304-5,
(New York, 1880).

With the first shock of grief and horror which stirred the nation when Garfield fell, there was mingled a feeling of deep resentment. It was held that indirectly the President was a victim of the Conkling faction, whose denunciations of him had worked upon the morbid mind of his assassin. Some, in their excess of feeling, went further still. Strange rumours flew about, and sinister accusations were made in private talk. Men even cherished a wild belief that a conspiracy had planned the murder of the President. In the first excited hours it was hinted that, either with or without his knowledge, a plot had been formed to place Mr. Arthur in the presidency, and in this way to deliver the administration into "Stalwart" hands. Few, even then, were willing to listen to so wild a charge; yet the feeling against Mr. Arthur for a time was very bitter. The newspapers, especially in the Eastern States, spoke of him in terms of rancour. They deplored the possibility that "this pot-house politician," as they called him, might take the place of Garfield, whom popular sympathy had already idealised as a martyr. Throughout these trying months, when the country hung upon the daily bulletins from Elberon, Mr. Arthur made no sign. Just what he suffered no man knew. But his dignified reserve was never broken; and when it was hinted that he might act as President during the period of Mr. Garfield's incapacity, he repelled the suggestion with indignant sternness. At last came the death of Garfield in September, 1881. Mr. Arthur assumed the office which thus came to him under circumstances so distressing. Before long the country learned to know the man as he really was. From the very outset he was the President of no faction, of no party, but of the entire people. Firm, wise, and vigilant, his administration was one of the very best in all our history. To his former political allies he showed no undue favour. To his former enemies he manifested no unfairness, but stood between them and the anger of Conkling, whose vindictive spirit led him in consequence to break off all relations with the President. Garfield's appointees were retained in office. Even the request of General Grant could not secure the displacement of the Secretary of the Navy and the substitution of a Stalwart.

Many of those whom Mr. Arthur thus protected repaid his generosity with the blackest ingratitude. All through his administration, they and other friends of Garfield carried on an underhanded warfare against him, a warfare of pinpricks rather than of blows delivered in the open. Calling themselves "the Garfield Avengers," they tried in every way to belittle Mr. Arthur's public acts and even to discredit his private life. In this manner, between the frank reproaches of his former friends and the treacherous enmity of his former foes, President Arthur's term of office afforded him no very pleasurable experience. Yet, at least, he never gave his ill-wishers the satisfaction of seeing that he winced. He was not one who wore his heart upon his sleeve, but he went on his way with an outward serenity that did honour to his strength of character. His political courage was shown in some very striking acts. Although there is no doubt that he desired a second term of office, he never flinched from what he held to be his duty, however unpopular the discharge of it might be. Thus, he vetoed the Chinese Exclusion Bill of 1882 in the face of the unanimous and excited demands of the Far Western States for its enactment into law. In the same year he vetoed a foolishly extravagant River and Harbour Bill appropriating some $19,000,000.

Again, although in former years he had himself been emphatically a spoilsman, as President he advocated and secured the passage in 1883 of an act reforming the Civil Service, and establishing an effective Civil Service Commission. He did all that was possible to secure the prosecution and conviction of those corrupt officials who had systematically robbed the Government through the notorious " Star-Route " contracts in the postal service. But his most enduring claim to honourable remembrance is found in his energetic efforts to build up an efficient navy in place of the grotesque collection of antiquated hulks on which the Grant administration had spent sums sufficient to have given the United States a modern fighting fleet. President Arthur was, in fact, the true creator of the new American navy, of which the first vessels—the *Chicago,* the *Atlanta,* the *Boston,* and the *Dolphin*—were laid down while he was President.

Upon its personal and social side his presidency was one to be long remembered. The honours of the White House were done with a graceful dignity, such as had never yet been known there. The President had lost his wife some years before; but his sister, Mrs. McElroy, an accomplished woman of great social charm, frequently presided at official functions. The diplomatic dinners were rescued from the smothered ridicule with which the foreign envoys had always viewed them; and the pungent epigram of Mr. Evarts, à propos of one of President Hayes's entertainments, suddenly lost its point.[2] As for the President himself, he must be regarded as the only man of the world, in the best sense of that term, who has ever occupied the

[2] To maintain the state which he regarded as necessary to the dignity of the presidential office, Mr. Arthur dipped deeply into his own private fortune.

White House. Jefferson might, perhaps, have been cited as another instance, were it not that, during his first term, he cultivated an ostentatious boorishness such as would have been impossible in a thoroughbred. President Arthur, however, was an ideal host both to his public and his private guests. Of a fine presence, courteous, witty, tactful, and possessing infinite *savoir vivre*, he was a living refutation of the taunt which Europeans sometimes level at us, to the effect that eminence in American politics is unattainable by one who is a gentleman at heart. Mr. Arthur kept the domestic side of his *ménage* a thing entirely apart from his official life. Coarse-minded, peeping correspondents, male and female, found scant material here for vulgar paragraphs of kitchen gossip. There were published no foolish, nauseating chronicles of the " daily doings " of the White House. The President's children were not photographed and paragraphed and made the subject of a thousand flat and fatuous stories. Beyond the veil of self-respecting privacy, which was drawn before the President's personal affairs, few ever penetrated. The only tale that reached the public was one that made even the Paul Prys of the press ashamed of their own curiosity. It became known that in one of the President's private apartments there was hung the portrait of a woman, before which every morning, by Mr. Arthur's personal order, great masses of cut flowers were heaped. Here was a rarely promising hint for the greedy journalist, eager to give his next despatch from Washington a touch of *sauce piquante*. With vast ingenuity and by bringing the resources of the press to bear, the secret was ferreted out at last, and the portrait was found to be that of the President's dead wife. It was very characteristic of the man who, to the world at large, was always the master of practical affairs with just a suggestion of the *viveur* about him, that he should in private have cherished this delicate sentiment which did him so much honour.

Perhaps it was precisely President Arthur's dignity and perfect taste that shut him out from the broader popularity which some other Presidents have enjoyed. Democracies prefer their idols to have feet of clay. Their ruler must not be too far above those whom he rules, and he must not show too markedly those finer traits which instinctively arouse the furtive suspicion and half dislike of the ignorant and unenlightened. The many-headed monster fawns only at the feet of those who flatter it by imitation, or who unconsciously partake of its uncouthness. The Orsons and Calibans of politics have an innate antipathy to a gentleman. It is not likely that even so great a man as Lincoln could have kept his powerful hold upon the masses had he not possessed some qualities which many of his truest friends deplored. His ultimate success was due, no doubt, before all else, to his sagacity, his perfect knowledge of human nature, and his infinite patience; yet much of it must surely be ascribed to the awkwardness of his appearance and the unconventionality of his manners. The Hoosiers and Suckers of the still untutored West could not rightly understand the consummate statecraft of which he was a master—his inborn genius for the task of government; but when they heard that he slapped his visitors upon the back and told indecent stories and received the ministers of foreign powers while sprawling in a wooden rocking chair, shoeless, and with his huge feet covered with blue yarn socks—then they felt that he was one of themselves, not President Lincoln, but "Good Old Abe." That which repelled a Sumner or an Adams gripped and held fast the hearts

of the men of Sangamon.[3] But Mr. Arthur had not been
bred in such a school. His type was one that neither likes
nor courts the familiarity of a mob's approval. He had
no eccentricities, no traits that were either crude or whim-
sical, no suggestion of self-consciousness or pose. He was
simply a dignified and courteous gentleman—*flos regum
Arthurus,* as one of his admirers quoted of him. And looking back upon his brave and honourable bearing under
the strain of incessant vexation and temptation, the American people have reason to be proud because the roll of
their chief magistrates contains the name of Chester Alan
Arthur.

At the time when Mr. Cleveland was inaugurated there
had been no Democratic President for a full quarter of
a century. A whole generation had been born and had
grown to manhood and to womanhood without ever having lived under any but Republican rule. This long continuance in power of a single party had led many citizens
to identify the interests of that party with the interests of
the nation. The Democrats had been so invariably beaten
at the polls as to make Republicans believe that the
defeated party had no decent reason for existence, and
that it was composed only of wilful obstructionists or of
persons destitute of patriotism. On the other hand, the
Republican party, identified as it was with success and
with so much creditable achievement, was held by them to

---

[3] The story is told that when President Lincoln first met Senator Sumner,
he called out: " Why, Sumner, you must be nearly as tall as I am!
Come, back up, and let's measure! " The effect of such a proposal upon
the glacial dignity of Sumner may be imagined.—Browne, *The Every-Day
Life of Abraham Lincoln,* pp. 451-2 (New York, 1886).—For the unfavourable impression produced by Lincoln upon Adams, see Adams, *Life of
Charles Francis Adams,* p. 146 (Boston, 1900).

monopolise all the political virtues of the American people. To criticise its leaders or to attack its policies seemed to many almost treasonable. To it were ascribed not only the successful conduct of a great war, the extinction of slavery, and the triumph of nationalism over the particularistic spirit of secession, but also the maintenance of the country's commercial credit and of its financial honour. Few remembered that without the support of loyal Democrats at the North, the Government must have yielded to the Confederacy. Few took the trouble to recall the fact that of the great Union commanders, Sherman, Sheridan, McClellan and Meade were Democrats, while Grant himself, though a resident of Lincoln's own State, had never voted for a Republican until after the war ended. Nor was it kept in mind that Stanton, the remarkable military administrator, and Chase, the great finance minister, had been Democrats; that Lincoln's second nomination to the presidency came to him not from the Republican party, but from a Union Convention composed of Republicans and Democrats alike. These things had been long forgotten. Partisan Republicans had come to look upon the existence of the Democratic party as a rather sorry joke, in the face of its long record of disaster and defeat. That it could ever return to power appeared to them not only an improbable, but even a ludicrous, assumption.

Among the ablest of the Republican leaders, however, a much saner view prevailed. These men were acutely conscious of certain facts of which their followers were ignorant. No political phenomenon, indeed, is more remarkable than the almost even balance between the two great parties from 1860 down to 1884. The large majorities which the Republican candidates had received in the Electoral College were utterly misleading as an indication of the comparative strength of the two parties throughout the country. A glance at the popular vote in each presidential election revealed a very interesting state of things, and showed that it was the distribution of the voters, rather than their numbers, which had given to the Republicans success. For example, in the election of 1860, as is well known, Mr. Lincoln, who had a clear majority of 57 electoral votes, was only a minority candidate in the popular vote; for had both wings of the Democracy been united, the ballots which they cast would have outnumbered those given to Mr. Lincoln by more than a quarter of a million. In the election of 1864, which took place at one of the most critical periods of the war, Mr. Lincoln had an electoral majority over General McClellan of 191 votes, and a popular majority of 407,000 votes; but in this election the eleven Southern States, being then outside the Union, took no part. At the election of 1868, out of a popular vote of nearly 6,000,000, General Grant, then at the very climax of his fame, received a popular majority of 305,000 votes, or almost one-quarter less than had been cast for Lincoln, while three Southern States were still unrepresented in the count.

In 1872, Grant's first administration had caused such widespread discontent that the Liberal Republican schism took place, headed by such well-known leaders as Senator Sumner, Carl Schurz, Charles Francis Adams, Horace Greeley, and Whitelaw Reid. Had the Democrats at this time made good use of the opportunity afforded them, they might have gained a signal victory. A candidate such as Charles Francis Adams, of high character and proved ability, could probably have won. But the nomination of Horace Greeley led to the lamentable fiasco which continued President Grant in office by a popular majority of 762,000 votes. This proved, however, in the end to be a Pyrrhic victory. The very fulness of their triumph removed all feeling of restraint from the Republican leaders, and there followed four years of government tainted by public scandal of every description. The Secretary of War resigned to avoid impeachment for bribery. The Navy Department was honeycombed with jobbery. The revelations in connection with the Whiskey Ring startled and disgusted honest men throughout the country. The President's own relatives and intimate friends were proved to have traded on their influence with him.[4] Mr. Colfax, the Republican Speaker of the House and afterward Vice-President, several Senators and a number of Representatives, were smirched by their connection with the Crédit Mobilier. Moreover, the

---

[4] Senator Hoar of Massachusetts said, in speaking on the proposed impeachment of Grant's Secretary of War, Belknap: "My own public life has been a very brief and insignificant one, extending little beyond the duration of a single term of senatorial office. But in this brief period, I have seen five judges of a high court of the United States driven from office by threats of impeachment for corruption or maladministration. I have seen the chairman of the Committee on Military Affairs in the House rise in his place and demand the expulsion of four of his associates for making sale of their official privilege of selecting the youths to be educated at our great military school. When the greatest railroad of the world, binding together the continent and uniting the two great seas which wash our shores, was finished, I have seen our national triumph and exultation turned to bitterness and shame by the unanimous reports of three committees of Congress—two of the House and one here,—that every step of that mighty enterprise had been taken in fraud. I have heard in the highest places the shameless doctrine avowed, by men grown old in public office, that the true way by which power should be gained in the Republic is to bribe the people with the offices created for their service, and the true end for which it should be used when gained is the promotion of selfish ambition and the gratification of personal revenge. I have heard that suspicion haunts the footsteps of the trusted companions of the President."—*Speech of May 6, 1876.*

use of Federal troops in sustaining the iniquities of " carpet-bag " government in the South had become more and more distasteful to the people of the North. The dissatisfaction of the country over such a state of things was shown at the election of 1876, when on the face of the returns the Democratic candidate, Mr. Tilden, had a clear majority of the electoral vote. This result was disputed, and the Electoral Commission created by Congress canvassed the returns in such a way as to give the Presidency to Mr. Hayes by a majority of one vote,—185 to 184,— Mr. Tilden having a popular majority of 250,000 votes. This election seemed to the more astute Republican leaders like the handwriting on the wall, presaging an end of Republican supremacy. The administration of President Hayes, however, considerably strengthened the party to which he belonged. A man of very moderate ability, he was, nevertheless, precisely the President that the country needed at the time. Henry Ward Beecher once described his administration as " a bread poultice "; and the description, though not wholly complimentary, was fairly just. Party feuds were healed. Governmental scandals came to an end. Federal troops were withdrawn from the South. Under the able management of Secretary Sherman, the Treasury resumed specie payments.[6] Hence, at the next election—that of 1880—the Republicans were again successful, and General Garfield had an electoral majority of 59 votes. Yet the record of the popular vote was exceedingly significant. Nearly 9,000,000 ballots had been cast, and out of these 9,000,000 ballots Garfield's majority over Hancock was only 815.[7] The numerical difference,

[6] January 1, 1879.
[7] The figures are those given in Johnston, *American Politics* (New York, 1900).

therefore, between the Republican and Democratic parties at this time was equal only to the population of an insignificant village. So extraordinary close a division had never before been known. It was obvious that Republican success at the next election hung, as it were, by a very slender thread.

It was while the political scales were in this state of almost perfect equipoise that the Republican Convention met in Chicago on June 3d, 1884, to nominate its candidates for President and Vice-President respectively. President Arthur hoped for a nomination, and on the first ballot he received 278 votes; but even at the outset he was outstripped by James G. Blaine of Maine, who led with $334\frac{1}{2}$ votes. This lead was steadily maintained in spite of the opposition of many distinguished Republican leaders; and on the fifth ballot Mr. Blaine received 541 votes, and was declared the nominee amid a scene of tumultuous enthusiasm. General John A. Logan of Illinois was nominated for the Vice-Presidency. The Democratic Convention, meeting in St. Louis on July 8th, took but two ballots. In the first of these, Grover Cleveland of New York led with 392 votes as against 170, cast for Mr. Bayard of Delaware; and on the second ballot he secured the nomination by 683 votes to $145\frac{1}{2}$ cast for Mr. Thomas A. Hendricks of Indiana. As soon as Mr. Cleveland had been nominated as the Democratic candidate for the Presidency, Mr. Hendricks was unanimously named for the office of Vice-President.

The nomination of Mr. Blaine produced an indescribable sensation throughout the length and breadth of the United States. No American statesman had ever had more ardent and intensely loyal friends than he, as none had ever had more virulent and bitter enemies. The former hailed his candidacy with intense enthusiasm; the latter began at once moving heaven and earth to compass his defeat. Mr. Blaine had already enjoyed a remarkable career. Born in Pennsylvania of Scotch-Irish parentage, he had been by turns a teacher and an editor, having taken up in 1854 his residence in Maine. In 1858 he had entered the State Legislature, where for two years he served as Speaker. In 1862, he was sent to Congress, and at once made his mark by his readiness in debate, his quick grasp upon political principles, and his exceptional fertility in resource. He had the impetuosity of the Celt and the clear reasoning brain of the Anglo-Saxon, besides that indescribable quality which, for want of a better name, is known as magnetism. His personal charm was indeed remarkable, and it was to this as much as to his other gifts that he owed the extraordinary devotion of his followers and friends. Early in his political life he had been compared to Henry Clay, to whose career his own was to exhibit a striking parallel. At first he was better known to his associates in Congress than to the country as a whole; but when, in 1869, he was elected Speaker of the House, he rose at once to the rank of a great party leader. It was not, however, until 1876 that he reached the climax of his parliamentary fame. Early in that year, owing to the approach of the centenary of national independence, it was felt that the time had come to hasten the growth of the kindly feeling which already was slowly uniting the sections of the country that had faced each other in the Civil War. To further this object, Mr. Randall of Pennsylvania, a distinguished Democrat, introduced in the House of Representatives a bill to relieve all persons in the United States from any disability imposed by the Fourteenth Amendment to the Constitution. Mr. Blaine was at once upon his feet to offer a substitute. It excepted from this amnesty Jefferson Davis, " late President of the so-called Confederate States." After some parliamentary fencing, an exciting debate began. Mr. Blaine, fluent and impassioned, set forth his reasons for excepting Mr. Davis from the amnesty offered by the Randall bill. His words were chosen with consummate art if it was his purpose to stir again the embers of sectional strife into a blaze and to exasperate the Southern Democrats whom he confronted on the floor.

" In my amendment I have excepted Jefferson Davis from amnesty. I do not place his exclusion on the ground that Mr. Davis was, as he has been commonly called, the head and front of the Rebellion, because on that ground I do not think the exception would be tenable. Mr. Davis was in that respect as guilty, no more so, no less so, than thousands of others who have already received the benefit and grace of amnesty. Probably he was far less efficient as an enemy of the United States, probably he was far more useful as a disturber of the councils of the Confederacy, than many who have already received amnesty. It is not because of any particular and special damage that he above others did to the Union, or because he was personally or especially of consequence, that I except him. But I except him on this ground: that he was the author, knowingly, deliberately, guiltily, and wilfully, of the gigantic murders and crimes at Andersonville."

Mr. Blaine then proceeded to describe in vivid language the sufferings of the Union soldiers confined in the prison-pen at Andersonville. He dwelt with all the power of a consummate orator upon the horrors of that loathsome place. He pictured the miseries of starvation and disease, the insults and ingenious cruelty of the jailer Wirz; and he stirred the indignation of his Northern hearers by painting the dreadful man-hunts in which savage bloodhounds had been set upon the track of escaping prisoners. He excepted from his condemnation the people of the South, and directly charged the crimes of Andersonville upon Jefferson Davis.

" The poor victim, Wirz, deserved his death for brutal treatment and the murder of many victims; but it was a weak policy on the part of our Government to allow Jefferson Davis to go at large and hang Wirz. Wirz was nothing in the world but a mere subordinate, and there was no special reason for singling him out for death. I do not say he did not deserve it. He deserved no mercy; but his execution seemed like skipping over the president, superintendent, and board of directors in the case of a great railroad accident and hanging the brakeman of the rear car. . . .

" It is often said that we shall lift Mr. Davis again into great consequence by refusing him amnesty. This is not for me to consider. I only see before me, when his name is presented, a man who, by a wave of his hand, by a nod of his head, could have put an end to the atrocious cruelties at Andersonville. Some of us had kinsmen there, most of us had friends there, all of us had countrymen there. In the name of those kinsmen, friends, and countrymen, I here protest, and shall with my vote protest, against calling back and crowning with the honours of full American citizenship the man who organised that murder."

Mr. Hill of Georgia replied to Mr. Blaine in a very able, temperate, and (as one reads it over now) convincing speech, so far as the complicity of Mr. Davis was concerned; but he and his associates from the South made the serious tactical mistake of charging that Confederate prisoners had been ill-treated in the North. This gave Mr. Blaine another chance; and, amid a scene of indescribable excitement, he returned to the attack, as brilliant and even more exasperating than before. The debate continued for several days, during which the House at times became a bear-garden. But through all the tumult Mr. Blaine was the one conspicuous figure. The whole country was stirred as it had not been for many years. The passions of the war revived and flamed up as fiercely as in the early sixties. The name of " Blaine of Maine " was in all men's mouths, and the North gloried in his victory, which was the victory of a partisan, but which was, nevertheless, magnificent. The feeling of his admirers was well expressed a few weeks later by Colonel Robert Ingersoll,[8] who with florid yet effective eloquence paid this tribute to his leader:

" Like an armed warrior, like a plumed knight, James G. Blaine marched down the halls of the American Congress and threw his shining lance full and fair against the brazen forehead of every traitor to his country."

From the moment of this spectacular exhibition, Mr. Blaine was an inevitable candidate for the presidency. But the fierce white light which beats upon a throne is no more fierce than that which beats upon a presidential aspirant. It was turned at once upon Mr. Blaine's whole past career. Every incident and every act of his were now subjected to minute investigation by his enemies and rivals. It was not long before a cloud was cast upon his personal integrity. Like a dank mist which rises at nightfall over marshy ground, there rose a vague, impalpable belief that in his public life he had not had a due regard for his own honour. Beginning with mere hints and ending with public accusations, a dozen stories grew until they filled

[8] In nominating Mr. Blaine at the Republican National Convention in Cincinnati, June 16, 1876.

the minds of everyone about him. It was said that Mr.
Blaine had pledged a number of worthless railroad bonds
to the Union Pacific Railway Company in return for a loan
of $64,000 which had never been repaid. It was also
charged that without consideration he had received bonds
of the Little Rock and Fort Smith Railroad. Still another
rumour said that while Speaker of the House he had left
the chair and asked one of the members to make a point
of order which would be sustained by him, and which would
be favourable to a railway company in which Mr. Blaine
was interested. Among a very few it began to be whispered
confidentially that there existed letters written by Mr.
Blaine to a business associate, which, if found, would
prove that the ex-Speaker had had corrupt transactions
with the Northern Pacific Company.

These reports obtained so widespread a currency that
Mr. Blaine was forced to rise in his place and bring the
matter to the attention of the House. He read a letter
from the treasurer of the Union Pacific and from Colonel
Thomas A. Scott, the president of that railway, denying
the story of the worthless bonds. He read another letter
from Morton, Bliss and Company, who were alleged to
have cashed the draft for $64,000, mentioned in the story,
but who now declared that no such draft had been presented to them. Mr. Blaine went on to say that he had
never owned the Little Rock and Fort Smith bonds which
he was said to have received without any consideration.
Apparently his name was cleared. He was, of course,
extremely anxious to avoid investigation at the hands of
Congress. The time for the National Republican Convention was drawing near. Many States had already instructed their delegates to support his candidacy. That
he should be the subject of an investigation for corrupt

transactions while his name was before the Convention would be fatal to his chances; and he desired above all things to stave it off. Nevertheless, the House, which was strongly Democratic, ordered its Judiciary Committee to make such an investigation, though in the resolution ordering it, Mr. Blaine was not specifically named. This was on May 2d; and at the first sessions of the Committee the evidence was corroborative of Mr. Blaine's assertions. On May 31st, however, a very curious incident occurred. There was brought before the Committee a man named James Mulligan. Mulligan had at one time been a clerk for Mr. Jacob Stanwood (the brother of Mrs. Blaine), and later a bookkeeper for Warren Fisher, Jr., a business man of Boston, who had had close relations with the management of the Little Rock and Fort Smith Railroad. While Mr. Mulligan was testifying, he chanced to mention very quietly that he had in his possession certain letters written by Mr. Blaine to Warren Fisher, Jr. At once it was observed that Mr. Blaine grew pale and gave every evidence of great excitement. A moment later, in a whisper, he asked a friend on the Committee to move an immediate adjournment. The gentleman in question did so on the plea of illness, and the Committee rose, to meet again the following morning. When it so met it listened to a most extraordinary story.

During the brief respite given by the adjournment of the Committee, Mr. Blaine had flashed his mind over all the possibilities of the situation. He knew that Mulligan had letters, which, if made public by Mulligan himself, would be interpreted by everyone in a sense extremely unfavourable to Mr. Blaine. He knew that these letters would surely be asked for by the Committee so soon as it should reconvene in the morning. To prevent this and to gain time he must act at once. He therefore went to the Riggs House, where Mulligan was staying, and met Mulligan, Fisher and one Atkins in a private room. There he first asked to see the letters which Mulligan had with him. When this request was refused, he pleaded with all the earnestness of a man whose future was at stake, that the letters might not be given to the Committee. Mulligan declined to surrender them. He said that he had no wish to injure Mr. Blaine, but that he must keep the letters in order to protect himself in case his testimony were impeached. Mr. Blaine asked to read the letters, promising on his word of honour to return them after reading. Mulligan then handed the letters to Mr. Blaine, who read them very carefully, put them into his pocket and carried them away with him.

Such was the story which Mulligan under oath told to the Committee when it met on the following morning.[9] Meanwhile, Mr. Blaine had secured advice from eminent

[9] Mulligan's story as told in his own words before the sub-committee was as follows: "After my examination here yesterday, Mr. Blaine came up to the hotel, the Riggs House, and there had a conference with Mr. Atkins, Mr. Fisher, and myself. He wanted to see those letters that I had. I declined to let him see them. He prayed, almost went on his knees— I would say on his knees—and implored me to think of his six children and his wife, that if the Committee should get hold of this communication, it would sink him immediately and ruin him forever. I told him I should not give them to him. He asked me if I would let him read them. I said I would if he would promise me on the word of a gentleman that he would return them to me. I did let him read them over. He read them over once and called for them again and read them over again. He still importuned me to give those papers up. I declined to do it. I retired to my own room and he followed me up, and went over the same history about his family and his children, and implored me to give them up to him, and even contemplated suicide. He asked me again if I wanted to see his children left in that state, and he then asked me again if I would not let him look over these papers consecutively (I had them

counsel (Senator Matthew H. Carpenter and Judge Jeremiah Black), to the effect that he was not bound to return
the letters. He therefore refused to do so at the request
of the Committee, and the matter for the moment rested
there. The case, however, looked very black for Mr.
Blaine. He had possession of the letters, to be sure, yet
his conduct was everywhere interpreted as giving evidence of guilt. Great excitement prevailed throughout
the country, and the friends of Mr. Blaine were everywhere dismayed. It soon appeared, however, that what
he had done was only part of a well-conceived plan which
did credit to his resourcefulness and audacity. On June
5th, Mr. Blaine rose in the House and claimed the floor
on a question of privilege. He at once proceeded to recite
the events which had led up to the incident just narrated,
and then, referring to Mulligan, he spoke as follows:

" This man had selected, out of correspondence running over
a great many years, letters which he thought would be peculiarly
damaging to me. He came here loaded with them. He came here
for a sensation. He came here primed. He came here on that
particular errand. I was advised of it, and I obtained those letters
under circumstances which have been notoriously scattered throughout the United States and are known to everybody. . . . I
claim I have the entire right to those letters, not only by natural
right, but upon all the precedents and principles of law, as the

numbered). I told him I would, if he would return them to me. He
took the papers, read them all over, and among them I had a memorandum
that I had made by way of synopsis of the letters, and referring to the
number of the letters—a synopsis containing the points of the letters. I
had made that memorandum so as to be able to refer here when questioned.
He asked me to let him read the letters and I showed him this statement
too. After he had read them, he asked me what I wanted to do with those
papers; if I wanted to use them. I told him I never wanted to use the
papers, nor would I show them to the Committee unless called upon to
do so. . . . Blaine has got them, and would not give them up to me."

man who held those letters in possession held them—wrongfully. The Committee that attempted to take those letters from that man for use against me proceeded wrongfully. They proceeded in all boldness to a most defiant violation of the ordinary private and personal rights which belong to every American citizen. . . . Then there went forth everywhere the idea and impression that because I would not permit that man, or any man whom I could prevent, from holding as a menace over my head my private correspondence, there must be something in it most deadly and destructive to my reputation. . . . Now, Mr. Speaker, I say that I have defied the power of the House to compel me to produce those letters. I speak with all respect to this House. I know its powers and I trust that I respect them. But I say this House has no more power to order what shall be done or not done with my private correspondence than it has with what I shall do in the nurture and education of my children—not a particle. The right is as sacred in the one case as it is in the other. . . . I am ready for any extremity of contest or conflict in behalf of so sacred a right."

Throughout this animated and even fiery justification of his right, the crowded House had listened in breathless silence, and with a tension of feeling which could almost be felt. There was abundant sympathy with Mr. Blaine. Even his adversaries were sorry for him. He seemed like a man driven into a corner and fighting for his very life. Yet the suppression of the letters looked only the more utterly damning. But at this moment, after a brief pause, Mr. Blaine dealt a master-stroke which he had planned with consummate art, and which he now delivered with a dramatic power that was thrilling. Raising his voice and holding up a packet, he went on:

"And while I am so, I am not afraid to show the letters. Thank God Almighty, I am not afraid to show them! There they are.

There is the very original package. And, with some sense of humiliation, with a mortification that I do not pretend to conceal, with a sense of outrage which I think any man in my position would feel, I invite the confidence of forty-four millions of my countrymen while I read those letters from this desk."

The tension was broken. The whole assembly burst out into frantic and prolonged applause. Then Mr. Blaine read the letters, one by one, with comments and explanations of his own. Having done so, he faced one of the Democratic members of the Committee, Mr. Proctor Knott, and in the course of a rapid dialogue brought out the fact that Mr. Knott had received a cablegram from a Mr. Caldwell, whose knowledge of the whole affair was very intimate, and that Mr. Knott had apparently suppressed it. The scene at the end of this exciting parliamentary duel baffled all description. The House went mad; and for fifteen minutes there reigned a pandemonium amid which the Speaker was helpless in his efforts to restore even a semblance of order. Mr. Blaine, for the moment, had won a brilliant triumph. He had restored and strengthened the faith of all his followers and had turned apparently inevitable disaster into victory.

He had not, however, laid the ghost of the railway scandals. Reading over the so-called Mulligan letters in cold type, a great number of Mr. Blaine's own party associates found in them evidence, if not of actual corruption, at least of so blunted a sense of official propriety as to make Mr. Blaine no longer seem a fitting candidate for the highest office in the land. From that time he had to face not only the opposition of the Democratic party, but the mistrust of thousands of Republicans, among whom were men of the highest character and influence.

The Mulligan letters showed that Mr. Blaine, in the years when they were written, had been suffering from what he called " very pressing and painful " pecuniary embarrassment. Writing to Mr. Fisher, he described himself as " left helpless and hopeless," and as " crippled and deranged in all my finances." A complicated series of financial transactions stood revealed, and also a willingness on the part of Mr. Blaine to secure especial consideration on the ground of his influence as an officer of the Government. The following letters are the two which were afterwards most often quoted. The first was dated June 29, 1869.

" My Dear Mr. Fisher: Your offer to admit me to a participation in the new railway enterprise is in every respect as generous as I could expect or desire. I thank you very sincerely for it, and in this connection I wish to make a suggestion of a somewhat selfish character. It is this: You spoke of Mr. Caldwell disposing of a share of his interest to me. If he really designs to do so, I wish he would make the proposition definite, so that I could know just what to depend on. Perhaps if he waits till the full development of the enterprise, he might grow reluctant to part with the shares; and I do not by this mean any distrust of him.

" I do not feel that I shall prove a deadhead in the enterprise if I once embark in it. I see various channels in which I know I can be useful.

" Very hastily and sincerely your friend,

" J. G. Blaine."

The second letter was marked " Confidential," and was dated at Washington, April 16, 1876.

" My Dear Mr. Fisher: You can do me a very great favour, and I know it will give you pleasure to do so—just as I would do for you under similar circumstances. Certain persons and papers are trying to throw mud at me to injure my candidacy before the Cincinnati Convention, and you may observe they are trying it in connection with the Little Rock and Fort Smith matter.

"I want you to send me a letter such as the inclosed draft. You will receive this to-morrow (Monday) evening, and it will be a favour I shall never forget if you will at once write me the letter and mail it the same evening.

"The letter is strictly true, and is honourable to you and to me, and will stop the mouths of slanderers at once.

"Regard this letter as strictly confidential. Do not show it to any one. The draft is in the hands of my clerk, who is as trustworthy as any man can be. If you can't get the letter written in season for the 9 o'clock mail to New York, please be sure to mail it during the night so that it will start first mail Tuesday morning; *but, if possible, I pray you to get it in the 9 o'clock mail Monday evening.* Kind regards to Mrs. Fisher.

"Sincerely,

"*Burn this letter.*   "J. G. B."

A third letter, dated October 4, 1869, made it evident that Mr. Blaine, while Speaker of the House, had sent his page to General Logan, suggesting a point of order, which, if made, would block a scheme unfriendly to a land grant in which Mr. Blaine's financial associates were interested.

Such, in brief, is the history of the famous Mulligan letters which sufficed to prevent Mr. Blaine's nomination for the Presidency in 1876 and 1880, and which now, in 1884, from the outset of his candidacy, were printed and scattered broadcast over the country by his political opponents.[10]

---

[10] In addition to the letters read by Mr. Blaine before the House, a number of others were made public by Messrs. Fisher and Mulligan, who deposited them with their lawyers in Boston. The authenticity of these letters was not denied by Mr. Blaine.

The Democratic candidate against whom Mr. Blaine had now to make his fight was a man of a wholly antithetical type. Mr. Cleveland was in no respect a brilliant man. The son of a clergyman, and early left to make his own way in the world, he had, like his rival, been a teacher, and had later taken up the practice of the law in Buffalo. There he had held some minor public offices. In 1863 he was Assistant District Attorney for the county, and from 1870 to 1873 he had served as Sheriff. He first attracted attention outside of his own city when, in 1881, he was elected Mayor of Buffalo by a combination of Democrats and Independents. In this office he instituted reforms and defeated various corrupt combinations, while his liberal use of the veto power maintained a wise economy. In 1882 he had received the Democratic nomination for the governorship of New York, and had been elected by the remarkable plurality of 192,000 votes.[11]

Mr. Cleveland was a type of man such as had not before come to the front as a presidential possibility. He represented the practical, every-day, usual citizen of moderate means and no very marked ambitions—a combination of the business man and the unimportant professional person, blunt, hardheaded, brusque, and unimaginative, and with a readiness to take a hand in whatever might be going on. His education was of the simplest, his general

[11] The size of this plurality was mainly due to the abstention from the polls of many discontented Republicans. At the Republican Convention held in Saratoga, Judge Folger, then Secretary of the Treasury, was nominated as Mr. Cleveland's opponent. It was felt that President Arthur had practically dictated this nomination in order to strengthen his own hold upon his party machinery in New York. Certain delegates were charged with having used forged proxies. Finally, the friends of Mr. A. B. Cornell, who was then Governor of the State, were indignant because he had not been re-nominated.

information presumably not very large; and his interest in life was almost wholly bounded by the limits of his own locality. As a practising lawyer he was well thought of; yet his reputation had not gone much beyond the local circuit. A bachelor, he had no need of a large income. His spare time was spent with companions of his own tastes. His ideal of recreation was satisfied by a quiet game of pinochle in the back-room of a respectable beer-garden; and perhaps this circumstance in itself is sufficient to give a fair notion of his general environment. He was, indeed, emphatically a man's man—*homo inter homines*—careless of mere forms, blunt of speech, and somewhat primitive in his tastes. But he had all the virile attributes of a Puritan ancestry. His will was inflexible. His force of character was extraordinary. He hated shams, believed that a thing was either right or wrong, and when he had made up his mind to any course of action, he carried it through without so much as a moment's wavering. So great was the confidence which his character inspired, that when a committee of the independent voters of Buffalo called upon him for the purpose of urging him to stand for the mayoralty, they asked him for no written pledges, but accepted his simple statement as an adequate guarantee. " Cleveland says that if elected he will do so-and-so," they told the people. And the people elected him, because they knew his word to be inviolable.

As Governor, Mr. Cleveland entered upon a wider field and one that must have seemed at first a place of limitless exactions. But his lack of imagination stood him in good stead. He bent his back to the burden and did each day's work as it came. A stranger to large responsibilities, and retaining much of the narrowness of the provincial business man, he viewed all questions as equally important, attending personally to all his correspondence, looking for himself into every item and detail of executive business, and giving hours of time each day to minutiæ which the merest clerk could have cared for with quite as much efficiency. This, however, was only one manifestation of the conscientiousness that showed itself far more commendably in higher matters. The rough, blunt, independence of the man made him indifferent to the insidious influences that rise like a malarial mist about the possessor of high political office. Subleties of suggestion were lost on this brusque novice, and anything more pointed than suggestion roused in him a cross-grained spirit that brooked no guidance or control. He forged ahead in his own way with a sort of bull-necked stubbornness, but with a power and energy which smoother politicians were compelled to recognise as very real. He cared nothing for popularity. He vetoed a bill requiring the street railways to reduce their fares, thereby offending thousands. He followed it up by a veto of another bill which granted public money to sectarian schools; and in consequence he estranged great masses of his Catholic supporters. He defied the Tammany leaders in the Legislature, and made still more powerful enemies. But when the people at large had come to understand him, they admired his independence and applauded this burly, obstinate, tactless, but intensely earnest man. They were pleased when the professional politicians were trampled on; and even the labour representatives, to whose dictation Mr. Cleveland had sturdily refused to bow, at heart respected him for his firmness and his honesty. In the end, his record as Governor of New York secured for him the nomination for the Presidency. Against the brilliant, subtle and magnetic

Blaine was pitted the plodding, incorruptible, courageous Cleveland.

The campaign opened immediately after the two candidates had been nominated. Those Republicans who were opposed to Mr. Blaine formed an organisation at a conference held in New York on July 22d, and prepared an address which was issued on the 30th by the so-called National Committee of Republicans and Independents, of which George William Curtis was the chairman, and George Walton Green the secretary. At once the movement assumed formidable proportions, and it was seen that thousands of Republicans were rallying to Cleveland, not because they had given up their party, but because they could not tolerate their party's candidate. Among them were men who had been identified with the Republican party from its earliest years—Henry Ward Beecher, William Everett, George Ticknor Curtis, Carl Schurz, and James Freeman Clarke. These Independents received the popular name of " Mugwumps," a word which, having been first employed in a semi-political sense by the Indianapolis *Sentinel* in 1872, gained its popular currency through the New York *Sun,* which began using it on March 23, 1884. These " Mugwumps," or political purists, had been described by Mr. Blaine four years earlier in a letter to General Garfield, in which he said: " They are noisy but not numerous; pharisaical but not practical; ambitious but not wise; pretentious but not powerful." This sentence was extremely characteristic of the man who wrote it.

Mr. Blaine was an old campaigner. He knew that his record would be violently assailed. He felt, however, that he had drawn all the enemy's fire in 1876 and 1880, and that in consequence their ammunition had been practically exhausted. He had no intention of conducting a defensive battle. With all his natural aggressiveness, therefore, he began to carry the war into the enemy's country. At first he trusted to the old sectional issue which had won so many elections for his party. The memories of the Civil War were again invoked. The perils of the " Solid South " and of " the South once more in the saddle " were pictured by a thousand party orators. But somehow or other this issue had, in sporting parlance, gone stale. The new generation which had grown up since the war cared little for these things, and the older generation had grown weary of them. Mr. Cleveland was sneered at because he had not enlisted in the army but had sent a substitute. To this it was answered that he was then the sole support of a widowed mother, and that neither had Mr. Blaine himself enlisted nor sent a substitute. A feeling of dismay affected the Republican managers when it was discovered that the war issue was no longer powerful. The tariff question was then taken up and hammered at industriously. This had proved sufficient to pull Mr. Garfield through in 1880, and much was hoped from it by Mr. Blaine. The Democratic platform, however, had been very wisely drawn, and its tariff plank decidedly appealed to the common sense of the American people. It said:

" Knowing full well that legislation affecting the occupations of the people should be cautious and conservative in method, not in advance of public opinion but responsive to its demands, the Democratic Party is pledged to revise the tariff in a spirit of fairness to all interests. But in making reductions in taxes, it is not proposed to injure any domestic industries, but rather to promote their healthy growth. . . . The necessary reduction in taxation can and must be effected without depriving American labour of the ability to compete successfully with foreign labour, and without imposing lower rates of duty than will be ample to cover any increased cost of production which may exist in consequence of the higher rate of wages prevailing in this country. Sufficient revenue to pay all the expenses of the Federal Government can be got under our present system of taxation, from custom-house taxes on fewer imported articles, bearing heaviest on articles of luxury, and bearing lightest on articles of necessity."

In this there was no suggestion of the favourite Republican bogey of Free Trade. It was instead a lucid definition of Protection as Protection had been understood by Lincoln and by the Republican financiers of his administration. Hence the tariff issue was another weapon which bent and broke in the hands of those who tried to wield it.

Seeing the futility of their efforts to rekindle the war spirit or to frighten the manufacturing interests, the Republican managers, in their desperation, descended to the lower plane of personal abuse, justifying themselves by citing the attacks which Democrats and Independents were making upon Mr. Blaine. From that moment the contest became shameful and indecent to an almost incredible degree. No such campaign of slander had ever before been waged. One is justified in thinking that no such campaign will ever again be known in American political history. To recall quite briefly some of its details may act as a deterrent in the future. Mr. Cleveland was then a bachelor, and so the Republican *condottieri* felt no such scruples as they might have entertained toward one who had a family to suffer. They thought him a fair target for every missile. An episode in his past and one that had been long since ended, was now revived, and made the basis for a charge of repulsive and habitual immorality.

When the story was first published, its substance was telegraphed to Mr. Cleveland, who immediately replied with the characteristic message, "Tell the truth." But the truth would not have been sufficient for the purposes of his opponents, and therefore the incident referred to was exaggerated and became the nucleus of a shameful structure of foul invention and filthy innuendo. It was charged that Mr. Cleveland had abducted a woman and imprisoned her in an asylum in order to suppress her story, and that he had kidnapped and secretly immured a child which claimed him as its father. Mr. Cleveland had made himself hated by the baser elements in Buffalo through his fearlessness in suppressing vice while he was Mayor; and now from every drinking-den and brothel there was sent forth a swarm of vile and slanderous stories which the partisans of Mr. Blaine greedily caught up and scattered recklessly throughout the land. It was a debauch of slander, and for a moment the Independents were staggered. But a brief investigation showed that, with the exception of a single incident, this prurient mass had oozed from the lewd imagination of the stews. It all resolved itself into the exaggeration of one episode in Mr. Cleveland's life, which had occurred years before and which long since had been atoned for by the rectitude of his after conduct. The following paragraph from a letter written by the Rev. Dr. Kinsley Twining, an eminent clergyman of Buffalo, who was conversant with all the facts, sets forth with sufficient clearness the truth which Mr. Cleveland desired to have told. This letter was indorsed by the most prominent citizens of Buffalo, and it was printed and circulated throughout the United States.

" The kernel of truth in the various charges against Mr. Cleveland is this, that when he was younger than he is now, he was guilty of an illicit connection; but the charge, as brought against him, lacks the elements of truth in these substantial points: There was no seduction, no adultery, no breach of promise, no obligation of marriage; but there was at that time a culpable irregularity of life, living as he was, a bachelor, for which it was proper and is proper that he should suffer. After the primary offence, which is not to be palliated in the circle for which I write, his conduct was singularly honourable, showing no attempt to evade responsibility, and doing all he could to meet the duties involved, of which marriage was certainly not one. Everything here was eminently to his credit under circumstances which would have seemed to many men of the world to justify him in other conduct than that which he accepted as his duty. There was no abduction, only proper legal action under circumstances which demanded it."

It is now believed by many that Mr. Cleveland chivalrously took upon himself the blame of this transaction in order to shield a personal friend who was himself the wrongdoer, but who had a family which would have suffered had the facts been brought to light. This belief suggested to the late Paul Leicester Ford a dramatic chapter in his political novel *The Honourable Peter Stirling*,[12] of which many incidents are understood to have been drawn from the life of Mr. Cleveland. Certain it is that there was no truth in the other stories. They were repeated on the stump with hideous unctuousness by an itinerant preacher who had been hired to proclaim them; but a move toward prosecuting him for slander brought him instantly to his knees. The wretched creature ate his words and grovelled and begged abjectly for forgiveness. He denied having any authority for what he had said, and confessed that he had simply repeated the loose stories which he had picked up in the street.

The opinion of the independent voters was very well

[12] New York, 1886. See chapter xxxiv.

expressed by the New York *Evening Post*. Taunted with its enmity to Blaine, who had been accused only of official dereliction, and with its support of one who had been confessedly unchaste, the *Post* replied that while an isolated instance of unchastity might affect the social reputation of a man, it had no relation whatever to his civic virtues; whereas the charges against Mr. Blaine, if true, disqualified him wholly for high office, since they were such as undermine the foundation of all civic honour.

As the campaign proceeded, its tone became almost frantic. Those who clung loyally to Mr. Blaine did so with a passionate intensity that made them quite incapable of reasoning. The attacks on Mr. Cleveland had filled his followers with the bitterest resentment. It was known that the scandalous stories about him had been published with Mr. Blaine's consent, and that in fact Mr. Blaine had sent the original copy of them to the Republican National Committee.[13] Therefore when certain industrious and not over-nice partisans unearthed a similar private scandal relating to Mr. Blaine, it was carried to Mr. Cleveland in the confident expectation that he would sanction its use in the campaign. To their surprise, he sternly forbade any such action, and notified the managers of his canvass to have nothing to do with it. This was early in the summer. A newspaper owner in the West, who had no such scruples as influenced Mr. Cleveland, resolved, on his own responsibility, to make the matter public. On August 8th, the Indianapolis *Sentinel* printed the story with sensational headlines. It asserted that the inscription on a headstone in the cemetery at Augusta, Maine, showed that a child had been born to Mr. and Mrs. Blaine within three months

---

[13] The authority for this statement is a well known Republican, Col. A. K. McClure.—See McClure, *Our Presidents*, p. 312 (New York, 1905).

after the date of their marriage. Upon this circumstance, the *Sentinel* made a series of editorial comments such as it is unnecessary to reprint, but which were insufferably frank and brutally explicit.

Mr. Blaine was stung to the quick by this shocking reflection upon his own honour and the virtue of his wife. He at once telegraphed to an eminent legal firm in Indiana, directing that a suit for criminal libel be brought at once against the *Sentinel*. On September 6th, he wrote a personal letter of explanation to Mr. William Walter Phelps, who gave it to the press. The essential portions of this letter may be quoted:

" At Georgetown, Ky., in the spring of 1848, when I was but eighteen years of age, I first met the lady who for more than thirty-four years has been my wife. Our acquaintance resulted, at the end of six months, in an engagement, which, without the prospect of speedy marriage, we naturally sought to keep to ourselves. Two years later, in the spring of 1850, when I was maturing plans to leave my profession in Kentucky and establish myself elsewhere, I was suddenly summoned to Pennsylvania by the death of my father. It being very doubtful if I could return to Kentucky, I was threatened with indefinite separation from her who possessed my entire devotion. My one wish was to secure her to myself by an indissoluble tie against every possible contingency in life; and on the 30th day of June, 1850, just prior to my departure from Kentucky, we were, in the presence of chosen and trusted friends, united by what I knew was, in my native State of Pennsylvania, a perfectly legal form of marriage."

He then stated that this marriage subsequently appeared to have been technically irregular, inasmuch as, through ignorance of the Kentucky law, he had not secured the proper form of license. Therefore, he had gone through a second marriage ceremony in Pennsylvania on March 25, 1851,—a date which had usually been accepted as that of his marriage to Miss Stanwood. He concluded:

" At the mature age of fifty-four I do not defend the wisdom or prudence of a secret marriage suggested by the ardour and the inexperience of youth; but its honour and its purity were inviolate, as I believe, in the sight of God, and can not be made to appear otherwise by the wicked devices of men. It brought to me a companionship which has been my chief happiness from boyhood's years to this hour, and has crowned me with whatever of success I have attained in life."

To the discredit of human nature, this perfectly frank and truthful explanation had no effect upon many of Mr. Blaine's enemies; and up to the day of the election, disgusting innuendoes regarding the affair continued to be heard upon the stump.[14]

[14] After the election, Mr. Blaine withdrew his suit against the *Sentinel,* publishing on December 10th, a letter to his counsel which contained the following passages:

" When I visited Indiana in October, I was repeatedly advised that six Democrats could not be found in the State who in a political suit would give a verdict against their leading party organ. I am perfectly able to fight the *Sentinel* newspaper in the Indiana court, but I would stand no chance whatever against the consolidated venom of the Democratic party of the State. With these surroundings and with this prospect, it is idle for me to go through the trouble and annoyance of a trial. . . . . Except from three members of the Democratic party of that State I have never heard that a word of dissent or disapproval was spoken; while the great mass of the Democratic speakers repeated the libel from every stump in Indiana with vituperative rancour, with gibes and ribald jest.

" As a candidate for the presidency I knew that I should encounter many forms of calumny and personal defamation, but I confess that I did not expect to be called upon to defend the name of a beloved and honoured wife, who is a mother and a grandmother, nor did I expect that the grave of my little child would be cruelly desecrated.

" Against such gross forms of wrong the law gives no adequate redress,

Political discussion, indeed, rapidly degenerated into personal abuse. Even the cartoonists of the different parties showed none of the humour which is usually to be found in the pictorial history of a campaign. Some of the caricatures were frightful in their malignity. It was at this time that Gillam drew his hideous pictures of Mr. Blaine as the Tattooed Man, which produced so painful an impression upon Mr. Blaine himself that his friends could with difficulty restrain him from instituting a criminal prosecution. On the other hand, the pages of *Judge* showed an almost equally offensive representation of the Democratic candidates. Many persons at that time had a very poor opinion of Mr. Cleveland's intellectual abilities and regarded Mr. Hendricks as much the abler man. Hence a cartoonist drew the Democratic ticket as a kangaroo with an extremely small head, but with an enormous, leech-like tail. The head, of course, was Cleveland, and the tail was Hendricks, whose face appeared upon it; and this conception, varied in a hundred different ways and published in crude colours, was worked out in a fashion that was most repulsive, as were also scores of other coarse cartoons, which to-day would be suppressed by the police.

Late in October it became evident that the vote of New York would decide the result of the election; and both parties concentrated upon that State their intensest energies. Mr. Cleveland as Governor had, as already described, offended the labour vote, the Roman Catholics, and Tammany Hall—three immensely powerful elements. Mr. Blaine, on the other hand, because of his Irish de-

and I know that in the end my most effective appeal against the unspeakable outrages which I resist must be to the noble manhood and the noble womanhood of America."

scent, his Catholic mother, and his professed sympathies with the cause of Ireland and the so-called Irish "patriots," was strong precisely where Cleveland was known to be most vulnerable. Yet in New York Mr. Blaine had made one venomous and implacable enemy. This was Roscoe Conkling, with whom, so far back as 1866, there had been established something like a personal feud. The two men had always been temperamentally antipathetic. Conkling was overbearing, proud of his personal appearance, and bore himself with a swagger which impressed the galleries of the House, but which was offensive even to many of his own party associates. In 1866, in the course of a debate, Blaine and Conkling came into parliamentary collision, and the former was goaded into a withering blaze of scorn. Turning upon Conkling, he said in measured tones and with an air of indescribable disdain:

"As to the gentleman's cruel sarcasm, I hope he will not be too severe. The contempt of that large-minded gentleman is so wilting, his haughty disdain, his grandiloquent swell, his majestic, supereminent, overpowering, turkey-gobbler strut, has been so crushing to myself and all the members of this House, that I know it was an act of the greatest temerity for me to venture upon a controversy with him."

Then, referring to a comparison which had been made of Mr. Conkling to Henry Winter Davis, he went on:

"The gentleman took it seriously, and it has given his strut additional pomposity. The resemblance is great; it is striking. Hyperion to a Satyr, Thersites to Hercules, mud to marble, dunghill to diamond, a singed cat to a Bengal tiger, a whining puppy to a roaring lion!"

This shock to his vanity Conkling never forgave, the less so as the cartoonists ever afterward depicted him as a turkey-gobbler. From that day the two men were enemies for life. It was Conkling who aided in preventing Blaine's nomination in 1876 and in 1880. It was Blaine who, as Garfield's Secretary of State, urged the President to defy the New York Senator and indirectly to secure his retirement into private life. Now it was Conkling's turn again, and he meant to feed his resentment to the full. His power in New York was great, and the Republican managers could do nothing with him. A political friend sought him out for the purpose of persuading him to make at least one speech in defence of Mr. Blaine. Conkling, who was sitting in his law office at the time of the interview, listened impassively to the earnest plea until the last word had been spoken. Then he looked up with a sardonic smile.

" Thank you," he said; " but you know I don't engage in criminal practice."

Blaine, therefore, took the stump himself and went about speaking to great crowds, and endeavouring to win them by that eloquence and charm of manner which had made him famous. He was, however, no longer the indomitable political gladiator of past years. The strain of the conflict had told on him severely. Though he let it be known to few, he was acutely sensitive to the attacks that were made upon him so unscrupulously and often so brutally. He suffered even when he seemed externally serene. Moreover, his fellow-candidate, General Logan, was not at all the associate whom Mr. Blaine would personally have chosen. Logan represented the opposing or " Stalwart " faction of the Republican party, and was in sympathy with Conkling and his friends. He was, besides a coarse-grained, illiterate sort of person, the precise antithesis of Mr. Blaine. Before the campaign had ended, a very marked coolness came to exist between the two men—a circumstance that inspired the following bit of doggerel, the syntax of which was supposed to represent General Logan's style of English:

> "We never speak as we pass by,
> Me to Jim Blaine nor him to I."

Mr. Blaine had also well-nigh reached the point of physical exhaustion. His health was already undermined. His vitality was failing. As he was dragged about from place to place, stared at by mobs, having always to appear affable and interested while haunted by a premonition of disaster, he almost experienced physical collapse. The acuteness of his mind must likewise have been somewhat dulled; for when, on October 29th, a few days before the election, he received at the Fifth Avenue Hotel in New York City a number of clergymen, he failed to notice a remark of one of them who made a brief address. This clergyman was the Rev. Dr. Samuel D. Burchard, who closed his speech with the following sentences:

"We expect to vote for you next Tuesday. We have a higher expectation, which is that you will be the President of the United States, and that you will do honour to your name, to the United States, and to the high office you will occupy. We are Republicans, and we do not propose to leave our party and identify ourselves with the party of Rum, Romanism, and Rebellion!"

These last words, so blazingly indiscreet when publicly addressed to a candidate who hoped to carry the pivotal State of New York by the aid of Catholic voters, were

heard by Mr. Blaine, but their significance was not instantly appreciated. As he afterwards told his friends in
private conversation, he was at the moment preoccupied
in thinking over the answer which he was to make. He
therefore took no notice of Dr. Burchard's peroration,
though it must have been personally offensive to him as the
son of a Catholic mother. He had, besides, himself just
returned from visiting his sister, who was the Mother
Superior of a convent in Indiana. Yet it was only after
the delegation had withdrawn that he fully realised the
serious blunder that he had made. He took immediate
steps to suppress the word " Romanism " in the reports
that were to appear in friendly newspapers. But it was
too late. The Horatian maxim, *Volat irrevocabile ver-
bum,* was to find a striking illustration of its truth. In less
than twenty-four hours, every Democratic paper in the
country had spread before its readers the Burchard allitera-
tion. Every Catholic voter in the State had read it upon
handbills, and had been told that Mr. Blaine had allowed
a slur upon his own mother's faith to pass unrebuked.

Still another political mistake was made by the Republican candidate on the evening of the same day. He attended
a dinner given in his honour at Delmonico's by a number
of prominent New York gentlemen. The list of guests
was a remarkably representative one, containing the names
of men prominent in every walk of life. But, unluckily
for Mr. Blaine, there were many present there who to the
popular imagination were associated only with great wealth
or with wealth used for oppression. Such, for example,
were Messrs. Jay Gould, H. H. Rogers of the Standard
Oil Company, Cyrus W. Field, Russell Sage, and H. D.
Armour, afterwards of the Beef Trust. As may be
imagined, Mr. Blaine's enemies were not slow in using this

so-called " Millionaires' Dinner " as a proof that Mr.
Blaine was the chosen candidate of the rich, and therefore devoid of sympathy with the poor and needy. Some
extracts from the New York *World* of the following day,
may be cited as typical, however absurd they may now
appear.

" Yesterday was Black Wednesday for Mr. James G. Blaine.
He will remember it with sorrow. . . . The Millionaires and
Monopolists banquet favourite candidates, but the People elect
Presidents, thank God! . . . Is there a workingman now
who believes that James G. Blaine is sincere when he pretends to
be the friend of labour? If so, why does he receive the homage
of Gould, Cyrus Field, and the millionaire enemies of the workingmen?

" While Blaine and his millionaire admirers were feasting at
Delmonico's last night, thousands of children in this great city,
whose fathers labour twelve hours a day, went to bed hungry and
many of them supperless. It was a Black Wednesday for James
G. Blaine. . . . Mr. Blaine was at home in the midst of the
Monopolists and Millionaires last night. He loves them and they
admire him. But the people witnessed the shameless exhibition,
and they will not elect to the presidency the defender of Jay
Gould's schemes and the partner of Cyrus Field.

" From Rum, Romanism, and Rebellion at the Fifth Avenue
Hotel, Mr. Blaine proceeded to the merry banquet of the Millionaires at Delmonico's, where champagne frothed and brandy spar-
kled in glasses that glittered like jewels. The clergymen would
have been proud of Mr. Blaine, no doubt, if they had seen him in
the midst of the mighty wine-bibbers. It was Mr. Blaine's Black
Wednesday.

" Beaten by the people, hopeless of an honest election, Blaine's
appeal at the banquet of the millionaires was for a corruption fund
large enough to buy up New Jersey, Connecticut, and Indiana, and
to defraud the people of their free choice for President. . . .

Every dollar subscribed at this late stage of the campaign, when all legitimate expenses have ceased, was given solely to purchase votes, to facilitate frauds, and to rob the people of a fair election. Every subscriber is an enemy of the Republic."

Still, the result seemed doubtful. Tammany Hall had not yet been won over. Its leader was John Kelly, a rough and ready politician, but an honest man, according to his lights. He had opposed Mr. Cleveland's nomination, pronouncing him no Democrat, and declaring that if elected he would prove a traitor to the party. Kelly held in his control the vote of Tammany Hall; and, as a last resort, Mr. Hendricks was summoned from Indiana to exert his influence. He made the journey of a thousand miles and conferred with Kelly until a late hour of the night. Hendricks was a party man of the straitest type, an old-time Democrat of the Middle West. He carried his point, and Kelly promised that for Hendricks's sake the Tammany vote should be cast for the party ticket.

Then came the day of the election on November 4th. Early on the following morning it was known that Cleveland had carried all the Southern States, besides New Jersey, Connecticut and Indiana. New York was still in doubt, but it seemed to have gone Democratic. The New York *Sun,* which had supported the farcical Greenback candidacy of General B. F. Butler, and which was bitterly opposed to Cleveland, conceded his election. The *Tribune,* on the other hand, kept its flag still flying, and declared that Blaine had won. It was evident that the result depended upon a few hundred votes in the outlying counties of New York. A very ugly feeling was manifested among the Democrats. They suspected that a plot was on foot to cheat them of their rights and to repeat the discreditable history of 1876. This suspicion was intensified when the Republican National Committee issued the following bulletin:

" There is no ground for doubt that the honest vote of this State has been given to the Republican candidate; and though the defeated candidate for the presidency is at the head of the election machinery in this State, the Democratic party, which has notoriously been the party of frauds in elections for years, will not be permitted to overthrow the will of the people."

Mobs filled the streets in the vicinity of the newspaper offices, watching intently every bulletin that was posted, and from time to time breaking out into savage cheers or groans. Violence was attempted in several cities, and bodies of men marched up and down as they had done at the outbreak of the Civil War. The excitement was most intense in the city of New York, where it was believed that Jay Gould, who controlled the Western Union Telegraph Company, was leagued with the more unscrupulous of the Republican managers to tamper with the delayed returns. Gould was one of the most sinister figures that have ever flitted, bat-like, across the vision of the American people. Merciless, cold-blooded, secretive, apparently without one redeeming trait, this man for many years had been the incarnation of unscrupulous greed. A railway-wrecker, a corrupter of the judiciary, a partner of the notorious Fisk, the author of the dreadful panic of Black Friday in 1873, when he drove hundreds of victims to ruin, to self-murder or to shame, Jay Gould, even at the present day, typifies so vividly all that is base and foul, as to cause even the mention of his name to induce the shudderings of moral nausea. No sooner was his repulsive personality associated with the belief that the election returns were being altered, than popular indignation broke loose from all restraint. An angry mob marched to the Western Union Building with shouts of "Hang Jay Gould!" Gould added to his other despicable traits the quality of cowardice. Fearing for his life, he besought police protection; and then from some inner hiding place he despatched a telegram to Mr. Cleveland, conceding his election and effusively congratulating him upon it.[15]

On the evening of the 18th of November, the official count was ended; and then the country knew that a plurality of 1149 votes in the State of New York had given the presidency to Mr. Cleveland. On that same night, Mr. Blaine appeared at the door of his house in Augusta, Maine, and said to a sombre, sullen crowd which had assembled there: "Friends and neighbours, the national contest is over, and by the narrowest of margins we have lost."

The election of Mr. Cleveland marks an epoch in our national history, the importance of which can only now be fully understood. It meant that, with the exception of the negro question, the issues springing from the Civil War had been definitely settled. It meant the beginning of a true re-union of all States and sections. It meant that the nation had turned its back upon the past, and was about to move forward with confidence and courage to a future of material prosperity, and to a greatness of which no one at that time could form an adequate conception. And it meant, although none then surmised it, that, as a result of new conditions, there was ultimately to be effected a momentous change in the whole social and political structure of the American Republic.

[15] See Breen, *Thirty Years of New York Politics,* pp. 695-697 (New York, 1899).

II

PRESIDENT CLEVELAND, from the very outset of his administration, was destined to confound the predictions of his political adversaries. The misrepresentations concerning him with which the country had been flooded during the campaign of 1884 had found lodgment in the minds of millions. Now that he was actually in office, a shiver of nervous apprehension ran through those Republicans who honestly believed that a Democratic administration meant ruin and disaster. They had been told that Mr. Cleveland was a man of limited intelligence, of low tastes, and of disreputable associations. Partisan newspapers had prophesied that his Cabinet would be made up of barroom politicians and old-time party hacks. It was said, for instance, that John Kelly would be appointed Secretary of the Treasury in return for the support which Tammany Hall had reluctantly given to Mr. Cleveland. Editorial writers let their imaginations run riot in suggesting other like appointments as not only possible but probable. At the North there were many who feared lest the results of the Civil War should be undone and lest the government of the United States should be given into the hands of " rebels." The negroes in the South were told that a Democratic President might seek to re-enslave them. Not a few timorous souls all over the country looked for immediate commercial panic and financial ruin.

In this respect, history was only repeating itself. Just

as the Federalists in 1801 had raised the cry that President Jefferson was an atheist, a satyr, a Jacobin, and an enemy to law and to the rights of property, and just as the Whigs,[1] in 1829 had thought to alarm the country by describing President Jackson as a gambler, murderer, and border ruffian, so Mr. Cleveland's accession to the presidency was declared to be the beginning of a political saturnalia. His brief inaugural address, however, surprised those persons who had thought of him as dull and as capable of nothing more than platitude. Not only was it dignified and wholly worthy of the occasion, but it contained more than one passage of grave and almost stately eloquence. The following sentences embody a spirit which will be found to have animated Mr. Cleveland's whole career of public service. It expresses the ideal principle of true democracy:

"But he who takes the oath to-day to preserve, protect, and defend the Constitution of the United States only assumes the solemn obligation which every patriotic citizen—on the farm, in the workshop, in the marts of trade, and everywhere—should share with him. The Constitution which prescribes his oath, my countrymen, is yours; the Government you have chosen him to administer for a time is yours; the suffrage which executes the will of freemen is yours; the laws and the entire scheme of our civil rule, from the town-meeting to the State capitals and the national capital, are yours. Your every voter, as surely as your Chief Magistrate, under the same high sanction, though in a different sphere, exercises a public trust. Nor is this all. Every citizen owes to the country a vigilant watch and close scrutiny of its public servants and a fair and reasonable estimate of their fidelity and usefulness. Thus is the people's will impressed upon the whole frame-work of

[1] The name "Whig" had not, however, yet come into general use by the party opposed to Jackson.

our civil polity—municipal, State, and Federal; and this is the price of our liberty and the inspiration of our faith in the Republic." [2]

At the close of the inaugural ceremonies, President Cleveland transmitted to the Senate the names of the men whom he had chosen to constitute his Cabinet. For Secretary of State he had selected Senator Thomas Francis Bayard of Delaware, a portly gentleman, who bore a name justly famous in American political history, since for five generations some member of the Bayard family had represented the State of Delaware in the national Senate, of which body Mr. Bayard himself had been temporary president in 1881. The new Secretary of War was Mr. William Crowninshield Endicott of Massachusetts, a very Brahmin of the Brahmins, being a descendant of John Endecott, who was one of the six gentlemen to whom the first royal patent for the Massachusetts Bay territory had been granted in 1628; and who was Colonial Governor in 1630 and 1664, and President of the United Colonies of New England in 1658. Mr. Endicott was a Harvard graduate, a lawyer of ability, and had served for ten years as a Justice of the Supreme Court of Massachusetts. He had taken an active part in political life and was an earnest advocate of reform in the Civil Service. For Secretary of the Navy, the President nominated Mr. William C. Whitney of New York. Mr. Whitney was sprung from old New England stock. Educated at Yale and Harvard, he had engaged in the practice of the law, and in 1871 had done effective work in destroying the Tweed Ring. Mr. Whitney was a man of wealth, an enthusiastic sportsman, possessed of a winning personality, generous, popular, and

---

[2] Quotations from presidential messages, inaugural addresses, and proclamations follow the text given in *Messages and Papers of the Presidents,* officially compiled by J. D. Richardson, 10 vols. (Washington, 1900).

widely known. He was also a most astute politician and had conducted Mr. Cleveland's campaign in New York with consummate skill.

Mr. Daniel Manning, of New York, received the Treasury portfolio, although usage was against giving two Cabinet offices to citizens of the same State. Mr. Manning had been better known as an active party manager than as a financier. He had been Mr. Tilden's trusted lieutenant, and had shown himself to be adroit and full of resource. He was the head of an important bank in Albany, and was soon to prove himself no less able in dealing with large financial problems than he had been fertile in political strategy. For Secretary of the Interior, the President named Senator L. Q. C. Lamar of Mississippi. Senator Lamar had drafted the ordinance of secession at the Mississippi Convention of 1861, and had served in the Confederate army for two years, and as Judge Advocate for a few months. He had, however, accepted the results of the war with frankness and sincerity, and was known to be as liberal-minded and patriotic as he was liked and respected.[3] Senator Lamar had the tastes of a scholar. He was fond of books and of philosophical researches, and was an admirable type of the

---

[3] An instance of his political liberality is to be found in the address made by Mr. Lamar in the Senate of the United States upon the occasion of Senator Sumner's death in 1874. Sumner was still an object of general detestation in the South, yet Senator Lamar had the courage to say of him:

"It was my misfortune, perhaps my fault personally, never to have known this eminent philanthropist and statesman. The impulse was often strong upon me to go to him and offer him my hand, and my heart with it, and to express to him my thanks for his kind and considerate course toward the people with whom I am identified. If I did not yield to that impulse, it was because the thought occurred that other days were coming in which such a demonstration might be more opportune and less

cultivated Southern gentleman. The new Attorney-General was Senator Augustus H. Garland of Arkansas, who had opposed secession in 1861, though subsequently he had been a member of the Confederate Congress, and later, after the war ended, Governor of Arkansas. President Cleveland chose for the office of Postmaster-General, Colonel William F. Vilas of Wisconsin, a Union soldier who had fought under Grant at Vicksburg. During the campaign he had served as chairman of the Democratic National Committee.

Altogether, the new Cabinet was one against which no reasonable criticism could be brought. More than that, it was a very remarkable body of administrators. For personal distinction it had had few, if any, superiors in the whole history of the Government. For ability it had not been equalled since the days of President Lincoln. Those deluded partisans who expected the new President to surround himself with a group of henchmen, unknown or only too well known, were put to silence. Those who had looked for a government of ex-Confederates had naught to say. There was even some significance in the fact that President Cleveland's first official act after making his Cabinet nominations, was to sign the commission of Ulysses S. Grant, restoring that illustrious but now impoverished soldier to the retired list of the army with the rank and pay of General.

Fortune soon gave the President a chance to show that in dealing with the foreign relations of the United States he could act with admirable energy and decision. Only a

liable to misconstruction. Suddenly and without premonition, a day has come at last to which, for such a purpose, there is no to-morrow. My regret is therefore intensified by the thought that I failed to speak to him out of the fulness of my heart while there was yet time."

few days after his inauguration, a revolt broke out upon the Isthmus of Panama, headed by a local incendiary named Pedro Prestan. Prestan raised a motley force, proclaimed a revolutionary government, took the City of Aspinwall (now Colon), levied contributions on the merchants, both native and foreign, and threatened to take possession of the Isthmian railway. Growing bolder, he seized an American steamship, the *Colon,* and imprisoned her officers. The United States Consul, who protested, was thrown into a dungeon (March 31). President Cleveland took instant action. Five vessels of war were ordered to the Isthmus. A strong body of marines, with Gatling guns and a battery of light artillery, were landed; and the armed forces of the United States soon held the whole line of the Panama railway. The *Colon* was taken from Prestan under the guns of the cruiser *Galena,* and his prisoners were rescued. The revolt collapsed. Colombian troops retook the city of Aspinwall, and Prestan himself was promptly hanged as a common malefactor. Not long after the South American republic of Ecuador received a needed lesson. The government of that country had imprisoned one Julio Santos, an American citizen, and had refused either to release him or to bring him to trial. President Arthur's Secretary of State had again and again protested, but in vain. President Cleveland took up the case with a sharp decisiveness which gave the Ecuadorians a shock. A man-of-war, the *Iroquois,* appeared at Guayaquil. A peremptory demand was made; and Mr. Santos was promptly set at liberty.

The country viewed with interest still another proof of the administration's capacity for action. In 1882, Congress had passed the so-called Edmunds Anti-Polygamy Bill, aimed against the plural marriages of Mormonism.

The enforcement of this law had greatly irritated the leaders of the Mormon Church, who had always secretly regarded Utah as outside the jurisdiction of the nation's laws. Perhaps they now accepted the Republican estimate of President Cleveland, and fancied that he would prove to be a second Buchanan, nerveless and irresolute. At any rate, the Mormons in Salt Lake City began to show a spirit of insolence and insubordination. Armed companies of them were formed and drilled by night. On the Fourth of July, the national flag was half-masted in derision by a Mormon officer. Threats were made that all Gentiles were to be forcibly expelled from Salt Lake City in defiance of the national Government. If such a *coup* had actually been planned, it was speedily made impossible. By orders from Washington, two batteries of United States artillery and a regiment of infantry were stationed at Fort Douglas, which dominated the city; and in the Military Department which included Utah, two thousand regular troops were held in readiness for instant service. Whatever plans for a Mormon outbreak had existed were crushed before they reached a head.

All these circumstances attending the early days of Mr. Cleveland's administration gave the country at large an entirely new conception of the President and of his capacity for government. Moderate Republicans recognised the fact that he well deserved the full measure of their respect. Partisans who hoped that he would justify the unfavourable pictures which they had diligently painted, were compelled to wait in sullen silence for some future opportunity of censure. The governmental departments were most efficiently conducted.[4] The country remained

[4] The only serious attempt by the Opposition to discredit a member of the Cabinet was directed against Attorney-General Garland in the matter

as prosperous as ever. The awful panic which had been predicted proved to be only another fiction of the campaign orators. Moreover, Republicans who had occasion to make the new President's acquaintance came away with nothing but pleasant words for his easy, unaffected and good-humoured ways. It was not many weeks, indeed, before Mr. Blaine himself appeared at the White House, to make a friendly call upon his late opponent. He was received with the greatest courtesy, and the two men chatted pleasantly together in the President's library. One of the unwritten laws of American public life permits a defeated candidate for the presidency to ask a political favour of his successful competitor, and Mr. Blaine desired to avail himself of this gracious little privilege. He requested the President not to remove from office Mr. Joseph H. Manley, who was postmaster at Augusta, Mr. Blaine's home city. Mr. Manley was an old friend and earnest supporter of Mr. Blaine, and the President very cordially granted the request, after which the interview terminated with every evidence of personal good feeling.[5] Some time after, a visiting delegation at the White House was found to

of the so-called Pan-Electric Scandal. Mr. Garland held stock in the Pan-Electric Company which owned a patent of which the Bell telephone was alleged to be an infringement. If this claim were sustained, the value of the Pan-Electric stock would be very great. Mr. Garland permitted the Solicitor-General to institute proceedings impugning the validity of the Bell patent. The Republicans charged Mr. Garland with an attempt to enrich himself by using the resources of his department for personal ends; though the decision of the case rested, of course, with the court and not with Mr. Garland or his Solicitor-General. A congressional committee afterwards exonerated both these gentlemen.

[5] President Cleveland showed another and more marked instance of courtesy to Mr. Blaine. A Democrat who had been appointed postmaster at Copiah, Mississippi, was found to have published a particularly offensive personal attack upon Mr. Blaine. When the facts became known to President Cleveland, he dismissed the man from office.

include among its members the redoubtable Dr. Burchard himself; and a smothered cheer went up, with not a little laughter, when the alliterative clergyman shook the President's hand and expressed his pleasure at finding him in such good health. Altogether, these days afforded as near an approach to an era of good feeling as Mr. Cleveland ever enjoyed throughout his years of public office. They represented the lull in political warfare that always follows an election in which passion has for the time exhausted itself and kindly feeling has resumed its normal sway. Americans are proverbially the best-natured people in the world; and in the case of a new President, they always feel disposed to let him orient himself before the din of party strife begins again.

Few Presidents have ever lived so completely under the microscope as did Mr. Cleveland during his first two years of office. That his countrymen should feel an intense curiosity regarding him was only natural. He had come so suddenly into prominence that, at the time of the election, he was scarcely known outside of his own State. To millions of those who had voted for him he was only a name and not a definite personality, as was Mr. Blaine, who had been conspicuous in public life for more than twenty years. Again, the very violence of the attacks that had been made upon him excited a lively interest in his ways and manners. Finally, he was a Democratic President, and no Democratic President had been seen for a quarter of a century. No wonder, then, that the Washington newspaper correspondents filled their letters with gossip about his goings and comings, his appearance, his opinions, and his daily acts. The slightest scrap of information regarding him was eagerly caught up and told and retold to interested listeners. In this universal curiosity, there was almost no unfriendliness. It was the expression of a very human wish to know just what manner of man it was who had so suddenly and unexpectedly come into the very highest office in the land.

Mr. Cleveland at this time was forty-seven years of age and in the full vigour of life. Somewhat over the middle height, he was powerful of frame, inclined to corpulency, and of a sanguineous temperament. Contrary to the unfriendly descriptions that had been widely circulated, his head was large and was well set upon a sturdy neck. A broad forehead projected slightly over a pair of deep-set clear blue eyes. His nose and chin were both indicative of a strong will, as were the firm lines of his mouth, which was partly covered by a drooping blond moustache. His complexion was ruddy with health, his broad shoulders were always vigorously squared, and he looked like one whom no amount of hard, exacting work could daunt. In his movements he was slow and almost sluggish, but the alertness of his mind impressed all who met him. His manner was one of perfect naturalness and simplicity. Now and then, in talking, a humorous gleam came into his eyes; and then one might expect some droll though dry remark, made more effective by the quiet manner of its delivery. His voice was of a tenor quality, not resonant or sonorous, yet one which had remarkable carrying power, so that in public speaking he could be clearly heard at a considerable distance. Those who made their first acquaintance with him at this time were almost always pleased, and were perhaps surprised to find that they were pleased. One of these visitors [6] who afterwards became a strenuous opponent of the President's policies, wrote of him:

[6] Mr. Henry Watterson.

" There is more to the President than even his friends are wont to allow; and he gains rather than loses on acquaintance. He has a deal of craft of the wiser and better sort, and needs only a little more training to foot it with the shrewdest of the politicians whom he affects to despise. He is a good listener and a good talker. His most obvious characteristics are straightforwardness and simplicity, both in speech and bearing. He seems to be extraordinarily frank. But to a close observer these appear to be outer aspects merely. He is not a man of confidences or effusions, is uncommonly self-possessed and self-contained, and emits on occasion a tough, dry humour, ready, relevant and illustrative."

Mr. Cleveland had a colossal capacity for work. He rose early and was at his desk by nine o'clock. He gave a close personal attention to details, wrote a good part of his correspondence with his own hand, and never spared himself in his endeavour to get at the bottom of every subject which came before him. He took nothing for granted, but delved into reports, documents and letters until he satisfied himself that he had mastered the case, as a lawyer masters a brief. The observer who has just been quoted wrote: " He is a wondrous worker. He has the poor man's love of work and trust in work. He wants to earn his day's wages; and there are some things which a President must do and ought to do which go against the grain, because they seem frivolous, belonging rather to play than to work." A keen but not unfriendly Republican critic [7] made some further interesting notes:

" Cleveland gets his power from his resoluteness. He is a self-contained, honest man, with strong indignations. He hates a liar and will not let down his attitude of self-respect to please somebody whom he does not like. His intellectual repulsions are de-

[7] G. A. Townsend in the *Cincinnati Enquirer*, March 25, 1885.

cided and irrevocable. The President gives more time to his office than is due to it, and he exacts of the subordinates that they give at least official hours to their tasks. Consequently, the Government at present carries less time-killers and triflers than formerly. His greatest happiness he probably derives from his own rough self-assertion and from his luck in reaching high stations in politics without much labour. . . . He comes of a fortunate stock. The old blood of Connecticut is about the best blood for government uses that we possess. Cleveland's personal composition is this old Connecticut basis somewhat flavoured by free living. He belongs to that class of preachers' sons who, for a period of time, fly the track and violate their parents' ethics, yet at bottom have a certain ethical truth, and are slightly harsh with infractions and infractors of rights. He observed that the Germans of Buffalo were, on the whole, about the best citizens; and he was happy sitting on a sanded floor with an old German landlady to refill his glass. Something of Martin Luther, therefore, became involved with the character of Jonathan Trumbull. . . . Nothing that has come from him seems to show that he is an adept in society, or art, or law, or literature. He is a pretty good writer as Presidents go, and makes his points concisely and impressively. Of imagination he seems to have none. But he is a good, stout, rough man-of-all-work who puts the establishment in running order and is as good as a watch-dog at the gate."

The domestic side of the White House was directed by the President's sister, Miss Rose Elizabeth Cleveland, whose personality interested the country almost as much as did that of the President himself. Miss Cleveland was then a lady of some thirty-nine years of age, who had been a teacher and a public lecturer on literary and historical subjects. She was a type of the *intellectuelle,* very carefully educated, very widely read, and a good deal of a personage in her way. She wore her hair cropped like a man's and had a touch of masculine decision in her bearing.

During her stay at the White House, she published a volume of criticism entitled *George Eliot's Poetry and Other Studies*,[8] that had a good deal of vogue, which it deserved on its own merits, for it was written in a crisp, nervous style and showed a good deal of intellectual acuteness.[9] Miss Cleveland did the social honours of the White House in a very satisfactory way, though her own tastes and ambitions were not social. She talked well, and very much as she wrote. In fact, her conversation must have seemed rather unusual to many of those who heard it, for it was decidedly allusive and was interspersed with classical quotations that were probably Greek indeed to the politicians who attended the President's receptions with their families. One can imagine with what feelings a group of typical Congressmen's wives would hear Miss Cleveland casually remark: " I wish that I could observe Washington life in its political phase; but I suppose I am too near the

[8] New York, 1886.

[9] The book went through twelve editions within a year, and Miss Cleveland was said to have received more than $25,000 in royalties. An English reviewer in the London *Times* wrote of it as follows:

" Miss Cleveland is far from being a deep and subtle thinker, but her sketches prove that she possesses the love of letters and history as well as an average power of expressing her views thereon. If there is now and then a feminine positiveness in her judgments we must condone it on the ground of her enthusiasm. The essays furnish pleasant reading enough, but scarcely anything more. Miss Cleveland· is extremely fond of quotations from the poets, but that is no reason why, in a comparatively small volume, a quotation from Longfellow should appear three times, with a serious difference between two of the versions. The inaccuracy of one passage quoted from Shakespeare is almost heartrending. The author gives it as follows: ' All the world's a stage, *and men and women are the actors*.' As though Shakespeare could have written the halting and unpoetical phrase printed in italics! There are several fairly interesting historical essays—studies in the Middle Ages—but Miss Cleveland's style is not one which would be appreciated by everybody."

centre to get an accurate perspective on that. Those who live on Mount Athos do not see Mount Athos." [10]

The first annoyance which the President was forced to suffer came, not from his political opponents, but from his own followers. The Democrats, no less than the Republicans, had found many of their expectations unfulfilled. There were two reasons for this, with one of which the President had nothing at all to do. Ever since the disputed election of 1876, a sinister belief had taken a firm hold upon the masses of the party. The desperation with which, in the year just named, the Republicans had fought to keep the presidency in their own hands had inspired a suspicion that something more than the mere spoils of office was at stake. Men then said that there were secrets which, if known, would show a frightful condition of affairs in the great departments of the Government, and especially in connection with the Treasury. It was whispered that the Republican party stood ready to initiate even a civil war rather than allow a Democratic President to be seated, with the power of bringing to light a mass of infamous transactions by which untold millions had been stolen. One of the documents most widely circulated by the Democrats in the Blaine-Cleveland contest was a pamphlet bearing on its cover in huge letters the words, " OPEN THE BOOKS! " It charged that the financial records of the Government had been falsified; that in the ledgers of the Registrar of the United States and the Secretary of the Treasury more than 2500 erasures and alterations had been fraudulently made; and that the official reports for two years alone (1870 and 1871) showed a discrepancy amounting to nearly a quarter of a billion dollars. A list of alleged defalcations was appended—affecting

[10] Poore, *Reminiscences of Sixty Years,* ii. p. 502 (Philadelphia 1886).

specifically the Pension Office, the Navy Department, the Post Office Department, and the Treasury. These charges were in part supported by extracts from the testimony taken by investigating committees of the House of Representatives in 1878, and by citations from official letters and reports. Mr. Hendricks, on July 12, 1884, addressing a large gathering in Indianapolis, had said with significant emphasis: "We want to have the books in the government offices opened for examination."

Among the ignorant stories still more extraordinary were rife. The Garfield-Hancock campaign of 1880 had been marked by a lavish use of money on the part of the Republicans, especially in Indiana. This money had, for the most part, come from the employés of the government departments, who had practically been forced to contribute through fear of dismissal.[11] But the rumour spread that the great sums spent in the purchase of venal voters had in reality come out of the United States Treasury. There were men who declared that the government printing-presses had, in 1880, been run all night, printing off sheets of treasury-notes of low denominations, and that the paper money thus fraudulently and secretly made had been turned over to the Republican campaign committee. It is odd that so absurd a tale should have been told, and still more strange that thousands should have implicitly believed it. But the fact serves to indicate how thoroughly convinced were the masses of the Democratic party that the new administration would at once unearth evi-

[11] Mr. Garfield himself, while a candidate, had written a note to Mr. J. C. Hubbell, who was chairman of the Republican National Committee, in which he said, among other things: "Please tell me how the departments generally are doing." This letter, which is known as the "My Dear Hubbell letter," was published later by one Brady who was implicated in the Star Route postal frauds.

dence of stupendous crimes committed during the long
Republican régime.

Of course, in this they were speedily undeceived. No
one who really understands the manner in which the Government is conducted could ever credit such impossible
assertions. The party in power does not try to conceal its
public acts from the leaders of the Opposition; and
the committees of Congress, made up of members of
both parties, are thoroughly informed of whatever hap-
pens. Indeed, the old and experienced party leaders in
both House and Senate work harmoniously enough
together in matters of administrative detail. They battle
fiercely in view of the galleries; but in the committee-rooms
they arrange matters with an eye to the general needs of
the public service, and with the sensible purpose of seeing
the Government properly carried on. Whenever a zealous
but inexperienced young member tries to make a stir upon
his own account, and to attack those measures which have
been arranged by his seniors, he is quietly suppressed by
the chiefs of his own party, and the business of the Government goes on unvexed.

And therefore, naturally enough, the so-called discrep-
ancies in the Treasury reports were found to be due simply
to varying modes of book-keeping; the awful revelations that had been looked for were never made; and with
a single exception, there was no real ground for an attack
upon the manner in which the Republicans had discharged
their trust. Even the figures published by the Democrats
themselves showed that the public service had been steadily improving in honesty and efficiency for many years.
Thus, during the first term of President Grant (1869-
1873), when the loose and careless methods of the Civil
War still partially prevailed, the Government had lost by

defalcations and in other irregular ways the sum of
$8,875,483. During his second term (1873-1877), how-
ever, this loss showed a diminution of nearly 50 per cent.,
being $4,547,247. Under President Hayes (1877-1881)
the amount had fallen to $1,775,996, and under Presidents
Garfield and Arthur (1881-1885), to $1,569,733. The
Democrats found nothing here to justify their dark sus-
picions and provide them with weapons for party use.

One department alone had been disgracefully misman-
aged, though of the fact the whole nation had long been
unpleasantly aware. This was the Navy Department.
Under President Grant, the Secretary of the Navy from
1869 to 1877, had been the notorious George M. Robeson of New Jersey, a man whose inefficiency and gross
neglect—to use no harsher term—had practically destroyed the fleets which at the close of the Civil War had
been the most formidable in the world. Robeson had
spent millions upon what he called " repairs "—these repairs sometimes costing more than the original value of
the ships repaired, and even then serving only to perpetuate types of vessels which had become obsolete and worthless in the face of naval progress in other countries. Secretary Whitney's first report summed the matter up with
terse impressiveness:

" The country has expended since July 1, 1868—more than
three years subsequent to the close of the late Civil War—over
$75,000,000 of money on the construction, repair, equipment, and
ordnance of vessels, which sum, with a very slight exception, has
been substantially thrown away; the exception being a few ships
now in process of construction. I do not overlook the sloops constructed in 1874, and costing $3,000,000 or $4,000,000, and to
avoid discussion they may be excepted also. The fact still remains
that for about seventy of the seventy-five millions of dollars which

have been expended by the Department for the creation of a navy, we have practically nothing to show. It is questionable whether we have a single naval vessel finished and afloat at the present time that could be trusted to encounter the ships of any important Power —a single vessel that has either the necessary armour for protection, speed for escape, or weapons for defence."

This, however, was an old scandal and related more especially to the days when Grant was President. Under President Arthur, there had been instituted a better order of things, and, consequently, political capital was not to be found in the condition of the navy.

The really serious grievance which many Democrats began to entertain arose from President Cleveland's position regarding the distribution of the public offices. At the time of his inauguration there were 52,609 ordinary postmasterships, 2379 so-called "presidential" postmasterships, 111 collectorships of customs, 224 places in the local land-offices, and 34 important diplomatic posts, besides scores of consulships, appraiserships, Indian agencies, pension agencies, territorial governorships and judgeships, positions in the revenue service, surveyorships, and superintendencies, many having attached to them a certain amount of petty patronage. Almost every one of these offices, some 110,000 in all, was occupied by a Republican. To secure them and to enjoy their emoluments was the hope of thousands upon thousands of Democratic party "workers," who now swarmed like locusts in the streets of Washington and besieged the governmental bureaus and the portals of the White House. Even when a Republican President had succeeded one of his own party, an invasion of office-seekers had invariably followed. New Congressmen always demanded changes in their districts;

members of the President's own faction always asked for removals and new appointments; party rivals had always to be propitiated. But if this had been true in the case of an ordinary change of administration, it can be imagined how enormous was the pressure for recognition now that not only had the administration been changed, but that a party which had been out of power for a quarter of a century had resumed control. President Cleveland, in fact, was in the same position as that occupied by Mr. Lincoln in 1861, when a critical observer, after visiting Washington, thus wrote home: "The nation is going to pieces; States are seceding; utter ruin is at hand; and here is Lincoln thinking of nothing except who shall be appointed postmaster in some little town, or gauger in some little port."

Every successive President had felt the annoyance of a system such as this, and would have been infinitely relieved could the burden of it have been lightened. A practical remedy was the institution of such a reform in the appointment system as would protect the President from incessant importunity. In 1867, a report had been made to the House of Representatives [12] recommending that a large class of appointments should be regarded as non-political and hence to be made upon the basis of competitive examinations and with fixity of tenure conditioned upon meritorious service. In 1871, Congress authorised the President to appoint a Civil Service Commission and to approve such rules as it might make for admission to government employ. This measure had the support of President Grant, who appointed the first Commission, of which Mr. George William Curtis was Chairman. But public sentiment, or at any rate party sentiment, was not yet ripe for a reform like this. All the influential party

[12] By Mr. Jenckes of Rhode Island.

leaders on both sides despised it, and it was contemptuously spoken of as " snivel-service reform." From 1872 to 1875, the rules made by the first Commission remained in force; but President Grant could not withstand the pressure brought to bear upon him; and so, somewhat reluctantly, he suspended their operation. After the assassination of President Garfield by a disappointed office-seeker in 1882, both houses of Congress enacted a law, usually known as the Pendleton Law,[13] which thoroughly satisfied the civil service reformers. This empowered the President to prescribe by executive order what classes of the public service should come under the operation of the merit system as framed by a new Civil Service Commission. Under President Arthur, some 14,000 government employés were brought within the so-called classified service.[14]

Mr. Cleveland was thoroughly in sympathy with the principle of this reform. In his letter of acceptance, (August 19, 1884) he had said:

" The selection and retention of subordinates in government employment should depend upon their ascertained fitness and the value of their work, and they should be neither expected nor allowed to do questionable party service."

This and other like declarations had done much to attract independent voters to Mr. Cleveland's side. After his election and before his inauguration, a number of these Independents addressed to him a letter asking his inten-

[13] From Senator George H. Pendleton of Ohio, a Democrat, who introduced it in the Senate.

[14] For an account of the movement for a reform of the Civil Service of the United States, see the Reports of the American Civil Service Reform Association.

tions with regard to Civil Service Reform. Replying to them (December 20, 1884), Mr. Cleveland wrote some very significant sentences, in which may be found an explanation of his subsequent course. They give evidence that he had already formulated very carefully a definite policy. After reiterating his former promise to uphold the Civil Service Law, he went on to say:

" I regard myself pledged to this because my conception of true Democratic faith and public duty requires that this and all other statutes should be, in good faith and without evasion, enforced, and because, in many utterances made prior to my election as President, approved by the party to which I belong and which I have no disposition to disclaim, I have in effect promised the people that this should be done."

Another paragraph shows that he did not underrate the difficulty of carrying out his pledge.

" I am not unmindful of the fact to which you refer, that many of our citizens fear that the recent party change in the national Executive may demonstrate that the abuses which have grown up in the Civil Service are ineradicable. I know that they are deeply rooted, and that the spoils system has been supposed to be intimately related to success in the maintenance of party organisation; and I am not sure that all those who profess to be the friends of this reform will stand firmly among its advocates when they find it obstructing their way to patronage and place."

A very important sentence, in the light of what afterwards happened, is the following:

" There is a class of government positions which are not within the letter of the civil service statute, but which are so disconnected with the policy of an administration that the removal therefrom of present incumbents, in my opinion, should not be made during the terms for which they were appointed, solely on partisan grounds, and for the purpose of putting in their places those who are in political accord with the appointing power; but many men holding such positions have forfeited all just claim to retention because they have used their places for party purposes in disregard of their duty to the people, and because, instead of being decent public servants, they have proved themselves offensive partisans and unscrupulous manipulators of local party management."

One sentence was obviously meant for Democratic perusal:

" While Democrats may expect a proper consideration, selections for office not embraced within the Civil Service rules will be based upon sufficient inquiry as to fitness, rather than upon persistent importunity or self-solicited recommendations on behalf of candidates for appointment."

One may add to these utterances a passage from a letter of his (September 11, 1885) to Mr. Dorman B. Eaton, a conspicuous civil service reformer:

" A reasonable toleration for old prejudices, a graceful recognition of every aid, a sensible utilisation of every instrumentality that promises assistance, and a constant effort to demonstrate the advantages of the new order of things, are the means by which this reform movement will in the future be further advanced."

By putting all these statements together, President Cleveland's policy in regard to appointments was clear enough for any one to understand. In the first place, he did not intend to reform the Civil Service over night, as some of the Independent doctrinaires expected him to do. In the second place, he did not intend to sweep all Republicans out of office before the expiration of their terms and without regard to the merit of the service which they had rendered. What he did mean to do was gradually to extend the operation of the Civil Service rules; and in the meantime, in filling vacancies with Democrats, to exact from them a reasonable standard of character and efficiency. This was a very sensible and very practical programme. It was certain, however, to subject him to a three-cornered attack—first, from the advanced reformers, who were impatient of all delay; second, from the Democrats, who had expected immediately to monopolise all the offices in the President's gift; and third, from his Republican adversaries, who were bound to find fault with him, whatever he might do.

Mr. Cleveland had a vigorous contempt for professional office-seekers,[15] and he had no mind to be subjected to their importunities. When approached by them he could make himself extremely disagreeable. He had two separate and distinct manners of showing his displeasure, either one of which was quite effectual. At times he would become ab-

[15] In 1885, while Governor, he had written to a young man a letter which contained the following sentences: "I judge from what you write that you now have a situation in a reputable business house. I can not urge you too strongly to give up all idea of employment in a public office, and to determine to win advancement and promotion where you are.

"There are no persons so forlorn and so much to be pitied as those who have learned, in early life, to look to public positions for a livelihood. It unfits a man or boy for any other business, and is apt to make a kind of respectable vagrant of him. If you do well in other occupations, and thus become valuable to the people, they will find you out when they want a good man for public service. I never sought an office of any kind in my life; and, if you live and follow my advice, I am certain that you will thank me for it some day."—Parker, *Writings and Speeches of Grover Cleveland*, pp. 337, 338 (New York, 1892).

solutely glacial. At other times his face would flush and he would pound the table with his clenched fist and give voice, with vigorous expletives, to an expression of his inflexible purpose. Some of his visitors who came on political errands found him anything but tractable. A somewhat rueful anecdote, ascribed to Mr. Henry Watterson,[16] may be cited as wholly characteristic of both men:

"We chatted and joked and laughed and were on terms of the most agreeable comradeship. I don't know what the President thought of me, but I marked him in my mental tablet as a splendid companion and a very jolly good fellow. After an hour pleasantly spent in the personal enjoyment of each other, and when the laughter had subsided that followed a story by the President, I thought it would be a good time to mention a little matter in which I felt interested. As soon as I began the recital, I could see the process of congelation; and before I had half finished my story, the President was a monumental icicle. I became so thoroughly chilled that I broke off, took up my hat and said, 'Good-night, Mr. President.' That's the kind of a good fellow Cleveland is."

Mr. Joaquin Miller, the poet, also had a little interview with the President, of which he subsequently published an account in the Chicago *Times*:

Here is my first interview, which I dotted down a few minutes after: "Mr. President, I—I—I want Captain Hoxie to be returned to Washington so as to complete our water-works." "Captain Hoxie," answered the President instantly, "is subject to the orders of the Secretary of War"—and he looked at me as if to say, "And you know it." Yes, I knew I had come to the wrong place and was boring the President and bothering for nothing, much as I had the matter at heart. So I gave up that subject and started on another equally important. "Mr. President, one thing more. I hear you are going to remove Commis-

[16] Philadelphia *Ledger*.

sioner Edmunds, the head of our Commissioners for Washington, and I—I——" The President looked hard at me and said promptly: "You have heard that! Well, I have not heard of it, and as I shall have to hear of it before he is removed, you can rest easy on that score for the present." By this time I felt that I had not the slightest business with the President, and so fell in with the band of shorn sheep that was passing on and out of the corral by another door.

Naturally, the expectant Democrats could not all at once believe that Mr. Cleveland really meant to carry out his pledges. The cynical assumption that political promises are made only to be broken, and that Jove laughs at statesmen's vows no less good-naturedly than at those of lovers, was firmly fixed in all their minds. Of course, the President had a little fad in the matter of the Civil Service. Of course, he really meant what he had said. But equally, of course, he would give way and thus make things more easy for himself. All other Presidents had done so. It was merely a question of bringing enough pressure to bear upon him. And so, thousands of place-hunters lingered in Washington, wasting their time, and depleting their resources, while they waited for the necessary "pressure" to be applied. But as the weeks slipped away, it gradually dawned upon them that here was a President who could not be coaxed or driven or coerced. His Cabinet officers were beset by Congressmen and local leaders from all over the country; but they were just as helpless as the rest. The one great hope of the famished Democrats rested in Vice-President Hendricks. He was a Western politician of the older type—a thorough partisan, narrow, intense, not squeamish about reforms, but a firm believer in Marcy's doctrine that in politics, as in war, the spoils belong of right to the victorious. Urged on by the almost frantic appeals that were made to him each hour of the day, Mr. Hendricks had a protracted interview with the President. Just what took place between them no one knows; but Mr. Hendricks came away with a long face; and the word was quickly passed that even he had failed.

All this soon placed the President in a new light before the country. It is rather remarkable that the lesson of his firmness while Governor of New York had made no real impression elsewhere. After his election to the Presidency and before he entered upon the duties of his office, speculation had been rife as to who would control the new administration. A writer whose identity was kept secret, but who aspired to be a·second Junius, had addressed to the President-elect a series of very bitter letters which were afterward collected and published in a book.[17]

These letters are very curious reading now; for they show how little Mr. Cleveland's character was understood at the time when they were written. They take it for granted that the President will be " a pigmy among giants." " It must move the heart of your most malevolent enemy to note with what a beggarly stock in trade you will open business in the White House." " You know that you have nothing to expect after the term which will so soon begin. You would like to float through its four years, softly and easily." " You are well aware that in your political career, you have been a pawn in the hands of stronger men." This was only what many persons had thought; but Mr. Cleveland had not been in office a week before his absolute mastery began to be understood. After his first Cabinet meeting had adjourned, a leading politician asked one of the Secretaries:

[17] Siva, *A Man of Destiny* (Chicago, 1885).

" Well, who is running things? " To which the reply was made with a significant shrug:

" Where MacGregor sits, there is the head of the table. You may be sure of that! "

It was, in fact, the same in Washington as it had been in Albany. There was no divided responsibility, no kitchen cabinet. Whatever blame and whatever praise the administration might receive, the President was entitled to them both. Mr. Watterson wrote of him: " We have at this moment as personal a government as we had under Grant."

That Mr. Cleveland had some of the defects of his qualities began also to appear. It was not sufficient for him to exercise the power which he possessed. He seemed almost morbidly desirous of impressing upon every one the fact that he alone was exercising it. Because it had been said that he would be a puppet, he thought it necessary to deal inconsiderately with those who were supposed to manage him. In this there was at times a touch of quite unnecessary arrogance. Thus, because Vice-President Hendricks had been credited with ability superior to the President's, Mr. Cleveland was never cordial to him. Because Secretary Manning was one of the men who had helped to make Mr. Cleveland both Governor and President, he found a personal enemy appointed postmaster in his home city of Albany. Mr. Tilden, who might have had the nomination in 1884 had he not declined it in advance, wrote to the President and asked for the appointment of Mr. Smith M. Weed as Collector for the Port of New York. He was met with a flat refusal. Mr. Cleveland's enemies called this sort of thing a jealousy of greater men; a fairer judgment would perhaps call it a jealousy of his own independence. But in any case, it caused bad feeling and added to the dissatisfaction excited by his failure to appoint more Democrats to office. Party discontent became outspoken. Men recalled the saying of John Kelly to Mr. Hendricks before the election: "Cleveland is no Democrat. If elected, he will prove a traitor to his party." Mr. Hendricks himself observed: "I had hoped that Mr. Cleveland would put the Democratic party into power in fact as well as in name." Senator Vance of North Carolina declared: "The President is not of my school of Democracy. We differ as widely as it is possible for two persons belonging to the same political party to differ." Senator Pugh of Alabama denounced the President's course in terms both metaphorical and profane. The newspapers, especially in the South and West, began openly to attack the President. Some of them advocated reading him out of the party altogether. "Brand President Cleveland traitor and kick him out of the party!" cried an Alabama editor. The rage of the disappointed office-hunters even found expression in verse. One hitherto mute, inglorious poet of the West got a wide hearing through some lines whose sincerity of feeling was more obvious than their elegance of diction:

> "A Democrat fool who serves as a tool
>   The men of his party to beat,
> Deserves to be thrashed and have his head mashed,
>   And kicked out into the street.

> "'Tis better to vote for some billy goat,
>   That butts for his corn and his hay,
> Than to vote for a man that has not the sand
>   To stand by his party a day!"

Of course it was inevitable that the President should have many offices to fill. The terms of thousands of Republican incumbents expired, and the places were given to Democratic successors. Other Republicans were summarily removed, presumably because, in Mr. Cleveland's famous phrases, they had shown themselves to be " offensive partisans " and guilty of " pernicious activity " while holding public office. Within a year, some 8000 fourth-class postmasterships had been allotted to Democrats. Yet these changes seemed infrequent and slow to the army of those whom Mr. G. W. Curtis had styled " a hungry horde." The President, perhaps, moved a little more cautiously than he would otherwise have done had he not discovered that in many instances his confidence had been abused. Members of Congress, in whose judgment he had trusted, induced him to appoint men who soon turned out to be utterly unfit. Some of them had most unsavoury records. A few had even worn prison stripes. This was the sort of thing which a President of Mr. Cleveland's temper could not forgive, and he became suspicious of all persons who urged the claims of friends. Toward those who had deceived him, his attitude became brusque to a degree.

On one occasion, a prominent politician signed a request for the appointment of a certain individual to a judgeship in one of the Pacific States. The appointment was made and the new judge was almost immediately seen to be absolutely unfitted for the office. The politician wrote to Mr. Cleveland explaining that he had signed the petition " not for one moment believing the appointment was possible." In answer to this frank confession the President wrote the following letter,[18] which must have made its recipient writhe:

[18] Parker, *op. cit.*

EXECUTIVE MANSION,
Washington, August 1, 1885.

DEAR SIR:

I have read your letter with amazement and indignation. There is one—but one—mitigation to the perfidy which your letter discloses, and that is found in the fact you confess your share in it. The idea that this administration, pledged to give the people better officers and engaged in a hand-to-hand fight with the bad elements of both parties, should be betrayed by those who ought to be worthy of implicit trust, is atrocious, and such treason to the people and to the party ought to be punished by imprisonment.

Your confession comes too late to be of immediate use to the public service, and I can only say that, while this is not the first time I have been deceived and misled by lying and treacherous representations, you are the first one that has so frankly owned his grievous fault. If any comfort is to be extracted from this assurance you are welcome to it.

GROVER CLEVELAND.

A certain Senator on another occasion came to him to complain about his policy regarding appointments.

"What do you want me to do?" asked the President, interrupting him.

"Why, Mr. President, I should like to see you move more expeditiously in advancing the principles of the Democracy."

"Ah," said the President, with a flash of the eye, "I suppose you mean that I should appoint two horse-thieves a day, instead of one."

The extreme advocates of civil service reform, on the other hand, complained because so many changes had been made. One act of the Executive exasperated them beyond all measure. This was the designation of Mr. Eugene Higgins of Maryland to be Appointment Clerk in the

Treasury Department. Mr. Higgins was the *bête noire* of all reformers. He was a protégé of Senator Gorman, and was known to be a spoilsman of the purest water. The Maryland Civil Service Association at once protested in vigorous terms against his appointment and asked for his immediate removal. This protest was taken up by the Independents all over the country, and Mr. Higgins was denounced in terms of extravagant abuse. It was said that this one act of Mr. Cleveland's had destroyed all confidence in his professions. He was declared to have broken his pledges, to have betrayed the cause of civil service reform, and to have gone over wholly to the enemy. Mr. Higgins, however, was not removed, and the clamour of the Mugwumps continued unabated.

Meanwhile, the Republicans had remained quiescent. It amused them to see the new President so roundly berated by his own supporters. The Republican party leaders were biding their time, and were making a very careful study of the man whom they were presently to confront. Looking over the situation, the shrewdest of them thought it best to let things take their course. It seemed good policy for them not to play an obstructive part when Congress should assemble. They decided that a resort to promiscuous filibustering would prove in the end unpopular with the country. They were confident, however, that in time the President would make some serious mistake of which they might take immediate advantage. When Congress met in December, the watchword was passed along the Republican ranks: " Just wait awhile and then put Cleveland in a hole! "

A fortnight or so before the opening of the session the Vice-President, Mr. Hendricks, died at Indianapolis.[19]

[20] December 8th, 1885.

As Congress was not sitting, and as, in consequence, there was no President of the Senate, there existed no constitutional successor to the presidency should Mr. Cleveland die during the interval before Congress met. Therefore, he felt that he ought not to take the long journey necessary to attend the funeral at Indianapolis. Malicious persons saw in his absence on that occasion a confirmation of his alleged unfriendliness toward the deceased Vice-President; but the country in general commended his refusal to run even the slightest risk of bringing about a condition which would leave the Government without a head.

President Cleveland's first message to Congress [20] was a long and carefully written document, which was received with general approval, both in this country and abroad.[21] The recommendations which attracted most attention had to do with (1) the development of the Navy, which in its existing condition Mr. Cleveland characterised as merely " a shabby ornament to the Government "; (2) a reform of the land laws, which should prevent immense tracts of territory from being acquired by single individuals or great corporations; (3) a reduction of tariff duties upon " the imported necessaries of life "; and (4) an extension of the reform of the Civil Service. In making this last

[19] November 25, 1885.

[21] The London *Standard* (December 9th) said: " The message is temperate and dignified and goes far to justify Mr. Cleveland's election." The *Daily News* remarked: " President Cleveland's message seems to place him in true succession to the greater men who have occupied the Presidential chair, rather than to the late Democratic line. It is conceived in a most just and friendly spirit towards all foreign powers and contains no word to tickle the ears of American Jingoes. The message expresses a sentiment of international good will. It is equally wise and prudent on all domestic topics."

recommendation, however, there were a few lines intended as a rebuke to some of the President's over-zealous critics. He wrote:

"Civil service reform does not . . . require that those who in subordinate positions should fail in yielding their best service, or who are incompetent, should be retained simply because they are in place. The whining of a clerk discharged for indolence or incompetency, who, though he gained his place by the worst possible operations of the spoils system, suddenly discovers that he is entitled to protection under the sanction of civil service reform, represents an ideal no less absurd than the clamour of the applicant who claims the vacant position as his compensation for the most questionable party work."

But there was something else in the message which, though it attracted little general attention at the time, possessed, in view of what happened in succeeding years, an extraordinary significance. More than five pages of the message were devoted to the question of silver. By the so-called Bland-Allison Law, enacted February 28, 1878, it had been provided that the coinage of the silver dollar of $412\frac{1}{2}$ grains should be resumed. This dollar was made a legal tender for public and private debts, and a provision directed its compulsory coinage at the rate of not less than \$2,000,000 or more than \$4,000,000 per month. The Bland-Allison Bill was passed by a Democratic House and a Republican Senate. President Hayes vetoed it, and it was at once passed over his veto by heavy majorities. The message which Mr. Cleveland now sent to Congress asked earnest attention to the working of this law. He pointed out that silver had steadily fallen in intrinsic value; that a so-called bimetallic conference with European nations, for the purpose of establishing internationally a common ratio between gold and silver had failed; and that if the coinage of silver should be continued under the Bland-Allison Act, the hoarding of gold would presently begin. The following sentences from this portion of the message are well worth recalling:

"The desire to utilise the silver product of the country should not lead to a misuse or the perversion of this power. . . . Up to the present time only about 50,000,000 of the silver dollars so coined have actually found their way into circulation, leaving more than 165,000,000 in the possession of the Government. . . . Every month, two millions of gold in the public Treasury are paid out for two millions or more of silver dollars to be added to the idle mass already accumulated. If continued long enough, this operation will result in the substitution of silver for all the gold the Government owns applicable to its general purposes. . . . The nearer the period approaches when it [the Government] will be obliged to offer silver in payment of its obligations, the greater inducement there will be to hoard gold against depreciation in the value of silver, or for the purpose of speculating. This hoarding of gold has already begun. When the time comes that gold has been withdrawn from circulation, then will be apparent the difference between the real value of the silver dollar and a dollar in gold, and the two coins will part company. Gold . . . will be at a premium over silver; banks which have substituted gold for the deposits of their customers may pay them with silver bought with such gold, thus making a handsome profit; rich speculators will sell their hoarded gold to their neighbours who need it to liquidate their foreign debts, at a ruinous premium over silver, and the labouring men and women of the land, most defenseless of all, will find that the dollar received for the wage of their toil has sadly shrunk in its purchasing power."

Mr. Cleveland quoted the words uttered by Daniel Webster in the Senate in 1834:

" The very man of all others who has the deepest interest in a sound currency and who suffers most by mischievous legislation in money matters, is the man who earns his daily bread by his daily toil."

He then proceeded to recommend that the compulsory coinage of silver dollars directed by the Bland Act be suspended.

These striking sentences received but scant attention at the time. Far greater interest was felt in the possibility of a conflict between the Democratic President and the Republican Senate which now elected Senator John Sherman to be its President *pro tempore*, and which had a Republican majority of 6. The House was Democratic by a majority of 42. With this division of power, it was obvious that no party measures pure and simple could be enacted. The field, therefore, was left clear for party skirmishing. It was not long before the Republican majority in the Senate made its first move toward " putting Cleveland in a hole." As has already been explained, the President had removed or suspended a number of Republican officials, and had appointed Democrats in their stead. In so doing, he had not made public his reasons for removal or suspension, other than in the general statement that this action was for the good of the public service. The Republican Senators sought now to bring him to an explicit and detailed accounting. Whether he refused or whether he acceded to their wish, they hoped to have it appear that he had removed Republicans solely from partisan motives. In this way his professed regard for civil service reform would be discredited; his Independent supporters would be es-

tranged; and the President himself would appear somewhat in the light of a hypocrite.

The case of Mr. George M. Duskin was selected as a
suitable one upon which to make the fight. Mr. Duskin
had been United States District Attorney for the Southern
District of Alabama. On July 17th he had been suspended by Executive order and Mr. John D. Burnett had
been designated to perform the duties of the office in
Duskin's place. When Congress met, the President nominated Mr. Burnett for appointment as Duskin's successor.
The Senate passed a resolution requiring the Attorney-
General to send to it all the papers relating to Mr. Duskin's suspension. The Attorney-General, by order of the
President, informed the Senate that it was not considered
that the public interests would be promoted by so trans-
mitting these papers and other documents. Thereupon
the Judiciary Committee of the Senate passed a resolution
censuring the Attorney-General and, by inference, the
President. It was evidently intended to make a formal
demand upon the President himself for these papers. Senators of the United States have an exalted opinion of their
own dignity. They are fond of calling the Chamber to
which they belong " the most august deliberative body in
the world." They claimed, moreover, in 1886, that inasmuch as the assent of the Senate was required to confirm
the appointment of certain officers, these officers were not
subject to removal by the President without the Senate's
permission. This claim was based upon the so-called Tenure of Office Act, passed in 1867 during the conflict between Congress and President Johnson. To be sure, the
more stringent features of the Act had been stricken out
in 1869, when General Grant assumed the Presidency.
Nevertheless, the Senate felt that, between its own over-

powering greatness and its somewhat tenuous legal right, it could overawe a new and inexperienced President.

Mr. Cleveland, however, did not wait for the issue to be fully joined between the Executive and the Senate. Like a good general, he attacked boldly, before his opponents had fully matured their plans. On March 1, 1886, he sent a message to the Senate in which he took high ground. "It is by no means conceded," wrote he, "that the Senate has the right in any case to review the act of the Executive in removing or suspending a public officer." Then he declared that the Attorney-General had acted solely under Executive direction. He said that the papers relating to the Duskin case were not public documents.

"I regard the papers and documents withheld and addressed to me or intended for my use and action, purely unofficial and private . . . and having reference to the performance of a duty exclusively mine. . . . If I desired to take them into my custody I might do so with entire propriety, and if I saw fit to destroy them no one could complain.

"The requests and demands which by the score have for nearly three months been presented to the different Departments of the Government, whatever may be their form, have but one complexion. They assume the right of the Senate to sit in judgment upon the exercise of my exclusive discretion and executive function, for which I am solely responsible to the people from whom I have so lately received the sacred trust of office. My oath to support and defend the Constitution, my duty to the people who have chosen me to execute the powers of their great office and not to relinquish them, and my duty to the Chief Magistracy, which I must preserve unimpaired in all its dignity and vigour, compel me to refuse compliance with these demands."

The message ended with the following haughty sentence:

" Neither the discontent of party friends, nor the allurements constantly offered of confirmations of appointees conditioned upon the avowal that suspensions have been made on party grounds alone, nor the threat proposed in the resolutions now before the Senate that no confirmations will be made unless the demands of that body be complied with, are sufficient to discourage or deter me from following in the way which I am convinced leads to better government for the people."

The boldness and vigour with which the President thus asserted his prerogative, astounded the Republican Senators. They found themselves in the very " hole " into which they had gleefully expected to put Mr. Cleveland. Just what to do they did not know. They had no means of coercing the President of the United States; and his calm indifference to the senatorial dignity was as unpleasant as it was novel in their experience. They argued and debated; but finally, in a sheepish, shamefaced way, they came to the conclusion that nothing whatsoever could be done but swallow the medicine which the President had administered.[22]

One of their number, however, took an oratorical revenge. This was Senator Ingalls of Kansas. Mr. Ingalls was a very brilliant, fluent speaker, possessing a voluminous vocabulary of bitterness. A tall, thin, cynical-looking man, with a power of emitting words which scorched like drops of vitriol, he never failed to command the attention of his colleagues and of the public. He let it be known that he was about to scarify the Administration with regard to its pretensions to reform. When he arose in his place on March 28th, both the floor

[22] See Cleveland, *Presidential Problems*, pp. 3-76 (New York, 1904).

of the Senate and the galleries were crowded. Speaking slowly, in order that every shaft might surely find its mark, he delivered an address which was a masterpiece of studied malice. First of all, he spoke of the attitude of his own party:

" They believe and I believe that for the past quarter of a century upon every vital issue before the American people, secession, slavery, coercion, the public credit, honest elections, universal freedom, and the protection of American labour, they have always been right and that their opponents have always been wrong; and, while they concede unreservedly patriotism and sincerity to their adversaries, temporary repulse has not convinced them that they were in error. There is neither defection nor dismay in their columns. They are ready, they are impatient to renew the battle. Animated by such impulses, it is not singular that they should feel that no Republican can hold an appointive office under a Democratic administration without either sacrificing his convictions or forfeiting his self-respect.

" Accordingly, sir, when a little more than a year ago a Democratic administration was inaugurated, those who were in public station began with one consent to make excuse to retire to private life. They did not stand upon the order of their going; they trampled upon each other in a tumultuous and somewhat indecent haste to get out of office. There was no craven cry for mercy; no mercenary camp-follower fled for shelter to the bomb-proofs of the Tenure of Office Act, no sutler crawled behind the fragile breastworks of civil service reform for protection. They lost their baggage, but they retained their colours, their arms, their ammunition, and their camp equipage, and marched off the field with the honours of war. If at the expiration of one year a few yet remain in office, *rari nantes in gurgite vasto,* it is because the victors have been unable to agree among themselves or been unable to discover among their own number competent and qualified successors."

Speaking of the President, he said:

"Sir, I am not disposed to impugn the good faith, the patriotism, the sincerity, the many unusual traits and faculties of the President of the United States. He is the sphinx of American politics. It is said that he is a fatalist; that he regards himself as the child of fate—the man of destiny, and that he places devout and implicit reliance upon the guiding influence of his 'star.' Certainly, whether he be a very great man or a very small man, he is a very extraordinary man. His career forbids any other conclusion."

Then he paid his respects to the advocates of reform. In his sentences were concentrated the hatred and contempt which the vindictive partisan feels for all who exercise an independent judgment in politics:

"Mr. President, the neuter gender is not popular either in nature or society. 'Male and female created He them.' But there is a third sex, if sex that can be called which sex has none, resulting sometimes from a cruel caprice of nature, at others from accident or malevolent design, possessing the vices of both and the virtues of neither; effeminate without being masculine or feminine; unable either to beget or to bear; possessing neither fecundity nor virility; endowed with the contempt of men and the derision of women, and doomed to sterility, isolation, and extinction. But they have two recognised functions. They sing falsetto, and they are usually selected as the guardians of the seraglios of Oriental despots. Geology teaches us that in the process of being, upward from the protoplasmic cell, through one form of existence to another, there are intermediary and connecting stages, in which the creature bears some resemblance to the state from which it has emerged and some to the state to which he is proceeding. History is stratified politics; every stratum is fossiliferous; and I am inclined to think that the political geologist of the future in his antiquarian researches between the triassic series of 1880 and the cretaceous series of 1888, as he inspects the jurassic Democratic strata of 1884, will find some curious illustrations of the doctrine of political evolution.

" In the transition from the fish to the bird there is an anomalous animal, long since extinct, named by the geologist the pterodactyl, or winged reptile, a lizard with feathers upon its paws and plumes upon its tail. A political system which illustrates in its practical operations the appointment by the same administration of Eugene Higgins and Dorman B. Eaton can properly be regarded as in the transition epoch and characterised as the pterodactyl of politics. It is, like that animal, equally adapted to waddling and dabbling in the slime and mud of partisan politics, and soaring aloft with discordant cries into the glittering and opalescent empyrean of civil service reform.[23]

A sufficient answer to the gibes of Mr. Ingalls was given a few days later by the organisation of the new Civil Service Commission which, aided by the President in every way, now entered upon its work. A definite plan for promotion was perfected. Rigorous investigations were conducted, and these unearthed many violations of the law. A Republican was appointed chief examiner. The bitter discussion in the Senate had served to rivet public attention upon this important question, and sentiment in favour of the reform was strengthened and extended every day.

Much feeling was excited in the spring of 1886 by the President's attitude toward private pension bills. That the military pension system had been grossly abused was perfectly well known to every one. Neither party, however, possessed the courage to eradicate these abuses. The Republicans had always officially posed as the friends of the veteran. The Democrats knew that if they took unfavourable action upon pension bills they would be accused

[23] *Congressional Record,* March 28, 1886.

of disloyalty and of hatred to the soldiers of the Union. The result was that disbursements for pensions had increased with startling rapidity. Thus, in 1866, the number of pensioners was 126,722, and the amount paid to them annually was $15,450,550. In 1875, there were 234,821 pensioners receiving annually $29,270,407. At that time, General Garfield declared in the House of Representatives that the expenditures for pensions had reached their maximum and thereafter might be expected to decrease. Congress, however, passed a so-called Arrears of Pension Act, giving to each pensioner " back-pay " from the time when his disability had been first incurred. At once the expenditures were almost doubled. In 1885, the pensioners numbered 345,125, and the annual sum paid them was $65,171,937. The Pension Bureau was administered in a spirit of extravagant liberality. Pensions were granted to individuals whose claims were ludicrous and at times outrageous. Men who had been dishonourably discharged were on the pension-list; others who had met with injuries from accidents while drunk were likewise favoured. Pensions had actually been bestowed upon malingerers who had shot off their own fingers in order to escape from service in the army. Yet even the Pension Bureau had felt that somewhere it must draw the line; and therefore many applications were rejected. Unsuccessful claimants, therefore, got into the habit of embodying their claims in private bills which were sent to Congress for special action. These bills were hastily rushed through both Houses without the slightest reference to their merits. It is recorded that on a single day the Senate once passed 500 private pension bills at a sitting. President Cleveland made up his mind that this sort of thing must stop.

He began to make a careful study of each private pension bill that came before him, going into all the evidence with the scrupulous care of a trained lawyer. It became at once apparent that many claimants for pensions were no better than swindlers; and therefore, on May 8th, he sent to Congress the first of a series of veto messages—a series which was continued throughout that session. These messages were brief, pungent, and often tinged with sarcasm, and when collected they made very interesting reading as throwing light upon the fraudulent character of many pension claims. "We are dealing," wrote Mr. Cleveland, " with pensions, not with gratuities "; and even had it been a question of gratuities, there was little reason for favourable action upon many of the bills. Some of the claimants were shown to have deserted from the army. One had fallen while getting over a fence, but had absolutely no trace of any injury upon his person. Another asked for a pension because he had hurt his ankle while *intending* to enlist. Another based his application upon the fact that, sixteen years after the conclusion of the war, he had fallen from a ladder and fractured his skull. Still another had broken his leg in a ditch while gathering dandelions, long after the war. A widow asked for a pension because her husband had died of heart disease in 1881—a circumstance which she ascribed to a wound in the ankle received in 1863. Absurd as were these and many other claims, the fact that the President rejected them was made the basis of a charge of hostility to the veterans of the Civil War. The merits of each case had little weight with those opponents who cared nothing for the truth, but who sought to bring discredit on the President. As a matter of fact, many of his vetoes were in the interest of the very persons whose claims he set aside. In

several instances, widows of soldiers had carelessly sought
relief through a pension bill, when the granting of such
relief would have cut them off from a far more liberal
treatment through the regular channels of the Pension
Bureau.[24]   The President, therefore, by his vigilance, not
only detected and exposed dishonesty, but he performed a
real service to many worthy persons.   In all, he vetoed one
pension bill in every seven, or about one hundred in the
aggregate; and only one of these bills was ever passed
over the President's veto.

Early in 1886, the rumour went abroad that Mr. Cleveland was about to end his bachelorhood.   This rumour
naturally excited widespread interest and caused a temporary cessation of party strife.   Only one President had
ever been married during his term of office,[25] and never had
the wedding of a President taken place in the White
House.   Before long it became known that the report was
true, and that an engagement existed between Mr. Cleveland and Miss Frances Folsom, the daughter of his former
law partner.   At the time when the engagement was announced, Miss Folsom was in Europe; but she presently
returned and became the object of an immense amount of
friendly curiosity.   Mr. Cleveland had been her guardian
after her father's death and it was said that the two had
begun to take a sentimental interest in one another after
certain gossips had spread a premature and quite un-
founded story of their betrothal.   Miss Folsom at this
time was twenty-two years of age.   She was a tall and

[24] See, for instance, the veto messages of July 9, 1886; February 3, 1887;
February 21, 1887; and February 23, 1887.
[25] President Tyler was married in New York toward the end of his
administration.

graceful girl, with manners that were at once dignified and winning. Her cordiality was sincere, and she was always tactful; and from the day when she first became known to the American people she remained deservedly a universal favourite. Following the usage which prevails with rulers of nations, the President was married in his official residence rather than at the house of his bride. The wedding took place on the evening of the second of June, in the Blue Room, in the presence of a small but distinguished company, including most of the members of the Cabinet. The ceremony was carried out with perfect taste; and the only incidents which suggested an official wedding were the presidential salute of twenty-one guns fired from the Arsenal, and a message of congratulation from the Queen of Great Britain, which was received just as the President and his bride were taking their departure.

They went by special train to a cottage which had been placed at their disposal at Deer Park in the mountains of Maryland. Public interest in the marriage was so great that the press of the country went far beyond the limits of what was permissible. On the following morning, the President was astonished to find that a pavilion had been reared directly opposite his cottage, and that a throng of newspaper correspondents were collected there, provided with field glasses, so as not to lose even the slightest detail which a bold-eyed curiosity could discover. This annoying espionage continued for several days, and fully justified some biting sentences which were written with regard to the editors who permitted such a breach of elemental courtesy.

" They have used the enormous power of the modern newspaper to perpetrate and disseminate a colossal impertinence, and have done it, not as professional gossips and tattlers, but as the guides and instructors of the public in conduct and morals. And they have done it, not to a private citizen, but to the President of the United States, thereby lifting their offence into the gaze of the whole world, and doing their utmost to make American journalism contemptible in the estimation of people of good breeding everywhere." [26]

Congress adjourned on August 5, 1886. It had of necessity enacted no measure regarding which there was a difference of opinion between the two parties. A tariff bill had been prepared by the Democrats of the House, but no action had been taken upon it. On the other hand, the question of the presidential succession had at last been definitely settled by a law which named the Vice-President, and the Secretaries of the Departments in the order of their establishment, to succeed in the event of the disability or death of those preceding them. Another bill, providing for an increase of the navy, passed both Houses and received the signature of the President. This Naval Appropriation Act was long afterwards pronounced " historic " by a Republican Secretary of the Navy.[27] It authorised the building of a battleship, the *Texas,* an armoured cruiser, the *Maine,* a protected cruiser, the *Baltimore,* a dynamite cruiser, the *Vesuvius,* and a torpedo boat, the *Cushing.* In this way, new and wholly modern types of warships were introduced into the American Navy; and of these vessels every one was destined to be remembered in the nation's history.

President Cleveland had by this time become thoroughly well known to all his countrymen. In some ways he had

[26] New York *Evening Post,* June 4, 1886.
[27] Long, *The New American Navy,* i., p. 41 (New York, 1904).

disappointed a section of his party. He had not altogether satisfied the expectations of the independent voters. But he had made no serious mistakes, and he had given to his followers a positive and definite policy to take the place of a purely negative, critical attitude which for twenty years had brought them nothing but disaster. Both as a man and as a statesman his fame had grown. Few doubted his sincerity of purpose, his integrity of character, or his indomitable courage.

In November, 1886, Harvard University celebrated the two hundred and fiftieth anniversary of its foundation. President Cleveland accepted an invitation to attend the ceremonies as a guest of the University and of the Commonwealth of Massachusetts. Accompanied by the Governor and escorted by a body of lancers, he proceeded to Cambridge, where he was received at the Sanders Theatre by President Eliot.[28] No such gathering had hitherto been seen upon this Continent, representing, as it did, all that was most distinguished in American art and literature, in statesmanship, in science, and in learning. In the presence of this brilliant assemblage, James Russell Lowell, the greatest of American men of letters then living, delivered an address which for its tone of rare distinction still remains a masterpiece, starred with felicitous allusions and pregnant with suggestive thought. Toward the close he spoke a few graceful words of welcome to the guests of the University, and then, at the last, turning to the most illustrious guest of all, he said:

"There is also one other name of which it would be indecorous not to make exception. You all know that I can mean only the President of our Republic. His presence is a signal honour to us all, and to us all I may say a personal gratification. We have no politics here; but

[28] November 8th.

the sons of Harvard all belong to the party which admires
courage, strength of purpose, and fidelity to duty, and
which respects, wherever he may be found, the

> " ' Iustum et tenacem propositi virum,'

who knows how to withstand the

> " ' Civium ardor prava iubentium.'

He has left the helm of State to be with us here; and so
long as it is entrusted to his hands we are sure that, should
the storm come, he will say with Seneca's pilot, ' O Nep-
tune, you may sink me if you will, you may save me if you
will, but whatever happen I shall keep my rudder
true! ' " [29]

[29] Winsor, *Record of the Celebration of the 250th Anniversary of the
Founding of Harvard College* (Boston, 1887).

III

THE REPUBLICAN RALLY

THE year 1886 was marked by serious disturbances arising from strikes and other labour movements, which recalled the events of 1877, when the industries of the country were paralysed, and when, at the great centres of traffic in twelve States, conditions existed that seemed to threaten civil war. In 1886, there was less violence, yet the social unrest was so widespread as to be at once significant and ominous. From the shipyards in Maine to the railways in Texas and the Far West, there was continual disorder in nearly every branch of industry. In New York City, the employés of the street-car lines began a strike on February 3d, which was ended on the 18th by a victory for the strikers. The disturbances, however, broke out again on March 2d and continued intermittently until September 1st, when the managers of the roads once more gave way. On one day, every line in New York and Brooklyn was "tied up" completely. In June, the elevated railways had a similar, though much more brief, experience. The mania for striking seemed to be in the very air; and on April 20th, in Boston, even the children in two of the public schools struck for a continuous session, and adopted all the approved methods of the conventional strike, stationing pickets, attacking such children as refused to join them, and causing a small riot which had to be put down by the police.[1]

---

[1] A nearly complete list of the strikes of this year will be found in *Appleton's Annual Cyclopædia* for 1887.

The storm centres of labour agitation were in St. Louis and Chicago. In St. Louis a demand was made by the employés of the Texas Pacific Railway for the reinstatement of a foreman who had been discharged. The receiver refused the demand, and a strike took place which very soon extended to the Missouri Pacific, and, in fact, to all the roads constituting the Gould system. Traffic throughout the whole Southwest was practically suspended, and before long the strike took on the form of riot and incendiarism. United States troops were sent to maintain order,[2] but their numbers were insufficient, and the rioters cared nothing for the special deputies who had been sworn in to keep the peace. A squad of these deputies fired upon a crowd, killing or wounding a number of persons (April 7th). This act inflamed the mob, which armed itself, and for a time was master of the city. The torch was applied to railroad property, factories were closed, and great losses were inflicted, not only upon the railways, but upon the entire population. The leader in these depredations was a Scotchman named Martin Irons, a typical specimen of the ignorant fanatic, exactly the sort of man who comes to the front whenever the populace is inflamed by passion and bent on violence. Sly, ignorant, and half an animal, he nevertheless was able to play upon the prejudices of his fellows, and to stimulate their class-hatred so artfully as to make them deaf to the counsels of their saner leaders. For a time he had his way; yet in the end this strike collapsed after those who shared in it had forfeited hundreds of thousands of dollars in wages, and after the railroads had incurred an even heavier loss.

In Chicago, the men in the Pullman works began a

[2] The Missouri Pacific was in the hands of a receiver appointed by one of the Federal Courts.

strike in May; and before long nearly fifty thousand labourers were out. In a conflict with the police a number of workingmen were shot. Chicago had for some time been the headquarters of a small but very active group of Anarchists, nearly all of whom were foreigners. The strikers had no sympathy with Anarchists, nor any affiliation with them. Nevertheless, the Anarchists believed that the proper moment had now come for them to strike a blow, and they hoped thereby to win to their support new followers from the ranks of the discontented. There were published in Chicago two newspapers, one in English (the *Alarm*), conducted by a man named Parsons, and the other in German (the *Arbeiter Zeitung*), conducted by one August Spies, both of them devoted to the anarchistic propaganda. About the time when the strike began, there appeared in the *Alarm* a most inflammatory article, of which the following is a part:

"DYNAMITE! Of all the good stuff this is the stuff. Stuff several pounds of this sublime stuff into an inch pipe, plug up both ends, insert a cap with a fuse attached, place this in the immediate neighbourhood of a lot of rich loafers who live by the sweat of other people's brows, and light the fuse. . . . The dear stuff can be carried around in the pocket without danger; while it is a formidable weapon against any force of militia, police or detectives that may want to stifle the cry for justice that goes forth from the plundered slaves."

On May 4th, a mass meeting of workingmen was held in the Haymarket Square to protest against the acts of the police. Late at night, after some rather tame addresses had been delivered, an Anarchist leader, an Englishman named Samuel Fielden, broke forth into a violent harangue. He denounced all government in the most savage terms, yelling out, " The law is your enemy! We are rebels against it!" Word had been sent to police head-quarters; and while Fielden was in the midst of his wild talk, a battalion of nearly two hundred policemen marched into the Square. Their captain commanded the gathering to disperse. Fielden replied, " We are peaceable." He was, however, arrested. A moment later, a pistol was fired, apparently as a signal, and at once a bomb was hurled into the ranks of the police. It exploded with terrible effect. Nearly fifty policemen were thrown to the ground, and seven of them were so badly wounded that they died soon after. With splendid discipline, the ranks were at once closed up and a charge was made upon the mob which scattered hastily in flight. Of the Anarchists arrested for this outrage, seven were sentenced to death by Judge Gary. Of these seven, four—Engel, Spies, Parsons and Fischer—were hanged; one—Lingg—committed suicide; and two—Schwab and Fielden—had their sentences commuted to im-prisonment for life. Eight years afterward, a Governor of Illinois, Mr. John P. Altgeld, moved partly by the appeals of sentimentalists, and partly by his own instinctive sympathy with lawlessness, gave a free pardon to such An-archists as had been imprisoned.

In June, 1886, in New York, the disturbed conditions were reflected in political agitation, though here, also, the Anarchists showed their heads. They were, however, dealt with before they could do mischief. One of their leaders, named Johann Most, and three of his companions, were imprisoned on the charge of inciting to riot. Most was a foul creature, at once murderous and cowardly. When arrested, he was found hiding under the bed of his mis-tress, and was taken away whimpering in abject terror. With him and with his kind, the workingmen of New York had no affinity, but sought to redress their grievances at the polls. In this year Mr. Henry George was nominated as the Labour candidate for the mayoralty of New York City against Mr. A. S. Hewitt, the Democratic candidate, and Mr. Theodore Roosevelt, the candidate of the Republicans. Although Mr. Hewitt was elected, it was only by a plurality. He received some 90,000 votes against 68,000 votes given to Mr. George; while Mr. Roosevelt stood at the bottom of the poll with a little more than 60,000 votes.

Wherever throughout the country the labour element had shown its discontent, the name of the Knights of Labour was, in one way or another, pretty certain to be heard. This organisation was one whose origin and evolution are of great significance in the social and economic history of the United States. Prior to 1866, such organisations of workingmen as existed were either societies for general purposes, not necessarily connected with labour questions, or else they were trade unions in the narrowest sense, confining their membership to men and women engaged in particular and special industries. In 1866, however, there was formed the National Labour Union, of which the purpose was to promote the solidarity, not only of skilled workmen, but of the masses in general, with a view to the amelioration of their condition. This body, unfortunately, almost from the first, fell into the hands of politicians, and in 1870 it died a natural death. Its aims, however, were adopted by a number of garment-cutters in Philadelphia, in 1869, who at first formed a secret order— secrecy being adopted because of the hostility of employers to labour organisations. This was the origin of the Knights of Labour, who admitted to membership in their body all persons above the age of sixteen, except saloon-keepers, gamblers, bankers, and lawyers. In 1882, it ceased to be a secret order; and thereafter it rapidly increased in membership until, in 1886, it was said to number more than seven hundred thousand persons. The principles which the order officially professed were distinctly socialistic. It advocated equal rights for women, the common ownership of land, and the acquisition by the Government of public utilities, such as railroads, telegraphs and telephones. It is here that we first find in the United States a large and influential body of men pledged to the support of what was in reality a system of State Socialism.[4]

In order to understand the significance of this movement, and to explain the rapid propagation of socialistic principles, it is necessary to recall a few important facts relating to American economic history of the preceding thirty years. One effect of the Civil War had been the rapid acquisition of great fortunes by individuals, and the growth of powerful corporations. Conspicuous among the latter were the railway companies. The period succeeding the war had been a period of railway building. Between 1860 and 1880, more than sixty thousand miles of railway had been constructed and put into operation. They represented an enormous amount of capital, and this capital represented an enormous amount of influence, both political and social. How much the nation owed to its railway system was very obvious. The easy distribution of its products brought prosperity to every section. Population was extended over new areas. Great cities sprang up in the remotest prairies at the magic touch of the railway builder. Moreover, in one sense, the unity of the Republic

---

[4] See Ely, *The Labour Movement in the United States* (New York, 1886).

itself was the work of the railway, which proved to be a great assimilator, annihilating distance, bringing one section into easy communication with another, and thereby creating not only common interests, but a common understanding. On the other hand, a moment's thought will make it clear that railways were essentially monopolies, and that their growth lodged in the hands of their owners the right to tax at will the people from whom they had received their charters, and whose interests they were supposed to serve. In 1870, when there were only 53,000 miles of railroad in the United States, the revenue collected by the railway companies from the public amounted to $450,000,000, representing a transportation tax which the owners of the roads imposed at their own discretion, and without the intervention or consent of any other authority. At that time Mr. Charles Francis Adams wrote:

" Certain private individuals, responsible to no authority and subject to no supervision, but looking solely to their own interests or to those of their immediate constituency, yearly levy upon the internal movement of the American people a tax . . . equal to about one-half of the expenses of the United States Government— army, navy, civil-list, and interest upon the national debt included." [5]

Even if the individuals to whom this irresponsible power was entrusted had been always wise, unselfish and public-spirited, the unregulated right of taxation would have been an anomaly in a free State. But as they were very human, serving their own interests, and naturally seeking their own enrichment, abuses, and very gross ones, were inevitable. Still, no hostile sentiment would have been

[5] Adams, *The Railroad System*, included in *Chapters of Erie and Other Essays*, p. 361 (Boston, 1871).

aroused against them had they levied their transportation tax equitably upon all and without discrimination. That they did not do so, and that in consequence they began, about 1870, to create and foster other still more gigantic combinations inimical to the public welfare, are facts which serve to explain the prevalence throughout the country of great social discontent, beginning in 1870 and growing deeper and more intense with each succeeding year. An instance—the most striking of all instances—of an abuse of corporate power by the railways, is found in the history of the Standard Oil Company.

In 1862, a partnership for the refining of petroleum was formed between John D. Rockefeller, his brother William Rockefeller, and an English mechanic named Samuel Andrews. This partnership grew into a corporation which, after 1870, became known to the country as the Standard Oil Company. From 1860 to 1868, the oil-wells in Pennsylvania and West Virginia had enriched the people of several States and had added very largely to the wealth of the entire country. By the year 1870, the production of oil had increased to such an extent that the United States exported to Europe not less than one hundred million gallons a year. A hundred new wells were drilled every month. The people of the oil region had in ten years created a new industry at the cost of patience, self-sacrifice and labour, supplemented by invention. New cities and towns had sprung up, humming with life, and full of hope and confidence in the future. Churches, schools, libraries, banks, and all the machinery of prosperity had been established, and these were supported by the oil wells and refineries. Presently, in some mysterious way, all this activity was checked. It was found that certain shippers of oil were obtaining from the railroads rates

so low as to enable them, by underselling other oil producers, to drive their competitors out of business. These
favoured shippers turned out to be a body of thirteen
men, among whom were the two Rockefellers,[6] who were
thus gaining a complete monopoly of the oil business.
They were united in what was known as the South
Improvement Company; and with the South Improvement Company the oil-carrying railroads[7] made a secret
contract which provided (1) that the freight rates should
be doubled to all other shippers; (2) that the increase
collected from competing shippers should be turned over
to the South Improvement Company; (3) that any other
changes in the freight tariff necessary to crush out
competition should be made; and (4) that the railroads should inform the South Improvement Company
of all the details of its rival's business. The result, of
course, was the ruin of the oil producers. They were faced
with the alternative of selling out to the South Improvement Company at a merely nominal figure, or else of
giving up their business altogether. Some of them went
to the officials of the Erie and the New York Central
roads in order to expostulate. They were told, " You had
better sell out. There is no help for it." Many did sell
out to the oil monopolists at fifty cents on the dollar. One
refinery, which produced annually an average profit of

[6] Before an investigating committee of the New York Senate (February
28, 1888), Mr. J. D. Rockefeller stated under oath that he had not been
a member of the South Improvement Company. On April 30th of the
same year, he admitted (also under oath) to a Congressional committee
that he and his brother had had an interest in that company.—Tarbell,
History of the Standard Oil Company, i., p. 138 (New York, 1904).

[7] These were the Erie, the Pennsylvania, and the New York Central and
Hudson River. The contract was signed on behalf of the railroads, by
Jay Gould, Thomas A. Scott, and William H. Vanderbilt.

$40,000 and which represented an investment of $150,-000, was abandoned to the monopoly for the sum of $45,000. The owner (Mr. Robert Hanna) said: "I would not have sold out if I could have got a fair show with the railroads." [8] The blow fell alike upon producer and refiner. Within two days after the secret contract went into effect, the prosperity of the oil region was at an end.

"The entire business of the oil regions became paralysed. Oil went down to a point seventy cents below the cost of production. The boring of new wells is suspended; existing wells are shut down. The business in Cleveland has stopped almost altogether. Thousands of men are thrown out of work." [9]

The annals of this time show a black record of ruin, despair and suicide. Naturally so great a wrong was not accepted with meekness. The law was tested in a great number of suits, some of them brought by individuals, and some of them technically in the name of the State of Pennsylvania. Indictments against the Rockefellers for criminal conspiracy were found by a Grand Jury, but with no result. The State officials seemed strangely unwilling to push these cases. Officers of the law became of a sudden wonderfully listless. Governor Hoyt of Pennsylvania refused to issue an order for the extradition of the Rockefellers. The highest court in Pennsylvania interfered to stay proceedings in the lower courts. The oil monopolists boasted with cool confidence that the case against them would never come to trial. Law having failed, a political agitation was begun, ac-

[8] Report of the Hepburn Committee, New York Assembly (1879), p. 2525.

[9] Titusville (Pennsylvania) *Herald,* March 20, 1872.

companied by outbreaks of disorder. Railway tracks were torn up; oil-tanks were destroyed. Popular sentiment justified an appeal to physical force against trickery and fraud. This state of things led to the calling of a Constitutional Convention in 1873. A very able lawyer, Mr. Samuel C. T. Dodd, addressing this Convention, used the following forcible language:

"In spite of the law we well know that almost every railroad in this State is to-day in the habit of granting special privileges to individuals, to companies in which the directors of such railroads are interested, to particular businesses, and to particular localities. We well know that it is their habit to break down certain localities, and to build up others, to break down certain men in business and to build up others, to monopolise certain business themselves by means of the numerous corporations which they own and control, and all this in spite of the law, and in defiance of the law. . . .

"The railroads took one of those charters which they got from the Legislature, and by means of that they struck a deadly blow at one of the greatest interests of the State. Their scheme was contrary to law; but before the legal remedy could have been applied, the oil business would have lain prostrate at their feet, had it not been prevented by an uprising of the people, by the threatenings of a mob, if you please, by threatening to destroy property, and by actually commencing to destroy the property of the railroad companies; and had the companies not cancelled the contract which Scott and Vanderbilt and others had entered into, I venture to say there would not have been one mile of railroad track left in the county of Venango—the people had come to that pitch of desperation. . . . Unless we can give the people a remedy for this evil, they will sooner or later take the remedy into their own hands." [10]

[10] Proceedings of the Constitutional Convention of Pennsylvania (1873), iii., p. 522.

As this subject will be more fully discussed hereafter, it need not, for the present, be treated in detail. Suffice it to say that the secret contract between the South Improvement Company and the railways was ostensibly cancelled. Yet the freight discriminations continued just the same. Furthermore, the example set by this one monopoly was copied and improved upon by other corporations in all parts of the country; and the railways lent their aid unscrupulously to combinations of all kinds in restraint of trade, and in discouragement of individual enterprise. In 1882, the same Mr. Dodd who had so bitterly denounced both the oil monopoly and the railways, but who soon after accepted a large salary as general counsel to the Standard Oil Company, invented a form of trust agreement under which the Standard Oil Company was reorganised in such a way as to provide that the stockholders of each of the companies composing it should assign their stock to a few trustees, thus giving them a permanent and irrevocable power of attorney. In return for the stock so assigned, the trustees distributed trust certificates to the stockholders of the separate companies. On these trust certificates the profits were divided.[11] This trust agreement was finally pronounced illegal by the courts; but for several years it was a favourite form of organisation with the great corporations, so that in popular language the word "Trust" came to be applied to every combination of capital which had a monopolistic tendency.

The long struggle between the Trusts and their less powerful competitors brought out very clearly one great central fact. The backbone of monopoly was to be found

[11] The full text of the Standard Oil Trust Agreement is given in E. von Halle, *Trusts . . . in the United States,* pp. 153-169 (New York, 1895).

in an abuse of the power which the railways of the country were exercising so oppressively. Unless, in some way, this power could be checked and regulated, the individual citizen was at the mercy of a comparatively few men whose command of money made them indifferent, because superior, to the ordinary processes of law. Popular sentiment then became so hostile to the railway interests as almost to justify the violence which had been shown in the strikes of 1886. It was during President Cleveland's first administration that Congress made a vigorous attempt to grapple with this subject.

The President's very long message of December 6, 1886, did not touch directly on the connection of the railroads with social discontent, though some passages spoke of the relation of capital to labour and to the public interests. The events of the preceding summer, however, were fresh in the minds of all; and, therefore, early in the session, a bill was reported in both Houses, intended to regulate and control the railways, under that clause of the Constitution (Article i. 8, §3), which gives Congress the right to regulate commerce among the several States of the Union.[12] This was not the first time that such an attempt had been made. Ten years earlier, a flood of petitions had poured in upon Congress, together with copies of resolutions passed by public meetings, chambers of commerce, and boards of trade. On May 16, 1876, Mr. Hopkins of Pennsylvania had asked unanimous consent of the House to introduce a resolution providing for a committee to investigate the charges against the railroads, and to report a bill

[12] During the preceding session, the Senate had proposed a mild sort of bill looking to the same end. The House framed a similar measure, known as the Reagan Bill. Upon the basis of these two bills, a conference committee drafted the document which was now reported.

for the regulation of interstate commerce. Immediately, Mr. Henry B. Payne of Ohio rose and made objection— an objection which he refused to withdraw at the request of other members. Mr. Payne subsequently went to Mr. Hopkins and explained that his objection was based upon considerations of economy. A special committee would be too great an expense, he said. He begged Mr. Hopkins to re-introduce his resolution and ask that it be referred to the Committee on Commerce. This was done. When the Committee on Commerce met to consider it, a representative of the Standard Oil Company (Mr. J. N. Camden) took his seat beside the Chairman, whispering suggestions in his ear and practically presiding. The treasurer of the Standard Oil Company, Mr. O, H. Payne, and Mr. Cassatt, the vice-president of the Pennsylvania Railroad, were summoned to testify. Both of them refused to answer questions. The Committee adjourned, ostensibly to consider means for compelling these witnesses to answer. It never again took up the subject; it never recalled the witnesses; it never made any report. When Mr. Hopkins afterwards asked to see the record of the testimony that had been taken, he found that it had been stolen.

The bill which was now reported by a conference committee, was much more stringent than either the Senate bill or the Reagan substitute of the preceding session. It provided for the appointment of a Commission of five members, to whom authority was given to inspect the books and other papers of all railways engaged in interstate commerce, and to summon witnesses and compel them to answer any questions relating to the railway management. It forbade discrimination in rates, and also the " pooling " of freight revenues by competing railways, or the division of such revenues between them. It forbade also a greater charge for a " short haul " than for a " long haul " over the same line and in the same direction. The Commission might appeal to the United States courts to enforce its mandates, either by injunction or by attachment, and the courts might impose a penalty of $500 for each offence, and a fine of $500 per day during such time as an offending railroad remained in contumacy. This bill was opposed by railway attorneys, both outside and inside of Congress. No one ventured frankly to defend the past conduct of the railways; but a vast amount of concern was expressed lest the proposed act might be unconstitutional. Congress, however, did not dare to reject the measure. The problem of the Trusts had already become a leading political issue, so that both parties were anxious to make a satisfactory record. A conference committee reported the bill to the Senate on December 15th, 1886, and it was passed by a vote of 43 to 15, fourteen Senators being absent or not voting. It was reported to the House and was passed (January 21, 1887) by a vote of 219 to 41, fifty-eight members being absent or not voting. The Interstate Commerce Act became law on February 4th, on which day it was signed by President Cleveland.

As will appear later, this law did not by any means attain the object sought by its framers. It established, however, an important precedent, and marked a long step forward in the direction of a complete national control of railway management. The President appointed to membership in the first Commission, Thomas M. Cooley, of Michigan, a very eminent jurist, with William R. Morrison of Illinois, August Schoonmaker of New York, Aldace F. Wheeler of Vermont, and Walter A. Bragg of Alabama.

This session of Congress was unusually fruitful in other salutary legislation. Very important was the Electoral Count Act, which definitely ended the possibility of such a dispute as that which followed upon the Hayes-Tilden contest of 1876-7. By the bill which now became law (February 3, 1887), each State must, through its own tribunals, determine the result of a disputed election. Only when it fails to do so, does Congress have jurisdiction, and even then no electoral vote shall be rejected except by the concurrent vote of both Houses. In the case of a disagreement between the Senate and the House, " the votes of the electors whose appointment shall have been certified by the Executive of the State, under the seal thereof, shall be counted." A stringent Anti-Polygamy Act was also passed, making polygamy a criminal offence. It became law without the President's signature. Other non-partisan measures which were passed provided for the withdrawal of the " trade-dollar " from circulation, for the extension of the free delivery system of the Post Office Department, for the reference of private claims to a Court of Claims, and for the granting of land in severalty to the Indians. Finally the Tenure of Office Act with which the Senate had attempted, as already told, to hamper the President's freedom in making removals from office, was repealed. The repealing bill was introduced in the Senate by a Republican, Mr. Hoar of Massachusetts. He very shrewdly perceived that in the contest between the Senate and President Cleveland, popular sympathy had been with the President. " The people, both Republicans and Democrats, expected that the political control of the most important offices would be changed when a new party came into power." [14] Senator Hoar's action irritated many of his Republican colleagues, especially Senator John

[14] Hoar, *Autobiography*, ii., p. 143 (New York, 1903).

Sherman, and only three of them voted with him; but with the solid support of the Democratic Senators, the repeal was carried, as it was also in the House; and thus was blotted out a law which, as the President observed had properly fallen into " innocuous desuetude." [15]

During this session, Mr. Cleveland continued to veto private pension bills, accompanying his vetoes, as before, with caustic words. Had he done nothing more in this direction, he would have continued to receive, from the country at large more gratitude than criticism. But on February 11, 1887, he returned without his approval a bill known as the Dependent Pension Bill, which granted a pension of twelve dollars monthly to every honourably discharged veteran of the war, who had served three months and who was dependent upon his own labour or upon others for his support. It gave a like relief to the dependent parents of all deceased veterans. This was, in effect, a general service pension, and the President vetoed it, saying in his message, among other things:

" I cannot but remember that the soldiers of our Civil War, in their pay and bounty, received such compensation for military service as has never been received by soldiers before, since mankind first went to war; that never before on behalf of any soldiery have so many and such generous laws been passed to relieve against the incidents of war . . . and that never before, in the history of the country, has it been proposed to render government aid toward the support of any of its soldiers, based alone upon a military service so recent and where age and circumstances appeared so little to demand such aid."

The veto of the Dependent Pension Bill and the terms which the President had employed in expressing his disapproval, brought upon him the loudly-voiced enmity of the

[15] Message of March 1, 1886.

Grand Army of the Republic. This organisation, established in 1868, was composed of veterans of the Civil War, and in 1887 it had a membership of more than four hundred thousand persons. Ostensibly non-political, it had always taken a keen interest in pension legislation; and the fear of its influence had been very powerful, alike with Congress and with the officials of the Pension Bureau; for, directly and indirectly, the " veterans " were believed to control not less than a million votes. The Grand Army men were now unrestrained in their abuse of the President. They called him an " enemy of veterans," and a friend of the Confederacy; and they asserted that his action on the pension bill had been taken to please his supporters, " the rebel brigadiers." Their wrath was not allayed by the comments which were published in the newspapers that defended Mr. Cleveland's veto. These journals pointed to the long list of pension frauds in the past, the extravagance of the Pension Bureau, and the tricks of the attorneys who made a specialty of pushing shady pension claims. It did not soothe the anger of the members of the Grand Army to be characterised as " blood-suckers," " coffee-boilers," " pension-leeches " and " bums." A very bitter feeling was engendered and was still intense when President Cleveland perpetrated a colossal blunder. There were stored in the custody of the War Department a number of Union flags captured by the Confederates during the Civil War and afterward recaptured by the Northern troops, and also a number of Confederate flags taken by the Union armies. On April 30th, after Congress had adjourned, Adjutant-General R. C. Drum addressed a letter to the Secretary of War, suggesting that all these flags, Union and Confederate alike, be returned to the respective States in which the regiments bearing the flags had been organised. Secretary Endicott submitted this letter to the President, and it was approved by him (May 26th), whereupon the Adjutant-General drafted letters to the governors of the different States, offering to return the flags in the name of the President.

No sooner had this action become known than a cry of indignation arose throughout the North and West. The "Rebel Flag Order" as it was called, was denounced in the most violent language and by men of every shade of political belief. Naturally, the Union veterans were the most deeply moved. Scores of Grand Army posts met and passed indignant resolutions. General Sherman in a letter said: "I know Drum. He has no sympathy with the army which fought. He was a non-combatant. He never captured a flag, and values it only at its commercial value. He did not think of the blood and torture of battle; nor can Endicott, the Secretary of War, or Mr. Cleveland." [16] Others pointed out that the President had exceeded his authority in approving such an order. These flags, they said, were the property of the nation, and could not be disposed of in any way except by the authority of Congress. Looking into the matter more carefully, Mr. Cleveland found that such was indeed the case; and so he was obliged to take the humiliating step of publishing an Executive Order (June 16th) admitting his mistake and annulling the action of the Adjutant-General. [17]

This did not end the affair, however. The President had been invited by Mayor Francis of St. Louis, to be

[16] *The Sherman Letters,* p. 375 (New York, 1896).
[17] It is interesting to note that eighteen years later (in February, 1905), a Republican Congress passed a bill identical in substance with President Cleveland's order, and that this bill having been signed by a Republican President, the "rebel flags" were returned.

present at the annual " encampment" of the Grand Army of the Republic, to be held in that city in July. He had accepted the invitation; but after the issuance of the " Rebel Flag Order " he began to receive threatening letters from all parts of the country. It was declared in them, and it was generally believed, that should he attend he would be publicly insulted. Facts seemed to bear out these assertions. A number of Grand Army posts held a meeting in the city of Wheeling, West Virginia. A street parade was one of the features of this meeting, and various banners had been suspended over the line of march. One of them bore the words: " God Bless Our President, Commander-in-Chief of Our Army and Navy." Nearly all the posts halted when they reached this banner. Then, refusing to pass beneath it, they folded and reversed their flags, and marched around it through the gutters. Soon afterwards, the President addressed a letter to Mayor Francis (July 4th), revoking his acceptance of the invitation to St. Louis, and saying:

" The threats of personal violence . . . which scores of misguided, unbalanced men, under the stimulation of excited feeling, have made, are not considered. Rather than abandon my visit to the West and disappoint your citizens, I might, if I alone were concerned, submit to the insults to which, it is quite openly asserted, I should be helplessly subjected if present at the encampment; but I should bear with me there the people's highest office, the dignity of which I must protect." [18]

The President at this time further exposed himself to a hot fire of criticism from his former supporters, the Independents and Civil Service reformers. He him-

[18] Parker, *Writings and Speeches of Grover Cleveland,* p. 398 (New York, 1892).

self had not altered his mind as to the value of the merit system; but in practice, the various departments had departed from his theory. There was a general relaxation of principle all along the line. A reformed Civil Service had become more and more unpopular among leading Democrats. In the Senate, the leaders of the President's party were openly hostile to him on this issue. Senator Vance of North Carolina, Senator Pugh of Alabama, and Senator Beck of Kentucky took the lead in this opposition within the party. Few of the Democratic Senators liked Mr. Cleveland personally.[19] Senator Vance even made an effort to have the appropriation for the Civil Service Commission discontinued. He failed in this; but the attempt seems to have nettled Mr. Cleveland and to have called out in him a certain petulance which was one of the noticeable traits of his character. Giving way to this mood, he let things take their course for a while, with the result that removals and appointments were made by his subordinates from strictly partisan motives. The most conspicuous instance of this was found in the Post Office Department. Mr. Adlai E. Stevenson of Illinois had been made First Assistant Postmaster-General. He was an old-school Democrat, a thorough believer in the spoils system; and he now set to work unchecked to sweep Republicans out of office. In the political slang of the time, " thousands of heads fell into the basket," and Democrats all over the country wrote and uttered panegyrics on " Adlai and his Axe." Had Mr. Cleveland allowed these removals early in his term, he would at least have won the gratitude of his own party leaders. Had he stood fast by the principle of reform, he would have kept his hold

---

19 " The Democrats in the Senate disliked him very much and gave him a feeble and half-hearted support."—Hoar, *Autobiography*, ii., p. 145.

upon the Independents. As it turned out, however, he had yielded too late to propitiate the former, while the latter were rabid in their denunciation of him. Mr. Stevenson won all the party applause, while the President received all the Mugwumps' abuse. Mr. Hale of Maine laid before the Senate a table showing the changes in office effected during two years of the Cleveland administration. A part of it may be quoted as illustrative:

Offices.	Number.	Changes.
Fourth-class Postmasters....................	52,609	40,000
Presidential Postmasters....................	2,379	2,000
Foreign Ministers.........................	33	32
Secretaries of Legation....................	21	16
Collectors of Customs.....................	111	100
Surveys of Customs.......................	32	all
Naval Officers............................	6	all
Internal Revenue Collectors...............	85	84
District Attorneys........................	70	65
Territorial Judges........................	30	22
Territorial Governors.....................	8	all
Local Land Offices.......................	224	190

Years afterward, in speaking of this time to a personal friend, Mr. Cleveland said with much feeling: "You know the things in which I yielded; but no one save myself can ever know the things which I resisted."

The President had the misfortune to alienate the sympathies of the press at large. He had always had a dislike for the newspapers, possibly because of the manner in which he had been attacked by them in 1884, and perhaps also because of the journalistic discourtesy which had been shown him at the time of his marriage. This dislike he took little pains to hide. The Washington correspondents, the élite of the profession, declared that he had snubbed them at public functions. On December 12, 1885, he wrote a letter to Mr. Joseph Keppler, the editor of *Puck,* in which he said, among other things:

"I don't think there ever was a time when newspaper lying was so general and so mean as at present; and there never was a country under the sun where it flourished as it does in this. The falsehoods daily spread before the people in our newspapers, while they are proofs of the mental ingenuity of those engaged in newspaper work, are insults to the American love of decency and fair play of which we boast."

On July 25, 1886, he addressed another letter to Mr. C. H. Jones, an editor in Jacksonville, Florida, in which he said:

"I am surprised that newspaper talk should be so annoying to you, who ought so well to understand the utter and complete recklessness and falsification in which they so generally indulge."

Again, in the speech which he made at the Harvard banquet (November 8, 1886) he spoke of

"the silly, mean, and cowardly lies that every day are found in the columns of certain newspapers, which violate every instinct of American manliness, and in ghoulish glee desecrate every sacred relation of private life."

The newspapers certainly did their best to justify these strictures. Pretty nearly every public or private act of President Cleveland was misrepresented and made to appear in a light that was either unfavourable or ludicrous.

When he went fishing on Memorial Day, this was interpreted by the press as a studied insult to the memory of the Union dead. When Secretary Manning lay ill of the malady from which he soon after died, it was reported that Mr. Cleveland never sent to inquire after his condition, but rather ostentatiously went down the river to attend a dinner given by a duck-shooting club. When the President made a short journey to the Middle West, delivering occasional speeches on the way, the New York *Sun* at once asserted that all of these speeches had been compiled, sometimes word for word, from an encyclopædia. The same paper professed to believe that Miss Cleveland had written her brother's messages to Congress, and that his famous phrases, " offensive partisans," " pernicious activity," " innocuous desuetude," and " ghoulish glee," had been coined by her. Reports were printed to the effect that the President had quarrelled with his sister because she had published a book, and that she had left the White House because she disapproved of his marriage. Three newspapers, the New York *Tribune,* the *Sun,* and the Washington *Critic,* took to inventing imaginary dialogues between the President and the members of his household, including his private secretary, Colonel Daniel S. Lamont. These dialogues were, for the most part, stupid and rather silly, but they were widely copied by the press throughout the country, and they annoyed the President far more than might have been supposed. One of the earliest of them shows fairly well a purpose to perpetuate the notion that the President's tastes were rather primitive:

Servant (to Mr. Cleveland). " The cook wants to know, sir, what you will have for dinner, sir? "

Mr. Cleveland. " Isn't Miss Cleveland in? "

Servant. " She dines out, sir."

Mr. Cleveland. " Oh, yes. I had forgotten that. Dinner—let me see. Rose dines out and Dan is at Old Point Comfort. Good enough. We'll have pig's feet, fried onions and a bottle of Extra Dry."

Another, published at the time of Congressional elections, derived its point from the spoilsmen's assertion that Mr. Cleveland was no Democrat.

" Daniel," remarked the President this morning, as he sat at his desk with two or three political almanacs and several tables of last year's figures spread out before him.

" Yes, sire," replied Daniel, who was pasting an editorial from the New York *Times* into the Presidential scrap-book.

" The election is in progress to-day, I believe? "

" Yes, sire."

" I remember it because I have $500 on it, Daniel."

" Yes, sire."

" Do you think we shall win, Daniel? "

" *We,* sire? " inquired Daniel, upsetting the paste-pot on the scrap-book.

" I said ' we,' Daniel."

" To whom do you refer by ' we,' sire? "

" The Democratic party, of course, Daniel," said the President, a little sharply.

" Oh! "

And Daniel slapped the scrap-book shut and went out of the room with a pernicious activity which surprised and shocked the President.

Toward the close of 1887, both parties began to look forward to the presidential contest of the following year. In spite of all the uproar that had been raised over the President's pension vetoes and over his partial failure as a reformer of the Civil Service, the Republicans felt that they had no genuine issue upon which to make a strong appeal to the country. The people, as a whole, seemed very well satisfied with the President; and while they recognised his mistakes, they had come to admire his sturdy independence. On the other hand, although the Democratic leaders personally disliked him, because they found him hard to manage and exceedingly plain spoken, there was really no other candidate possible for the party. The congressional elections of 1886 showed a slight falling off in the Democratic vote; but the party still retained control of the House, while the Senate was almost evenly divided. If the President acted with discretion, so his friends told him, and precipitated no new issue, he might be fairly certain of a re-election. The Republicans were secretly depressed. The theory of their invincibility had been shattered in 1884, and they had no great confidence in their immediate future. Mr. Blaine was in Europe. His health was said to be very bad. The party lacked at once a leader and an issue. If the Democrats raised no new question, their prospect of success seemed good. But the President would not take advice. He had made up his mind that something must be done with regard to the national finances. For the coming year, it was estimated that the surplus in the Treasury would be, in round figures, $140,000,000. That so much money should be withdrawn from general circulation and locked up in the Treasury seemed to him certain to disturb business, to diminish the circulating medium of the people, and at the same time to offer a perpetual temptation to extravagance in Congress. Inasmuch as this huge surplus, wholly unnecessary for the needs of the Government, was due to the operation of the tariff, he made up his mind that the tariff ought to be revised. In this he was only following good Republican precedent. General Garfield, in a speech of July 13, 1868, had declared that there must be " a rational and considerate adjustment of the tariff." President Grant, in his message to Congress in December, 1874, had said: " Those articles which enter into our manufactures and are not produced at home should be entered free." A Republican Tariff Commission appointed by President Arthur in 1881 had, in its report, recommended " a substantial reduction of existing duties." The Commission advised such a reduction to the extent of an average of twenty per cent. Finally, the Republican national platform of 1884 had specifically pledged the party " to correct the inequalities of the tariff and *to reduce the surplus*."

President Cleveland, therefore, prepared a message which he purposed to transmit to Congress at the opening of its session in December. Departing from an unbroken line of precedent, he resolved to devote his entire message to the single subject of tariff reform. His intimate friends to whom he disclosed this purpose were aghast. They thoroughly believed in the measure which he advocated, but they told him that the time was inopportune. The presidential election was at hand. The message would be styled by the Republicans a free trade document. The protected manufacturers would be alarmed. The people would not understand. To send such a message at this time would mean the loss of the election. Mr. Cleveland, however, stood firm. He admitted that the election might be lost, but he said that he had a duty to perform and that it must be performed regardless of any personal consequences to himself. " It is more important to the country that this message should be delivered to Congress and the people than that I should be elected President." [20]   The

[20] A. K. McClure, *Recollections*, p. 129 (Salem, 1902).

message would at least give to the party and the people a living issue for the future, and one which would ultimately lead to victory.

Congress met on December 6th, and the message was transmitted to it. After speaking of the condition of the Treasury, the President went on to recommend a reduction of the duties on raw materials, and especially upon wool—a recommendation which had been made by President Grant in 1874. Toward the close of the message occurred the following sentences:

"Our progress toward a wise conclusion will not be improved by dwelling upon the theories of Protection and Free Trade. This savours too much of bandying epithets. It is a condition which confronts us, not a theory."

The reading of this message created an immense sensation. The Republicans now felt that they had a fighting chance. The Democrats, on the other hand, saw that their one prospect of success lay in accepting the doctrine of the President, in closing up their ranks, and in presenting a united front. The party lines were very closely drawn. The word was passed that Democrats who would not speak and vote for tariff reform were no longer to be considered members of the party. A tariff measure was introduced in the House by Mr. Roger Q. Mills of Texas. It removed the duty upon raw wool and made other changes intended to reduce the annual customs revenue by some $50,000,000. The average reduction in the tariff contemplated by this bill was seven per cent., or less by half than the reduction proposed by the Republican Commission of 1881. The House of Representatives passed the Mills Bill by a party vote. The Senate proposed, as a substitute, a bill reducing the duty on sugar by one-half, and repealing altogether the internal revenue tax upon tobacco. Republicans intimated that they were willing to abolish the internal revenue taxes entirely rather than lower the customs duties. Debate waxed hot. The Republican proposal was jeered at by the Democrats. They said that it meant free whiskey and free tobacco while their own proposal simply meant free wool. The Republicans retorted with the alarm-cry of "Free Trade and the destruction of American industries!" The battle for the next presidency was already on.

There was a general feeling among the Republicans that Mr. Blaine was entitled to receive the nomination. No other candidate could make so strong an appeal to his own party; and there was felt, besides, a great deal of sympathy with him because of his defeat in 1884. It was believed that the old charges against him would no longer affect the masses of his party. Mr. Blaine, however, on January 25, 1888, addressed a letter from Florence, Italy, to the Chairman of the Republican National Committee, saying that because of "considerations entirely personal to myself," his name would not be presented at the next National Convention. Many were unwilling to accept this as a final withdrawal; but a second letter, from Paris, to Mr. Whitelaw Reid (May 17th), made it practically certain that Mr. Blaine was out of the running. Putting him aside, the names most often heard as of probable candidates were those of Senator John Sherman of Ohio, for whom a number of Southern States presently instructed their delegates to vote; Mr. Walter Q. Gresham of Illinois; General Russell A. Alger of Michigan; and ex-Senator Benjamin Harrison of Indiana.

The Democratic Convention met at St. Louis on June

5, 1888, and nominated Mr. Cleveland by acclamation, an honour not previously given to a Democratic candidate since Jackson's time. As the nomination was uncontested, the proceedings were unusually tame and lacking in incident. For the Vice-Presidency, the nomination went to Mr. Allen G. Thurman of Ohio. Judge Thurman was an old-fashioned Democrat who had been a Senator, and whose popularity in the West was reckoned upon to carry the doubtful State of Indiana. It was thought possible, too, that he might succeed in his own State of Ohio, which had given Mr. Blaine a rather small majority at the last election. Judge Thurman was a somewhat picturesque figure in politics and was popularly styled the "Old Roman"; but he was now advanced in years, feeble in health, and belonged wholly to the past. The average voter knew little about him except that he was in the habit of carrying and frequently brandishing a large red bandanna—a fact which gave point to a remark made by Senator Riddleberger of Virginia soon after the Convention. Some one asked the Senator what he thought of the nomination for the Vice-Presidency.

"Think?" said he. "Why, I think that you've simply nominated a pocket-handkerchief."

The Republican Convention met in Chicago on June 19th. It was not until the third day and after seven ballots that it chose its candidate. Senator Sherman led with a vote of 249 out of 830. Gradually, however, his following fell away, while that of General Alger and of Mr. Harrison increased. Mr. Sherman afterwards declared that the Southern delegates who had been instructed for him were brought over by the Alger interest. If so, Alger did not profit by the bargain. After the third ballot General Harrison's vote rapidly grew, until at last he obtained a clear majority.   Mr. Sherman charged that this was due to a secret and corrupt arrangement made with a member of the New York delegation (presumably Mr. Thomas C. Platt) and that friends of Mr. Harrison had made pledges on his behalf in order to secure the New York delegates.[21] For the Vice-Presidency, the Convention nominated Mr. Levi P. Morton, a New York banker, who had served a term in Congress and had been United States Minister to France.

Mr. Harrison was descended from Governor Benjamin Harrison of Virginia, a signer of the Declaration of Independence, and was the grandson of President William Henry Harrison.   By profession he was a lawyer, and he had served in the Civil War under General Sherman.   He was an excellent public speaker, a man of unblemished character, and a citizen of the State of Indiana, the vote of which was thought to be necessary to Republican success.

The campaign was comparatively a quiet one.   No bitter personalities marred it.   The contest turned mainly upon the issue presented by Mr. Cleveland in his tariff message. The Republican canvass was conducted with a feeling akin to desperation.   Speakers sought to alarm the manufacturing interests by the cry of "British Free Trade," and in this they were successful.   Large sums of money flowed into the campaign treasury and were spent like water.   It was in this campaign that the old-time torchlight processions were generally given up.   Political clubs were organised in their place, and did effective work.   As in the Harrison campaign of 1840, party songs were sung to stimulate enthusiasm, and at all Republican meetings this crude minstrelsy held an important place.   There was something almost fanatical in the spirit with which the

21 See Sherman, *Recollections*, ii., p. 1029 (Chicago, 1895).

Republicans strove for victory. They were not very hopeful; yet all that unlimited money and careful organisation
could do for them was done. The people at large admired
the courage with which President Cleveland had raised an
issue of principle, even when it jeopardised his own political prospects. Early in October, it seemed quite certain that
in addition to the solid vote of the Southern States he could
count upon that of Connecticut and New Jersey. The only
two States that were really doubtful and that were needed
to re-elect him, were Indiana and New York. Both parties
recognised this fact, and the supreme efforts of each were
concentrated upon these two States. As Mr. Harrison was
a citizen of Indiana, he was thought on the whole to have
the better chance; but the Republicans left nothing to mere
luck. They proceeded to pour great sums of money into
Indiana and to arrange quite openly a scheme for the purchase of voters on an elaborate scale. A letter, said to have
been written by Mr. W. W. Dudley, the treasurer of the
National Republican Committee, and unquestionably ema-
nating from that Committee, was sent to the party leaders
in Indiana. It contained the following memorable
sentence:

" Divide the floaters into blocks of five and put a trusted man in
charge of these five, with the necessary funds, and make him responsible that none get away, and that all vote our ticket."

In New York, which was President Cleveland's own
State, he might have looked for a majority had the political
conditions there not been peculiar. A large number of
Democrats who represented the Tilden wing of the party
were very hostile to Mr. Cleveland. They accused him
of gross ingratitude to Tilden. According to their story,

Mr. Cleveland's nomination in 1884 was due to Mr. Tilden's favour. They asserted that in June, 1884, Daniel Manning had gone to Mr. Tilden and had asked for his aid, promising in return to give to Mr. Tilden "any assurances he required in regard to the naming of Mr. Cleveland's Cabinet, should he be elected.[22] After Mr. Cleveland became President, he neglected to consult Mr. Tilden until every Cabinet place but one had been filled. He then asked Mr. Tilden to advise him as to the appointment of a Secretary of the Treasury. On Mr. Tilden's recommendation, Mr. Manning was appointed. He found himself, however, in an unfriendly atmosphere, as his letters to Tilden show. He wrote (December 21, 1885):

" I am living in an atmosphere that is full of mischief, and where the whirl is so great that one is inclined sometimes to doubt whether he comprehends his associates or fully understands anything of what he is about."

It is quite evident that Tilden had hoped, as Mr. Bigelow expresses it, that the Cleveland administration would be " a continuation of the Tilden dynasty," with Mr. Tilden himself as the power behind the throne. One can scarcely blame the President if he resented this assumption of control, though he might, doubtless, have been more tactful in declaring his independence. Practically, however, he proscribed all of Mr. Tilden's friends; he ignored Mr. Tilden's recommendations; and he made Mr. Manning feel that he was regarded with unfriendliness because of his relations with Tilden. Between the President and such a man as Mr. Tilden, indeed, there could be in any case little real sympathy. They had no more natural affinity than has a mastiff with a fox; and the result of this tempera-

22 Bigelow, *Tilden,* ii., p. 280.

mental antipathy was an unfortunate one for Mr. Cleveland. When Secretary Manning finally left the Cabinet in 1886, his friends felt that he had been greatly injured; [23] and his death, which soon after followed, was even ascribed to the harshness with which the President had treated him. Consequently, in New York there were many Democrats who were not unwilling to punish the President by helping to defeat him at the polls. Even so staunch a Democrat as Mr. A. S. Hewitt, then Mayor of New York, let his long friendship for Mr. Tilden estrange him from the present leader of his party whom he had cordially supported in 1884. "I shall not make a speech nor spend a dollar in the campaign," said he. "Cleveland is no statesman and I don't believe in his re-election." [24] Tammany Hall was also disaffected. Its leaders had never

---

[23] An evidently inspired editorial in *Leslie's Weekly* of January 27, 1887, said: "In the party view, Mr. Manning was squeezed out because he was not sufficiently a creation of the President's to be willing to supply all the subserviency essential to obtain office without any of the ambition for real power involved in the independent possession of its opportunities. He was neither a partner, adviser, nor dividend-drawer, though he supplied nearly all the brains and will-power, and no small share of the capital required for the enterprise, the President contributing only his reticence, his obscurity, his powers of absorption and his luck. Thus the time had come when the President and his ladder must part. The ladder is therefore shoved from under, and the President is up the tree. The ladder politely says: 'Considered as a ladder, I think I will take a rest!' The President replies: 'Considered as a ladder, you have my thanks. Rather than admit that you have been more or less than just a convenient ladder, I will provide myself with another ladder by the first of April, until which time please remain. Also permit me to express the hope that in any new post to which you may be called, your merits as a ladder for others will be as conspicuous as they have here been in my behalf.' So the President and Mr. Manning part on as good terms as the gourmand who eats an orange parts with the rind which he throws away."

[24] Breen, *Thirty Years of New York Politics,* p. 714.

liked Mr. Cleveland, and they had come to like him even less. As it happened, too, there now arose in New York politics a personality which sought to profit by Democratic dissension.

When Mr. Cleveland became President he had resigned the governorship of New York. The Lieutenant-Governor succeeded him. This was Mr. David Bennett Hill, a sublimated type of the practical politician. Mr. Hill had regarded Mr. Cleveland's efforts to reform the Civil Service as disloyal to the Democratic party. He posed as being a partisan through and through, and was fond of uttering in public addresses the emphatic declaration: " I am a Democrat ! " significantly intimating that the President was not. Mr. Hill was now a candidate for Governor, and he, or his friends for him, appear to have entered into an alliance with the Republicans under an arrangement by which Democratic votes were to be cast for Mr. Harrison in exchange for Republican votes to be given to Mr. Hill. The campaign in New York had, in consequence, some peculiar features. Flags bearing the words " Harrison and Hill " were displayed all over the State; meetings were held and were addressed by speakers who urged the election of Hill and said nothing about Cleveland. On the whole, the Democratic prospects in New York grew more and more unfavourable.

Toward the end of October, the Republicans prepared and executed a genuine *coup*. Mr. Cleveland's tariff position had been described by the campaign orators as essentially pro-British. It was difficult, however, to represent Mr. Cleveland as a partisan of England; for in dealing with the Canadian fisheries question, he had urged Congress to pass measures which would have brought the country within appreciable distance of a war with Great

Britain. Hence, the Republicans resorted to a trick to place the President in a false light on this issue. On September 4, 1888, a letter dated at Pomona, California, was addressed to Sir Lionel Sackville-West, the British Minister at Washington. This letter, which was signed "Charles F. Murchison," but which was actually written by a man named Osgoodby, purported to come from an Englishman, naturalised in the United States, and asked Sir Lionel for information as to whether Mr. Cleveland's policy toward Canada was sincere, and whether he was not at heart a friend of England. The following sentences, very artfully framed, deserve quotation:

"I am unable to understand for whom I shall cast my ballot, when, but one month ago, I was sure that Mr. Cleveland was the man. If Cleveland was pursuing a new policy toward Canada, temporarily only and for the sake of obtaining popularity and the continuation of his office for four years more, but intends to cease his policy when his re-election in November is secured, and again favour England's interest, then I should have no further doubt, but go forward and vote for him. I know of no one better able to direct me, sir, and most respectfully ask your advice in the matter. . . . Mr. Harrison is a high tariff man, a believer on the American side of all questions and undoubtedly an enemy to British interests generally. . . . As you . . . know whether Mr. Cleveland's policy is temporary only and whether he will, as soon as he secures another term of four years in the presidency, suspend it for one of friendship and free trade, I apply to you privately and confidentially for information which shall in turn be treated as entirely secret. Such information would put me at rest myself, and if favourable to Mr. Cleveland, enable me, on my own responsibility, to assure many of my countrymen that they would do England a service by voting for Cleveland and against the Republican system of tariff."

To this letter Sir Lionel Sackville-West was indiscreet enough to make the following reply:

" SIR: I am in receipt of your letter of the 4th inst. and beg to say that I fully appreciate the difficulty in which you find yourself in casting your vote. You are probably aware that any political party which openly favoured the mother country at the present moment would lose popularity, and that the party in power is fully aware of the fact. The party, however, is, I believe, still desirous of maintaining friendly relations with Great Britain, and still desirous of settling all questions with Canada which have been, unfortunately, reopened since the restriction of the treaty by the Republican majority in the Senate and by the President's message to which you allude. All allowances must, therefore, be made for the political situation as regards the presidential election thus created. It is, however, impossible to predict the course which President Cleveland may pursue in the matter of retaliation should he be elected; but there is every reason to believe that, while upholding the position he has taken, he will manifest a spirit of conciliation in dealing with the question involved in his message. I enclose an article from the New York *Times* of August 22d, and remain yours faithfully,

"L. S. SACKVILLE-WEST."

The Republicans held back this correspondence until October 24th, when they published it both in the newspapers and in millions of handbills. A shout went up that Mr. Cleveland was now undoubtedly " the British candidate." Sir Lionel's letter was interpreted as meaning that the President was especially friendly to British interests; that his apparently rigorous attitude toward Canada was adopted solely for electioneering purposes; and that in case of his re-election he would pursue a very different policy. Mr. Blaine, who had now returned from Europe in improved health, went about addressing great gatherings of Irish-American voters, and using everywhere the Murchison letter as a text. President Cleveland at first paid no attention to this matter, and was obviously disposed to treat it with contemptuous silence; but his party managers insisted that something should be done to neutralise the effect of the letter. A telegram informed him that " the Irish vote is slipping out of our hands because of diplomatic shilly-shallying. See Lamont at once. Something ought to be done to-day." The clamour increased, and President Cleveland then showed the one and only trace of weakness that can be detected throughout his whole career. To gain votes he demanded that the British Government recall its Minister. Lord Salisbury demurred. Naturally enough he did not see why the diplomatic relations of the two countries should be strained because of the exigencies of an American political campaign. Thereupon the President ordered that Sir Lionel's passports be given him, and he left Washington soon after." [25]

Had this action been taken so soon as the Murchison letter was published, it might have saved some votes. Had no action at all been taken, the President's dignity and his reputation for political courage would not have been impaired. As it was, he had obviously yielded to expediency and, therefore, he gained nothing whatsoever. At the election, Mr. Harrison won by a majority of sixty-five electoral votes. He carried both Indiana and New York, though in the latter State Mr. Hill was elected Governor.[26] Cleveland carried the South and also New

[25] The dismissal of Sir Lionel was naturally resented by Lord Salisbury, who appointed no successor to him until after Mr. Cleveland's term had ended.

[26] Harrison had a majority in New York State of 12,096 votes; Hill had a majority of 18,481 votes.

Jersey and Connecticut. The Republicans were successful in the congressional elections, having a majority of ten in the next House. An analysis of the vote showed that Mr. Cleveland had been defeated by a very narrow margin. Even in Mr. Harrison's own State he had come within 2000 votes of a majority, and had obviously lost New York only through the treachery of his own party. In the popular vote, as against Mr. Harrison, he had a majority of over 100,000 ballots. The sentiment of the country as a whole, therefore, still seemed to be on his side.

But the victorious Republicans in their rejoicing took small account of these considerations. They had won, and they believed that their party had come back to stay. They spoke of Mr. Cleveland as of one politically dead. On the night before the inauguration of Mr. Harrison, Washington was filled with civic and military organisations which had come to celebrate the glorious victory. Late in the evening, a motley crowd proceeded to the grounds of the White House. The windows of the executive mansion were darkened as though to symbolise defeat. Then the crowd of revellers, composed of "marching clubs," drunken militiamen, and hooligans of the city, lifted up their voices and chanted in discordant tones the ditty which had been most popular of all, in the late campaign:

> "Down in the cornfield
> Hear that mournful sound;
> All the Democrats are weeping—
> Grover's in the cold, cold ground!"

IV

THE PRESIDENCY OF BENJAMIN HARRISON

BENJAMIN HARRISON was inaugurated in the midst of a violent rainstorm, which, continuing all through the day, converted the streets of Washington into a muddy lake. While the oath of office was being administered, Mr. Cleveland good-naturedly held his umbrella over the bared head of his successor; and when the new President stepped forward to pronounce his inaugural address, the torrential splashing of the rain made his words inaudible to the sixty thousand men and women who were huddled about the Capitol, drenched to the skin, and shivering in the raw east wind. Superstitious persons spoke of "the Harrison hoodoo," and recalled the fact that President William Henry Harrison had died within a few weeks after his inauguration, as the result of a chill contracted on that day. There was much criticism of the ceremonial arrangements, which had been unintelligently planned. Members of the House of Representatives complained bitterly of the insolence with which they were treated by the employés of the Senate, and they even discussed the subject afterwards in a heated debate upon the floor of the House. The procession from the Senate Chamber to the East Front of the Capitol was so badly managed that it degenerated into an unseemly scramble. The customary review, in which nearly forty thousand men defiled before the President, was shorn of its impressiveness by the condition of the streets and the bedraggled appearance of the paraders. Altogether, the inefficiency of man seemed to combine with the disfavour of the elements to render this day of Republican triumph inauspicious.

Mr. Harrison's very long address contained, in addition to the usual rhetorical passages, several paragraphs that were of interest as foreshadowing his future policy. He spoke of the development of the new navy, and said that " the construction of a sufficient number of modern warships and of their necessary armament should progress as rapidly as is consistent with care and perfection in plans and workmanship." A general approval was given to the protective theory of the tariff, but on this head he probably thought it unnecessary to speak at length. There were a few sentences relating to the Trusts.

" The evil example of permitting individuals, corporations or communities to nullify the laws because they cross some selfish . . . interest . . . is full of danger, not only to the nation at large, but much more to those who use this pernicious expedient to escape their just obligations or to obtain an unjust advantage over others. They will presently themselves be compelled to appeal to the law for protection ; and those who would use the law as a defence must not deny that use of it to others. If our great corporations would more scrupulously observe their legal limitations and duties, they would have less cause to complain of the unlawful limitations of their rights or of violent interference with their operations."

Regarding the matter of appointments to office, Mr. Harrison was very frank. Though he pledged himself to enforce " fully and without evasion " the Civil Service law, he added, for the encouragement of good party men :

" Honourable party service will certainly not be esteemed by me a disqualification for public office. . . . It is entirely creditable to seek public office by proper methods and with proper motives; and all applicants will be treated with consideration. Persistent importunity will not be the best support of an application for office. . . . I hope to do something to advance the reform of the Civil Service. The ideal, or even my own ideal, I shall probably not attain. Retrospect will be a safer basis of judgment than promises."

The President established himself very quietly in the White House. He was far from being the object of that sort of public interest and curiosity which Mr. Cleveland had experienced. This was due, of course, partly to the fact that he was not, in politics, altogether a *novus homo*. Though not particularly well known in the East, his public career had been a long and honourable one. As colonel of an Indiana regiment in the Civil War, he had served with conspicuous gallantry, heading a bayonet charge at Resaca, and commanding a brigade at Kenesaw Mountain. Because of his share in the operations about Nashville in 1864, he had been breveted a brigadier-general of volunteers " for ability and manifest energy." After the war he practised law and was elected official reporter to the Supreme Court of Indiana, publishing subsequently a volume of judicial decisions. In 1876, he made his first appearance in politics as the Republican candidate for Governor, failing, however, to secure an election. In 1880, he was sent to the United States Senate, where he served upon several important committees, and won some reputation as a clear and forceful reasoner. With this record, and because his personal character had not been an issue in the presidential campaign, it was natural that he should, as President, be made the subject of fewer " pen-pictures " and anecdotes than his predecessor. But still another reason was to be found in the fact that his personality was less remarkable.

At the time of his inauguration he was in the fifty-sixth year of his age. Almost abnormally short of stature, he seemed, nevertheless, to be taller than he actually was, owing to the length of his body and the dignity of his manner. Sturdy of frame, he enjoyed vigorous health. A greyish beard, cut nearly square, covered a goodly portion of his face. His neck was so short as to give his head the appearance of being set directly upon his shoulders, and he usually held his chin down and partly drawn back upon his somewhat protuberant chest—a circumstance which led the irreverent to liken his appearance to that of a pouter-pigeon. If, however, he was not particularly impressive, his bearing was nevertheless the bearing of a gentleman, and he was one with whom not even an intimate friend would have dreamed of taking liberties.

Mr. Harrison, unfortunately for himself, had two separate and distinct manners. With the members of his own household and a very few others he was genial, hearty and spontaneously cordial. But to the rest of the world he exhibited a wholly different and most unsympathetic demeanour. His tone and manner were as cold as ice. He lacked that most delightful of all personal gifts— responsiveness. To strangers, and even to political friends who had to do with him, he appeared almost ungracious in his aloofness and indifference. Those who talked with him were met with a frigid look from two expressionless steel-grey eyes; and their remarks were sometimes answered in a few chill monosyllables devoid of the slightest note of interest. The President had also some rather unpleasant little personal traits and habits which offended many of his visitors; so that, on the whole, an unfavourable impression got abroad with regard to Mr. Harrison as an individual. The whole matter was rather strikingly summed up by one who knew him well, in these two sentences: "Harrison can make a speech to ten thousand men, and every man of them will go away his friend. Let him meet the same ten thousand men in private, and every one will go away his enemy."

President Harrison was a man of much intellectual ability. He had the mind of a trained lawyer—acute, penetrating and analytical. Something of the casuistry of the advocate at times appeared in what he wrote and said; but in the main he was eminently fair. An uncompromising adherent of his own party, he accepted its policy without question and defended it without reservation.[1] This he could do the more readily in that his intellect, though cultivated, lacked breadth, so that his views of public questions were often narrow ones. He showed, indeed, during the first year of his presidency a certain absorption in minor interests, and a fondness for fussing over questions relating to petty patronage and to all the minutiæ of politics. This tendency he afterwards largely overcame; for in him, as in most American presidents, the pressure of great responsibility gradually broadened and developed his whole nature. His integrity was never questioned, and this inherent honesty often made it hard for him to endure the companionship of many whose good will it was politic to conciliate. He felt, indeed, a strong personal dislike for some of the most influential leaders of his party; and though, in his official intercourse with them, he tried hard to treat them with cordiality, he did it with

---

[1] Senator Sherman wrote to him soon after the election: "The President should touch elbows with Congress. He should have no policy distinct from that of his party; and this is better represented in Congress than in the Executive." Mr. Harrison lived up to this admonition all through his term of office.

so bad a grace that his actual sentiments became perfectly well known.

As a public speaker, President Harrison attained to an unusual degree of excellence—in fact, more truly so than any other President since Garfield. While in the Senate he had always been listened to with interest; but at that time he had not yet matured his powers. There were invariably traces of formality and heaviness; and while he was always dignified, he was seldom graceful. His phraseology sometimes suggested the lay exhorter, the Presbyterian elder, or the leader of a prayer-meeting. One of his locutions was, " I lift up a prayer "—an expression which some of the newspapers caught up and rang the changes on with malicious glee. After his nomination, the party managers, who at first regarded him somewhat in the light of a respectable figure-head, urged him to be silent during the campaign.[2] But to this cautious advice he paid no attention; and when delegations visited him at his home, he made short, off-hand speeches which were so neat and telling as to be regularly reported in the press, and to furnish many effective texts to his followers. In all he delivered ninety-four of these impromptu addresses, and surprised even those who knew him, by his facility and felicity. As President, he never made a flat or feeble speech, nor one composed of platitudes. His oratory was marked by ease and finish, and a certain geniality of tone which by no means belonged to his ordinary conversation. In 1891, he made a journey through the South, and often addressed the throngs that greeted him. Here he was surrounded by those who were politically his opponents, and against whom he had fought at the time of the Civil War. It was no easy matter to speak off-hand under con-

2 McClure, *Recollections*, p. 140.

ditions such as these without saying something that would give offense, or without descending to the most obvious banality. Yet President Harrison never once did either; but rose above all criticism in a series of little speeches that were gems of occasional oratory—graceful, winning, suggestive and tactful to a degree.[3] In the longer addresses which he made while he was President, the same qualities were noticeable; and sometimes there was revealed a touch of that higher eloquence which combines dignity and reason with sincere, unstudied feeling.

The new Cabinet, with two exceptions, was one of no very marked distinction or ability. The exceptions were Mr. Blaine and Mr. Tracy. President Harrison had been more or less reluctant to give Mr. Blaine a place in his official household. So brilliant, ardent and magnetic a personality was not likely to lend itself to subordination. The President felt that he might himself be overshadowed by it. In fact, his attitude toward Mr. Blaine resembled that of Mr. Cleveland toward Tilden. The President wished to be master in his own house, and it did not please him to hear Mr. Blaine spoken of continually as " the uncrowned king." Nevertheless, he had no choice. Precedent required that he should appoint to the chief Cabinet-office the man who might have had the nomination had he wished it, and who, it was said, had really given it to Mr. Harrison. Mr. Blaine had sent a telegram to his friends while the Chicago Convention was in session; and although its contents were kept secret, the Blaine leaders had given Mr. Harrison their support immediately after its receipt. It was claimed that, in return, Mr. Harrison had promised to make Blaine his premier. This was undoubtedly untrue,

---

[3] These speeches were collected and published by Hedges, *Through the South and West with President Harrison* (New York, 1892).

since such a pledge was quite unnecessary. The President practically had no choice in the matter; and therefore, as it appeared, with reluctance and somewhat sullenly, he offered the portfolio of State to Mr. Blaine.

Mr. Benjamin F. Tracy of New York, who became Secretary of the Navy, was an eminent lawyer, a veteran of the Civil War. He had been United States District-Attorney in New York, and for two years an Associate Justice of the highest court in that State. Surprise was expressed that he should be chosen for the Navy Department rather than for the Attorney-Generalship. He was, however, so intelligent an administrator as fully to justify the President's selection of him; and during the next four years he did admirable work in building up a modern fleet. Mr. William Windom of Minnesota, the Secretary of the Treasury, was a safe man of moderate ability. He had been for a few months a member of President Garfield's Cabinet, retiring at the accession of Mr. Arthur, and entering the United States Senate for a second time. The new Secretary of War was Mr. Redfield Proctor of Vermont, a wealthy gentleman who had been Governor of his own State. Mr. Harrison's Secretary of the Interior was Mr. John W. Noble of Missouri, a veteran of the war and subsequently a practising lawyer. At the time of his appointment he was little known outside of his own State. The new Postmaster-General was Mr. John Wanamaker of Pennsylvania, a rich business man. To the Attorney-Generalship the President called his former law partner, Mr. W. H. H. Miller of Indiana. Congress had established a Department of Agriculture in addition to the existing executive offices, and this post was now filled by Mr. Jeremiah M. Rusk of Wisconsin, a State of which Mr. Rusk had been Governor for seven years.

Mr. Rusk was a somewhat picturesque personage. He had been in his early years a farmer; and his quaint and often racy speech still smacked of the soil. He had served all through the Civil War, and had displayed remarkable gallantry at Atlanta and during Sherman's march to the sea, where, like Mr. Harrison himself, he had been breveted a brigadier-general. Next to Blaine, Mr. Rusk was the most popular member of the Cabinet. He had a bluff, hearty, unconventional manner; he administered the new Department with great success; and his frank honesty and quaint utterances endeared him to the masses, who spoke of him with affectionate familiarity as " Uncle Jerry."

The appointment of Mr. Wanamaker was one that called forth a certain amount of criticism. Mr. Wanamaker was the proprietor of a large shop in Philadelphia, and he was also conspicuous as a religious leader and a promoter of Young Men's Christian Associations and Sunday schools. But during the campaign of 1888, Mr. Wanamaker had both himself contributed, and had collected from the rich protected manufacturers of Pennsylvania, an immense campaign fund, which he turned over to Senator Matthew S. Quay, whose political methods were notoriously objectionable. Mr. Quay was then chairman of the Republican Executive Committee, conducting the campaign; and the cash provided by Mr. Wanamaker had formed a part of the funds which, in Indiana, had influenced the " floaters," and consolidated the " blocks of five." The contrast between Mr. Wanamaker's piety and the purposes for which his money had been given was a little too glaring to pass unnoticed by his political opponents; though there was no reason for holding Mr. Wanamaker accountable for the use made of the fund by others.

Nevertheless, under the circumstances, his appointment to a Cabinet office distinctly savoured of a commercial transaction. His acceptance of the post, therefore, was held to indicate conditions which, as was said by one critic, " President Harrison must know, and, knowing, must deplore and feel ashamed of."

" That Mr. Wanamaker will administer the office respectably we have little doubt; and that this will after a while be used as an argument, even by clergymen and religious newspapers, in favour of allowing Cabinet offices to be purchased by contributions to campaign funds, we have just as little. Nearly all corruption begins under some harmless guise. Votes are always bought for the good of the cause; decisions are always sold to the right side; and we finally get to the comfortable conclusion that not only is God with the big battalions, but that He makes political debauchery one of His instruments for good." [4]

Some adverse criticism also arose in certain quarters from the fact that Mr. Wanamaker did not always appear to keep his high political office distinct from the interests of his business. As head of the nation's postal system he was the absolute chief of thousands of country postmasters. These men were kept reminded by circulars and otherwise that the Postmaster-General was also a great retail merchant. When the Pan-American Congress, composed of delegates from all the American Republics, was in session, its members visited Philadelphia; and, as a matter of courtesy to the Postmaster-General, they made an inspection of his " emporium." Upon leaving, each of these gentlemen was presented with a " souvenir volume," ornately printed and containing a description in florid rhetoric of the glories of the Wanamaker shop. Following the description was this request, with which, however, Mr. Wanamaker, probably, had nothing to do:

[4] *The Nation*, March 7, 1889.

"DEAR SIR: Confident of our commanding position in the mercantile world as leaders in retail commerce, and believing that we have reached the highest point yet attained in our country in the science of retail trading, we beg leave to ask your acceptance of this souvenir of your visit to our place of business, *in the hope that it contains information sufficient to warrant its submission to your Government as a portion of your report upon the honourable Congress to which you are accredited.*"

Because of these and similar occurrences, the whole country was amused when the New York *Sun* gave an exhibition of its impish cleverness at the expense of Mr. Wanamaker. Picking out day by day the flamboyant advertisements of his wares which appeared over his signature in the newspapers, it treated them with great gravity, professing to believe that they had been personally composed by him as serious literary productions, and discussing in terms of æsthetic criticism Mr. Wanamaker's Essays on Ladies' Underwear, his unrhymed Poems on Walking Skirts, his Reflections on Flannels, and his philosophical Musings upon Muffs.[5]

But while the Postmaster-General contributed nothing to the prestige of the Administration, the new Secretary of State won laurels for himself and for his chief. The State Department was a post admirably suited to the tastes and intellectual qualities of Mr. Blaine. Like Disraeli, whom in some respects he strikingly resembled, Blaine loved administration on a large scale. He had long been the most conspicuous figure in national politics, and it gratified alike his ambition and his imagination to appear in the still more spacious theatre of international affairs. His friends shared his enthusiasm and spoke with proud anticipation of the "spirited foreign policy" which was presently to be carried out. Mr. Blaine's opponents, on

[5] See, for instance, the *Sun* for March 15, 1889.

the other hand, professed a feeling of disquietude. They said that, with regard to the foreign relations of the United States, safety rather than brilliancy was to be preferred in the conduct of affairs. They prophesied that Mr. Blaine —restless, aggressive, and with a love of dramatic effects— would involve the country in some dangerous complication; and to justify this belief, they recalled what had occurred in 1882, when for nine months Mr. Blaine had been Secretary of State in President Garfield's brief administration, and until President Arthur relieved him.

The reminder of that time was an interesting one. Peru and Chile were then at war with one another; and Secretary Blaine had used his influence to preserve the territorial integrity and the independence of Peru, both of which were threatened by the triumphant Chileans. This action had given great offence to Chile and it had been severely criticised in the United States. It was Mr. Blaine's misfortune to have excited a suspicion that his motives were not disinterested. He had had some casual interviews with an adventurer named Shipherd; and in the course of the negotiations over the Chilean affair, he had taken up certain claims against Peru, known as the Landreau and Cochet claims, in which Shipherd was pecuniarily interested. Mr. Blaine wrote a despatch (August 4, 1882) to the American Minister in Peru, directing him to notify both the Chilean and Peruvian governments that no treaty of peace between the two countries must be made until the Landreau claim should be settled.[6] This despatch deeply angered Chile, as did the further activities of the Secretary at that time. Many thought that had not Mr. Arthur become President when he did, and had he not taken the matter out of the hands of Mr. Blaine, war might

[6] Senate Exec. Documents, No. 79 (Forty-seventh Congress), p. 507.

have occurred. The whole matter was investigated afterwards by the House of Representatives. Mr. Blaine appeared before a committee of the House, and his appearance led to an exciting scene.[7] A Democratic member, Mr. Perry Belmont of New York, took a leading part in examining Mr. Blaine; and he asked such searching questions, and seemed so sceptical, that at last Mr. Blaine was nettled. Mr. Belmont was a new member of Congress and was, besides, a young and unknown man, while Mr. Blaine was the most eminent of American statesmen. He therefore tried to overawe his youthful cross-examiner by assuming the grand manner. The phrasing of a certain telegram was under discussion. Mr. Blaine declared that the words had been garbled. Mr. Belmont stuck to his own interpretation. "I am not in a police-court to be badgered!" said Mr. Blaine; and he went on to say that Mr. Belmont had intentionally altered the despatch and was persisting in a falsehood. Belmont's face grew white to the lips, and then flamed red with anger. He looked Blaine straight in the eyes. Then he said:

"I believe you are a bully and a coward!"

It was these incidents—the Shipherd connection, the so-called "guano claim," and the strained relations with Chile in 1882—which Mr. Blaine's opponents now brought up again; but most persons regarded them as ancient history, and waited with interest to see to what the new Secretary of State would first turn his hand. As a matter of fact, at the very moment when President Harrison was taking the oath of office, there existed in a far quarter of the globe a condition of affairs so critical that it might at any moment plunge the United States into a

[7] See House Report, No. 1790 (Forty-seventh Congress).

war with the foremost military power of Europe. To understand this situation one must recall the succession of events which had made it possible.

Ever since the humiliation of France at the hands of Germany in the war of 1870, the latter power had arrogated to itself a sort of supremacy over other nations. Allied with Austria and Italy, the German Empire set no bounds to its pretensions. Russia was quiescent; England was isolated; France was prostrate. Prince Bismarck, as he sat in his chancellery on the Wilhelm-Strasse, felt that there indeed was the true *omphalos* of earthly power. He had despoiled Denmark in 1864. He had humbled Austria in 1866. He had crushed France in 1870. He was now treated with almost servile deference by ambassadors and statesmen. A frown of his, an impatient speech, or a curt despatch, was enough to send the shivers down the back of every Foreign Minister in Europe. No wonder that he had grown arrogant, and that all official Germans, taking their tone from him, cultivated a swaggering insolence which paid no heed to others' rights or feelings. In the early eighties, the Chancellor was pushing his scheme of planting German colonies in distant lands; and any unconsidered trifles of territory which he chanced to find unclaimed were promptly visited by German men-of-war and recorded on the official map as being German soil. This policy was quite openly directed against England as the great colonising power; but England was under the spell of Germany's enormous self-assertiveness; so that Downing Street seemed timidly anxious to avoid a clash with the autocrat of the Wilhelm-Strasse. In course of time, Prince Bismarck cast his acquisitive eye upon the Samoan Islands.

The Samoan Islands are twelve in number, lying in the track of vessels which ply between the American seaports on the Pacific Coast, and Australia. They have, therefore, a certain commercial importance, and to a naval power a definite strategic value. Upon the principal island, Upolu, where the chief town, Apia, is situated, a number of Germans, Americans and English had settled. A Hamburg trading firm was established there, besides a thriving American business house and a company of Scotch merchants. In 1878, a treaty was made by which the Samoan chief or " king " of that time gave to the United States the use of the harbour of Pago-Pago for a naval station.

As was natural, the small foreign community in Upolu, isolated from the greater world outside and thus thrown in upon itself, was rent by the small jealousies, intrigues and bickerings which arise when petty interests clash in a petty sphere. Race prejudice intensified the feeling, until Apia fairly seethed with pent-up enmities. Gradually, however, two distinct factions were formed, when the Americans and English made common cause against the Germans, who were the more numerous and who were also unpleasantly aggressive. By the year 1884, it had become clear that Germany intended by hook or by crook to get control of the Islands, and in doing so to ignore the rights of the English and American residents. The German consul, one Herr Stübel, began to manifest extreme activity. He had all the *morgue* and frigid insolence of the true Prussian official, and moreover he had at his beck several German ships of war, which always appeared most opportunely whenever Stübel was carrying things with a particularly high hand. The German residents assumed a most offensive bearing toward the other foreigners as well as toward the natives. In April, 1886, Stübel raised the German flag over Apia and in a proclamation declared that only the Government of Germany should thereafter rule over that portion of the islands. The British consul hesitated to act without instructions; but the American representative hoisted the colours of the United States and proclaimed an American protectorate.[8] This conflict of authority was serious, and led Secretary Bayard to energetic action. A conference at Washington between the representatives of Germany, Great Britain and the United States, agreed that the action of both consuls should be disavowed and that the *status quo ante* should be preserved in Samoa pending further negotiations.

Bismarck, however, had no intention of abandoning his ultimate purpose, or even of abiding by his agreement. A new consul, Herr Becker, was sent out from Berlin and proved to be as obnoxious as his predecessor. He planned a stroke that was delivered with prompt efficiency. The native king, Malietoa, was favourable to the English and Americans. Becker, seizing upon the pretext afforded by a drunken brawl between the German sailors and a few Samoans, declared war upon Malietoa, "by order of His Majesty, the German Kaiser." Martial law was proclaimed in Apia; German marines were landed; Malietoa was seized and was deported in a German ship; while a native named Tamasese, a creature of the Germans, was set up in his place. From that moment events tended rapidly toward a crisis. The American consul, Mr. Harold M. Sewall of Maine, wrote vigorous despatches to Washington and sent emphatic protests to Herr Becker, who answered him with sneering incivility. The Samoans refused to acknowledge the German puppet king and took to the bush, where the English and Americans furnished

[8] May 14, 1886.

them with arms. But in Apia, a German judge was set over the local courts, the captain of a German cruiser was made Prime Minister, and the German flag again flew over the soil which Germany had pledged itself to regard as neutral territory. A writer of genius, Mr. Robert Louis Stevenson, who was a resident of Samoa throughout these troublous times, has left a minute account of the intolerable bearing of the Germans and of the indignities to which other foreigners were subjected by them.[9] Mr. Sewell, single-handed, resisted their aggressions. The British consul sympathised with him; but the spell of Germany's predominance in Europe seemed to paralyse his will. At last, to punish those Samoans who were in arms against Tamasese, the German corvette *Adler* was ordered to shell the native villages, and thus to inspire the people with a wholesome dread of German power.

Just prior to this time, there had arrived in Samoan waters the United States gunboat *Adams,* under the orders of Commander Richard Leary. Commander Leary was to his very finger-tips a first-class fighting man. His name, as Stevenson remarked, was diagnostic. It told significantly of a strain of Celtic blood in the man who bore it. Leary had, indeed, a true Irishman's nimbleness of wit, an Irishman's love of trouble for its own sake, and even more than an Irishman's pugnacity. When he had learned just how things stood in Apia, and when he had noted the bullying demeanour of the Germans, his blood grew hot. Until now the notes of protest addressed to Becker had been couched in formal phrases. From the moment when Leary took a hand in the correspondence these notes be-

---

[9] Stevenson, *A Footnote to History: Eight Years of Trouble in Samoa* (London, 1891). See Callahan, *American Relations in the Pacific* (Baltimore, 1901).

came suddenly pungent with a malicious and most ingenious wit which made the sacrosanct emissaries of His Imperial and Royal German Majesty fairly gasp with indignation. The diabolical cleverness with which Leary followed up their every move was utterly infuriating, and no less so was his supreme indifference to what they thought or wanted. When the German warship fired rocket-signals at night, Leary used to sit on his after-deck and send up showers of miscellaneous rockets, which made the German signalling quite unintelligible. He refused to recognise their appointed king, and in a score of ways he covered them with a ridicule which seemed likely to make them ludicrous even in the natives' eyes. Meanwhile, a German night attack upon the Samoan "rebels" had been repulsed and several Germans had been killed. Very eagerly, then, did Herr Becker urge the captain of the *Adler* to bombard the "rebel" position at Apia. Surely the sound of the *Kanonendonner* would bring the natives, and also the insolent Yankees, to their senses. Captain Fritze of the *Adler* therefore ordered up his ammunition and prepared for the bombardment.

Leary's ship, the *Adams,* was a wooden vessel whose heavy armament consisted of smooth-bores, only a few of which had been converted into rifled guns. The German corvette was also wooden, but her guns were of the latest pattern turned out by Krupp. Nevertheless, at short range, this superiority would count for little; and the *Adams* was commanded by a sailor who would rather fight than eat. At the appointed hour, the *Adler* steamed out with the German ensign flying at her peak. The *Adams* followed close upon her heels, as if for purposes of observation; but it was noticed that her deck was cleared for action. Soon the *Adler* slowed down and swung into position, so as to bring her broadside guns to bear upon the helpless village. Instantly volumes of black smoke poured from the funnel of the *Adams,* the long roll of her drums was heard as they beat to quarters, and the American ship dashed in between the *Adler* and the shore, where she, too, swung about, her guns at port and trained directly on the Germans. Presently, Commander Leary in full uniform and accompanied by his staff boarded the *Adler.* His colloquy with the German captain was short and sharp: " If you fire," said he, " you must fire through the ship which I have the honour to command. I shall not be answerable for the consequences ! " So saying, he took his leave and returned to his own vessel.

Captain Fritze could scarcely believe his ears. Such audacity had never yet confronted him. He could not fire on the village unless he fired through the *Adams.* He knew that his first shot would be answered by an American broadside, and that this would be the signal for a war between his country and the American Republic. He faltered, shrinking from so terrible a responsibility; and then, his heart swelling with humiliation, he turned tail and steamed sullenly away. That night there was joy in Apia; and the Germans, lately boastful, went about with shamefaced looks.

Soon afterwards, Leary set sail for Honolulu, whence he might send despatches to his Government. In his absence, the Germans tried to accomplish on land what they had failed to do on water. It was known that the Samoans had gathered in large numbers in the interior of the island, and that they were in arms against the king whom Germany had tried to force upon them. A dare-devil American named Klein, a correspondent of the New York *World,* was with them, and acted as a sort of military leader. The Germans laid a plan to surprise them and to seize their chiefs. On December 18, 1888, long before daylight, a battalion of marines was disembarked from the German cruiser and marched stealthily through the forest. An hour later, the Samoans fell upon them and whirled them back to the seashore with a loss of fifty men and several officers. The fury of the Germans was unrestrained. Vice-Consul Blacklock telegraphed to Washington soon after:

"Germans swear vengeance. Shelling and burning indiscriminately, regardless of American property. Protest unheeded. Natives exasperated. Foreigners' lives and property in greatest danger. Germans respect no neutral territory. Americans in boats, flying. American flag seized in Apia harbour by armed German boats, but released. Admiral with squadron necessary immediately."

Up to this time, the situation in Samoa had aroused but little interest in the United States. Samoa was very far away. Most Americans had never even heard of it. But this stirring cablegram, followed as it was by detailed accounts of German aggression and of insults to the American flag,[10] roused the people to a warlike mood. To this mood President Cleveland's Government responded. The warships *Nipsic*[11] and *Vandalia* were hurried off to Apia, followed shortly by the *Trenton,* the flagship of Admiral Kimberly, a fine old sea-dog of the fighting type. The

[10] The German sailors had taken a flag from an American named Hamilton, and had trampled on it and torn it to shreds. Stevenson wrote: "These rags of tattered bunting occasioned the display of a new sentiment in the United States; and the Republic of the West, hitherto so apathetic and unwieldy, leaped to its feet for the first time at the news of this fresh insult."—*Op. cit.,* p. 527.

[11] Klein took refuge on the *Nipsic,* whose commander flatly refused to surrender him to the German naval officers.

British Government at last took heart of grace and ordered the cruiser *Calliope* to Samoa. The Germans were no less active; and early in March there were anchored off Apia, besides the vessels just enumerated, a German squadron consisting of the *Adler,* the *Eber,* and the *Olga,* all with their decks cleared and their crews ready for immediate battle. A single rash act might provoke a mighty war.

Such was the situation when President Harrison took office on March 4th. Four days later it was rumoured in Germany that the *Nipsic* had fired on the *Olga.* On March 10th, a despatch from Kiel, which was supposed to have come by way of Australia, reiterated the report, and added that the American vessel had been sunk by a torpedo from the *Olga.* A wave of excitement swept over the whole country. In San Francisco, great crowds filled the streets and massed themselves about the newspaper offices to await the posting of further bulletins. The tone of the press was one of intense hostility to Germany. The Government at Washington began preparing for any emergency that might arise. All the vessels of the Pacific Squadron were notified to be in readiness. The new steel cruiser, *Philadelphia,* was hastily equipped for service. But the news, when it came, was very different from that for which men waited. It told of a fearful battle, not with human forces, but with the elements. A fierce typhoon had struck the Samoan Islands on March 16th, and within a few hours, six of the warships that had been anchored in the harbour of Apia were driven from their moorings. The *Eber* was dashed against a coral reef and sunk. The *Adler* was capsized. The *Olga* and the *Nipsic* were hurled upon the sand; while the *Trenton* and the *Vandalia,* shattered and dismantled, settled to their gun-decks in the tremendous waves. The British ship,

Calliope, alone escaped. Her captain with high courage staked the safety of his vessel upon the chance of reaching the open sea. Crowding on every pound of steam until her boilers were almost bursting, and with her machinery red hot, the British cruiser fought her way out inch by inch against the hurricane. As she passed the American flagship, Admiral Kimberly led his sailors in three hearty cheers, which were answered by the British seamen amid the shrieking of the storm. When the typhoon subsided, it was found that few lives had been lost; and Admiral Kimberly, parading the band of the *Trenton,* took temporary possession of Apia to the strains of the national anthem.[12]

The news of this disaster dispelled all thoughts of war in Germany and in the United States. Prince Bismarck proposed a conference at Berlin to deal with the Samoan situation. He was confident that he could win by his strenuous diplomacy what he had failed to gain by bluster and a show of force. He felt perhaps that his personal presence and the greatness of his fame would overawe the untrained American commissioners, as it had invariably overawed the skilled diplomatists of Europe. He had dealt with Americans before. In 1883, a Minister of the United States at Berlin, Mr. A. S. Sargent, had displeased him by one of his despatches. Bismarck therefore ordered the officials at the Foreign Office to speak only German to Mr. Sargent whenever he called. As Mr. Sargent spoke nothing but English, he was placed in a very humiliating position, and for a whole year was obliged to transact all his official business through a secretary

[12] See, in addition to the description of Stevenson, *op. cit.,* the account by an eye-witness, J. Lyon Woodruff, attached to the *Trenton,* in the *Cosmopolitan Magazine* for November, 1895.

of legation. During Mr. Cleveland's administration, Germans naturalised in the United States were expelled from Germany with only twenty-four hours' notice. Mr. Bayard had tried to resent this breach of amity and of treaty rights, but he had proved to be no match for Bismarck. On the whole, then, the Chancellor felt quite easy in his mind.

The conference began on April 29, 1889. The United States was represented by Mr. J. A. Kasson, Mr. William Walter Phelps and Mr. G. H. Bates, Mr. Bates having already visited Samoa and made himself familiar with the conditions there. Prince Bismarck's object was to make a treaty which should recognise the political predominance of Germany in Samoa. After he had set forth his views, the American commissioners opposed them absolutely. They insisted that the United States, Great Britain and Germany should share alike, and that the rights of each should be recognised as equal. Bismarck was a great actor. He could assume at will a tremendous indignation, and work himself into a rage which his huge bulk of body made really awe-inspiring. He now resorted to this device, and frowned portentously as he growled out sentences that seemed full of menace. The Americans were thoroughly impressed by his manner, and they cabled to Secretary Blaine, informing him that the Chancellor was very irritable. Mr. Blaine at once flashed back the terse reply: "The extent of the Chancellor's irritability is not the measure of American rights." [13]

This message so stiffened the backbone of the American commissioners that they held to their point with unyielding pertinacity. Their British colleagues, heartened by their

[13] Hamilton (Dodge) *Biography of James G. Blaine*, p. 659 (Norwich, 1895).

example, united in supporting the American position. Bismarck found that he could accomplish nothing, either by threatenings or by cajolery; and at last the man of blood and iron backed down squarely, and conceded every point. Malietoa, whom the Germans had seized and exiled, was restored as King of Samoa. A general act was signed under which the three powers established a *condominium* in the islands.[14] This was the first diplomatic reverse which Bismarck had encountered in all his great career, and he had met it at the hands of the United States. It was a signal triumph for Mr. Blaine and for the nation. The incident made a profound impression in Europe, and most of all in England. The London *Saturday Review,* an organ usually known for its hostility to everything American, summed up the events in Samoa and then added: " It has been left for the navyless American Republic to give us a lead in the path of duty and of honour."

Taken by itself, this Samoan affair was but a trifling incident and might well be chronicled in a single paragraph. But in the light of subsequent events its ultimate significance is seen to have been very great. First of all, it revealed to the American people their need of a more powerful navy; and Congress soon after provided the sum of $25,000,000 for the building of new ships, a sum which was presently augmented by a further appropriation of $16,500,000. By the end of the year 1890, the United States had under construction five battleships of the first class, an armoured cruiser and an armoured ram, besides ten steel cruisers and six vessels intended for coast defence. Another and very far-reaching result was found in the growth among official Germans of an intense animosity toward the United States, for having, at every move of the

14 This continued until 1898.

Samoan game, thwarted and humiliated Germany.   This feeling grew with the lapse of time; and nine years later, in another island of the sea, it was destined once more to drive the two nations to the very brink of war.

Even more impressive was the Samoan episode as the revelation of a new temper in the people of the United States.   This has been well described by Mr. John Bassett Moore in the following words:

" The chief historical significance of the Samoan incident lies less in the disposition ultimately made of the Islands, than in the assertion by the United States, not merely of a willingness, but even of a right, to take part in determining the fate of a remote and semi-barbarous people, whose possessions lay far outside the traditional sphere of American political interests.   The tendency thus exhibited, though to a certain extent novel, was by no means inexplicable.   The intense absorption of the people of the United States in domestic affairs, which resulted from the Civil War and the struggle over Reconstruction, had ceased. . . .   The old issues were no longer interesting.   The national energy and sense of power sought employment in other fields.   The desire for a vigorous foreign policy, though it jarred with tradition, had spread and become popular." [16]

Mr. Blaine was less successful in his attempt to establish for the United States the claim that Bering Sea was practically a *mare clausum*.   The object of this claim was to secure to American sealers the sole right to take seals in Bering Sea.   Seal catching was immensely profitable and was engaged in by Russians, Canadians and Americans. These sealers made their catches in so indiscriminate a manner, killing alike the females and the males, as to make

[16] *The Cambridge Modern History*, vii., p. 663 (New York, 1903).   See also Henderson, *American Diplomatic Questions*, p. 251 (New York, 1901).

it probable that before many years all seals would be exterminated. The Cleveland administration had tried to establish American jurisdiction over Bering Sea and had seized several British sealing vessels in the open waters. These vessels were subsequently released; but the whole question still remained unsettled when Mr. Blaine began a correspondence with Lord Salisbury in support of the American claim. In this correspondence it must be said that the American Secretary did not appear to the best advantage. The traditions of diplomacy require the tone of all formal communications to be ceremonious and courtly to the last degree. However burning the question at issue may appear, the diplomatic duellists must everywhere observe the most punctilious etiquette, and never either in word or phrase overstep the limits of a stately self-restraint. These traditions Lord Salisbury on his side followed absolutely. His immensely able argument was couched throughout in terms of the finest courtesy, suggesting in every line the urbanity and graceful deference which mark the intercourse of high-bred gentlemen. Mr. Blaine's despatches, on the contrary, however plausible, were marked at times by a certain swagger, a tone of lurking insolence and an offensive assumption that his opponent's argument was one of conscious duplicity and falsehood.[17] This perhaps was due to the fact that in his heart of hearts, Mr. Blaine was quite aware of the weakness of his case. Certain it is that he accomplished nothing; and at last he betook himself from diplomacy to methods based on force. Instructions were issued to American revenue

---

[17] "One who reads the Bering Sea correspondence must admit the dialectic skill of Mr. Blaine, and yet feel on the whole that he was hurting his cause by being, in the phrase of his critics, 'too smart.' . . . This was perhaps the most conspicuous instance of Blaine's failure in tact."—Stanwood, *James G. Blaine*, p. 361 (Boston, 1905).

cutters to capture British sealing vessels even when found
in open waters. The British Minister at Washington at
once informed his Government, and immediately Lord
Salisbury despatched a vigorous protest (June 14, 1890),
which ended in the following very ominous words:

" The undersigned is . . . instructed formally to protest
against such interference, and to declare that Her Britannic
Majesty's Government must hold the Government of the United
States responsible for the consequences that may ensue from acts
which are contrary to the established principles of international
law."

What this really meant was that if American cruisers
should molest British vessels in Bering Sea outside of the
three-mile limit, British ships of war would forcibly resist
them. The gravity of the crisis was sufficiently apparent;
and Mr. Blaine, though he seems to have weighed the
question of war and peace, decided presently for peace.
In a very characteristic private note to the President
(March 6, 1891) he said:

" If we get up a war-cry and send naval vessels to Bering Sea it
will re-elect Lord Salisbury. England has always sustained an
administration with the prospect of war pending. Lord Salisbury
would dissolve Parliament instantly if we made a demonstration
of war. On the other side I am not sure—or rather I am sure—
that war would prove of no advantage to you. New York and
Massachusetts are steadily against war with England unless the
last point of honour requires it. Again, I think you will bitterly
disappoint Lord Salisbury by keeping quiet. We should have all
the fuss and there would be no war after all. Not a man in a
million believes we should ultimately have war." [18]

The whole question was subsequently referred to arbitration. A mixed tribunal met in Paris in 1893 and de-

[18] Hamilton, *op. cit.,* p. 671.

cided that the American case was defective, and it was therefore lost upon every legal point involved. The final decision held: "That the United States have no right to protection of, or property in, the seals frequenting the islands of the United States in the Bering Sea, when the same are found outside the ordinary three-mile limit."

While Secretary Blaine was confronting Bismarck, President Harrison was busying himself with the much less noble task of parcelling out the offices. The significant sentence in his inaugural, which declared that honourable party service would not be a disqualification for appointment, had been accepted by party "workers" as a special invitation. These now descended upon the capital and overwhelmed the President with their importunities. Questions of petty patronage occupied his entire time, and they seem, moreover, to have greatly interested him. His activities for several months were those of an office-broker, and the spectacle was not altogether edifying. He observed the Civil Service law as it stood upon the books; and within the range of the classified service no changes were made from partisan motives. But elsewhere, what was practically a clean sweep was carried out. It cannot be said that that result strengthened Mr. Harrison even with his own party; since for every office-seeker who was gratified by an appointment, at least three or four expectant ones were disappointed, while the majority of the people viewed this office-mongering with something like contempt. It will be remembered that, according to Senator Sherman,[19] Mr. Harrison had received the Republican nomination, as the result of a bargain with Mr. T. C. Platt of New York. It was reported that to Mr. Platt had been promised the Secretaryship of the Treasury. If such a bargain had

[19] Sherman, *Recollections*, ii., p. 1029.

actually been made, it was undoubtedly made without Mr. Harrison's consent; for Platt was not appointed. Nevertheless, to console him, he was allowed to have a large share of Federal patronage; and the same concession was made to Mr. Quay of Pennsylvania. President Harrison likewise looked very carefully after the interests of his own relatives. Offices were given by him to his father-in-law, to his son's father-in-law, to his daughter's brother-in-law, to his own brother, and to several of his son's college chums. He also brought upon himself much criticism by bestowing important places on the editors of newspapers which had supported him in the late campaign. Mr. Whitelaw Reid of the New York *Tribune* received the mission to France. Mr. Thorndike Rice, who, as editor of the *North American Review,* had published an outrageously personal attack upon Mr. Bayard, was made Minister to Russia. Mr. Enander, a Chicago editor, became Minister to Denmark. An Oshkosh editor received the Peruvian mission, and an Indianapolis editor the English consul-generalship. One J. S. Clarkson, editor of the *Iowa State Register,* was allowed to distribute the fourth-class postmasterships. The editor of the Utica *Herald* became Assistant United States Treasurer at New York. Mr. Robert P. Porter of the New York *Press* was appointed head of the Census Bureau. Mr. Porter was an Englishman by birth, a Free Trader who had with suspicious suddenness become a convert to Protectionism. One of these appointments fell through. It was that of Mr. Murat Halstead of the Cincinnati *Commercial Gazette* to be Minister to Germany. Mr. Halstead was rejected by the Senate for an interesting reason. During the Cleveland Administration the Ohio Legislature had elected as United States Senator, Mr. Henry B. Payne, a warm friend of the Standard Oil Company.   Subsequent investigation showed that Mr. Payne's election had been due to the most barefaced bribery.   Another Ohio legislature secured the necessary evidence of this fact and forwarded it to Washington, accompanied by a resolution asking the Senate to investigate the case of Mr. Payne with a view to unseating him.   Senatorial courtesy was held to demand that Mr. Payne himself should welcome such an investigation and should ask for it, as an honourable man might have been expected to do.   But Mr. Payne held his tongue, and though lashed by Senator Hoar with indignant sarcasm, he said no word.   The Senate, therefore, declined to investigate the matter.[21]   Mr. Halstead in his newspaper had declared that this refusal was due to improper influences; and the Senate now took its revenge by rejecting the editor's nomination.

All these circumstances—the attempt to subsidise the press, the Wanamaker affair, the partisan removals and appointments, the affiliation of the President with such men as Platt and Quay, and the proofs of a petty nepotism—excited throughout the country a feeling of disgust which found expression in a most unexpected place.   On April 29th and the two following days, there was celebrated in New York City the one hundredth anniversary of the first inauguration of President Washington.   The details of the old-time ceremonies were carefully reproduced. Like Washington, President Harrison was entertained by the Governor of New Jersey, and then proceeded to Elizabethport, whence he was conveyed by water to the foot of Wall Street, landing at the very place where Washing-

---

[21] Cf. Lloyd, *Wealth against Commonwealth,* pp. 373-388 (New York, 1898).

ton had disembarked a hundred years before. A squadron of warships thundered a salute as the President came ashore. There were given two public receptions and, in the evening, a gala ball. On the 30th, the President was escorted, as Washington had been, to St. Paul's Church, where, in the pew which Washington had occupied, he listened to a religious service conducted by the Bishop of New York, the Rt. Rev. H. C. Potter. When the Bishop entered the pulpit in which Bishop Provoost had preached before Washington, the presidential party settled themselves down comfortably, expecting to hear a polished historical address, lightened here and there by a few graceful compliments to Washington's successor. It came to them with something of a shock when the Bishop, far from pronouncing a bland discourse, replete with pleasant things, spoke out with something of the fire of an ancient prophet. In words that burned, he contrasted the simplicity, integrity, and honour of George Washington and of the nation's founders, with the vulgar display, the self-seeking, and the shamelessness of men in high places at the end of a hundred years.

" The growth of wealth, the prevalence of luxury, the massing of large material forces, which by their very existence are a standing menace to the freedom and integrity of the individual, the infinite swagger of our American speech and manners, mistaking bigness for greatness and sadly confounding gain and godliness—all this makes it impossible to reproduce to-day either the temper or the conduct of our fathers."

And then the Bishop spoke two sentences which struck home:

" The conception of the national government as a huge machine existing mainly for the purpose of rewarding partisan service—this is a conception so alien to the character and conduct of Washington and his associates that it seems grotesque even to speak of it. It would be interesting to imagine the first President of the United States confronted with some one who had ventured to approach him upon the basis of what are now commonly known as 'practical politics.'" [22]

This sermon caused a great sensation throughout the country. Some said that the Bishop was guilty of bad taste in choosing an occasion such as this for a rebuke so pointed and so personal. Others said that the whole discourse was on the very highest plane, and that the Bishop had shown himself a true priest of God, speaking out boldly the lesson which the hour and the place demanded, and undeterred from his duty by those considerations which too often influence the time-serving and timid ecclesiastic. Certain it is that his words were caught up and repeated all over the land, and that they voiced the sentiment of millions.

When Congress met on December 3d, the President's message took up the question of the surplus in the Treasury. At the end of the Cleveland administration this had amounted to very nearly $97,000,000; and, as Mr. Harrison had pointed out, it was more likely in the ordinary course of events to increase rather than to diminish. He recommended, therefore, a revision of the tariff and the removal of the internal tax upon tobacco. Congress, however, in both houses of which the Republicans had a working majority, took a very cheerful view of the surplus, holding, in the naïve words of Colonel Frederick Grant, that "a surplus is easier to handle than a deficit." The Senators and Representatives felt that if the surplus

[22] New York *Herald; Sun; Evening Post,* for May 1, 1889.

in the Treasury proved embarrassing, the easiest and simplest way to reduce that surplus was to spend it. Hence, Congress promptly passed the Dependent Pension Bill which President Cleveland had vetoed. At once the number of pensioners rose from about 350,000 to nearly 550,000, and steadily increased until, ten years later, it had reached 1,000,000; while the yearly payments grew from $65,000,000 to $150,000,000, representing pretty nearly half the entire annual budget of the United States.[23] Heavy appropriations were made for the Navy and for an exposition in Chicago to celebrate the four hundredth anniversary of the discovery of America. Money was also poured out lavishly for various public works; until this Congress in its two sessions had made itself responsible for an expenditure which exceeded that of any other Congress by $170,000,000. The total amount of money voted for various purposes was roughly computed at $1,000,000,000. Hence, the Fifty-first Congress was generally spoken of as "the Billion-Dollar Congress." When this name was uttered in the presence of Mr. Speaker Reed he remarked casually, "Yes, but this is a billion-dollar country."

The saying was very characteristic of the man, who now began to play a somewhat spectacular part in national legislation. Mr. Thomas B. Reed was a native of Maine,

[23] Mr. Harrison appointed to be head of the Pension Office, an active politician, James Tanner, commonly known as "Corporal" Tanner,—a favourite of the Grand Army of the Republic. Tanner began "re-rating" the pensions illegally and bestowing "back-pay" at a lavish rate. Wealthy men, among them United States Senator Manderson, were thus made the recipients of large sums from the Treasury, simply by Tanner's mandate. Called to account by Secretary Noble, Tanner replied insolently that he was the Secretary's superior officer in the matter of pensions. The President had finally to remove him, so great became the scandal of his conduct.

who had been a member of Congress for twenty-three years. He was a very striking figure. Fully six feet in height, of huge girth, and impressing the beholder with a sense of great reserve power, he was both physically and mentally a giant. A keen reasoner, alert, audacious, and absolutely self-possessed, his party recognised in him a leader who could neither be outwitted nor outfaced. His speech was caustic, his wit keen; and he took delight in destroying shams, sometimes even those shams in which his associates pretended to believe. He had a nasal Yankee drawl, and the eyes which peered out of his large round face twinkled with an irrepressible humour. He was now elected Speaker of the House, and he was counted upon by the Republicans to force through some very controversial legislation against a minority which was both large and decidedly pugnacious.

The measure which threatened to meet with the bitterest opposition was a Federal Elections Bill, intended to give the Federal Government power to supervise Congressional elections, and if necessary to use military force for the protection of every legal voter. This measure was directed against the South, where the negro vote had practically been suppressed. The fact was perfectly well known. The South was unanimous against any interference which would once more tend to restore the negro to political importance. Over the proposed bill, therefore, the fight was certain to be acrimonious and protracted. It was believed that the minority, by making use of filibustering tactics, by introducing dilatory motions and by demanding the roll call upon each of these, could wear out the endurance of the majority and thus prevent the passage of the bill. By refusing to vote, the Democrats could, under the existing rules, prevent a quorum of the

House unless practically all the Republican members should be present. Speaker Reed and his party friends decided to thwart such obstructions. They drew up and adopted a set of rules empowering the Speaker to refuse to entertain motions obviously intended to delay the business of the House, and also to " count a quorum "— meaning by this that the Speaker could direct the Clerk of the House to record as " present and not voting " all members who were actually there and who refused to answer to their names at roll-call.

It required strong nerves and complete presence of mind to enforce these rules to the letter; but Mr. Reed was fully equal to the task. The sessions of the House soon resembled pandemonium. Member after member on the Democratic side would rise and make a series of motions, shouting out the words at the top of their lungs; but the Speaker paid no more attention to them than if they had been miles away. While he counted his quorums, members sought to escape from the hall, but found that the doors were locked.[24]   Then they raged up and down the aisles, denouncing the Speaker in unmeasured language, yelling, shrieking, and pounding their desks, while the Republicans added to the din by cheering and whistling with delight. Passion waxed so hot that even the correspondents in the press-gallery shared in it; and many of them leaned over the railing, shaking their fists at the Speaker, and pouring forth a torrent of profanity which was quite inaudible amid the uproar. Through it all, Mr. Reed sat tranquilly in his chair, serene as a summer morning, unheeding the deluge of denunciation which

[24] Mr. Kilgore of Texas, popularly known as " Buck " Kilgore, gained a transient fame by kicking down the door and making his escape at one of these sessions.

descended on him, while he would say slowly in his most exasperating drawl:

" When—the ex-ci-ta-ble gen-tle-man from Tex-as has come to or-der, the Chair will—rule—upon the point."

These tempestuous sessions continued day after day, and under the guidance of " Czar Reed," as he was called, the Federal Elections Bill ultimately passed the House. In the Senate, however, it died a peaceful death; because there existed in the upper House the right of unlimited debate; and an alliance was formed between the Democrats and a number of Republican Senators to prevent the passage of the bill. There was, as a matter of fact, little real desire in the North for its enactment into law. That the negro vote was suppressed throughout the Southern States was not denied; yet most fair-minded men had come to feel that the enfranchisement of the negro had been a political error; and no one liked to contemplate even a partial return to the hideous scenes of the Reconstruction Period, when ape-like blacks had leagued themselves with the vilest whites in a repulsive and disgraceful political orgy.

Under the Reed rules were passed the Dependent Pension Bill, already mentioned, a bill for the admission of Idaho and Wyoming as new States, and bills to repeal the Bland-Allison Act and to substitute in its place the so-called Sherman Silver Law. This last act provided that thereafter the Government should purchase every month 4,500,000 ounces of silver, and issue against this bullion, up to its full value, legal tender notes redeemable on demand in coin. As the genesis and the operation of this new law will be discussed more fully in a subsequent chapter, it may be passed over here without especial comment. The most important legislation of the session was a tariff bill, framed by the Committee on Ways and Means, of which the chairman was Mr. William McKinley of Ohio. The passage of this bill marked a new stage in the development of protective legislation in the United States.

Prior to the Civil War, the tariff system of the United States had, as a whole, been primarily devised to produce revenue, and only secondarily to protect domestic industries against foreign competition. Thus, the acts of 1824, of 1828, and of 1832, which represent the high-water mark of protective sentiment in ante-bellum days, were at the most intended to give American manufacturers of iron, cotton and woollen goods and a few other commodities, some temporary assistance until they should have established themselves upon so firm a basis as to stand alone. The protectionists of those days were of the old school, regarding a high tariff on imported goods only as a means to a definite end, and not as an end in itself. The " infant industry argument " was the one which writers and speakers upon the subject most often used and which most appealed to the popular intelligence. " Give us help for a while, until our factories are built, our machinery installed, our business organised, and our experience acquired, and then we can hold our own against the world." This was quite in accordance with the independent, individualistic spirit of the native American of the early nineteenth century, who asked only for an opportunity to make a fair start and who, after that, had a sturdy confidence in the sufficiency of his own brain and his own hands. By 1842, in fact, the country at large had begun to experience a reaction from even so much of protectionism as was embodied in the acts just mentioned. To be sure, in 1842, a new tariff bill, passed by the

Whigs, was professedly a protective measure; but its life was short; and under President Polk the duties were scaled down by the tariff of 1846 to a point where many of the articles about which protectionist writers have the most to say were subjected to an average duty of only thirty per cent. These rates were lowered still further by the act of 1857—a purely non-political measure—and when the Civil War broke out, the tariff system of the United States represented an approximation to Free Trade in that it was intended to produce revenue for the needs of the Government and not especially to shelter or build up any industries which without protection would be unprofitable. Agitation on the subject of the tariff had at that time practically ceased. Both political parties were satisfied to leave things as they were. The country had been extraordinarily prosperous. Manufactures flourished, and the " infant industries " which had appeared to require assistance in 1832 were well past the period of infancy. When, therefore, in 1860, with a view to the coming election, the Republicans introduced into Congress a new tariff bill with a higher scale of duties,[26] they were rebuked by one of the ablest of their own number, Mr. Sherman, who declared:

" When Mr. Stanton says the manufacturers are urging and pressing this bill, he says what he must certainly know is not correct. The manufacturers have asked over and over again to be let alone." [27]

In fact, the instinctive dread of any change whatever, which in after years led business men and producers gener-

[26] The object was to benefit certain special interests in Pennsylvania and in two or three other States, of which the electoral votes were indispensable in the next election.

[27] *Congressional Globe*, p. 1867 (1859-60).

ally to dread a lowering of the tariff, operated in 1860 to make them dread an increase in the duties.

The Civil War, however, brought with it an insistent and incessant demand for money to meet the drain upon the Treasury. Every species of taxation that could be devised by the harassed Chase was legalised by Congress. When at last the expenses of the Government had risen to something like $3,000,000 a day, there came a climax to the financial agony in the passing of measures of taxation, direct and indirect, more sweeping than any modern people had ever known. Incomes were taxed; the excise imposts grew heavier and heavier; cheques, notes, drafts, wills, deeds, mortgages, business agreements, insurance policies, and almost every form of legal document, were valid only after they had paid their tribute in the form of revenue stamps. The barest necessities of life—even medicines, salt, and matches—yielded great sums to the tax-gatherer. Specific or *ad valorem* duties were heaped upon a vast number of products and manufactures. Transportation by rail or boat was taxed, and so was the business of the telegraphs and of the express companies. A multitude of ordinary callings had to pay heavy license fees. More than this, not only were manufactures subjected to a general tax, but at each stage of production a separate tax was levied on every article—first while it existed only as raw material and then again when it had been turned out as a finished product. Nothing escaped the eye of the inquisitor. Many persons ruefully recalled the pungent words in which Sydney Smith had depicted the miseries of tax-ridden England at the close of the Napoleonic wars.[28]

---

[28] " Taxes upon every article which enters into the mouth, or covers the back, or is placed under the foot; taxes upon everything which it is pleasant to see, hear, feel, smell, or taste; taxes upon warmth, light and

It was the manufacturers who suffered most; and in order that they might not be absolutely ruined, some compensatory legislation was needed in their interest. " I shear my sheep; I do not flay them," said the Emperor Tiberius on one occasion; and in the same spirit the financiers at Washington sought to preserve the manufacturing industries from extinction, so that they might continue to be a source of revenue. " If we bleed manufacturers," said Mr. Morrill of Vermont in 1862, " we must see to it that the proper tonic is administered at the same time." The " tonic " was administered in the shape of a high tariff on imported manufactures. This largely shut out foreign competition, and so gave to the American producers a monopoly of the home market as a compensation for the heavy burdens which they were bearing in time of war. The measure was understood to be distinctly a war measure. It was avowedly a temporary arrangement, a part of the whole abnormal, exceptional legislation which Con-

locomotion; taxes on everything on earth, and the waters under the earth; on everything that comes from abroad, or is grown at home; taxes on the raw material; taxes on every fresh value that is added to it by the industry of man; taxes on the sauce which pampers man's appetite, and the drug that restores him to health; on the ermine which decorates the judge, and the rope which hangs the criminal; on the poor man's salt, and the rich man's spice; on the brass nails of the coffin, and the ribands of the bride; at bed or board, couchant or levant, we must pay. The schoolboy whips his taxed top; the beardless youth manages his taxed horse, with a taxed bridle, on a taxed road; and the dying Englishman, pouring his medicine, which has paid 7 per cent., into a spoon that has paid 15 per cent., flings himself back upon his chintz bed, which has paid 22 per cent. and expires in the arms of an apothecary who has paid a license of a hundred pounds for the privilege of putting him to death. His whole property is then immediately taxed from 2 to 10 per cent. Besides the probate, large fees are demanded for burying him in the chancel; his virtues are handed down to posterity on taxed marble; and he is then gathered to his fathers to be taxed no more."— *Works of Sydney Smith,* ii., p. 117 (London, 1848)

gress enacted in order to meet an extraordinary crisis in the struggle for national existence. Its advocates never dreamed that it was to be perpetuated, any more than the tax upon the telegraph, or the license to carry on an ordinary business.

After the war had ended, nearly all these unprecedented expedients for wringing money from the people were speedily abandoned. The floating debt was funded. Stability and order brought renewed prosperity; and when the need of maintaining half a million men in arms ceased to exist, Congress repealed tax after tax. At last every one of the exceptional burdens from which the manufacturers had suffered was removed. Logically, then, the protective duties which had been imposed to enable them to bear those burdens should also have been abolished. This, however, was not done. Leading Republican statesmen, even those who were protectionists, admitted that the high duties were no longer necessary, and, therefore, that they were no longer just.[29] Many attempts were made to remove or modify them, as in the abortive measure of 1867, which had a majority in both houses of Congress, but which failed to pass because, owing to a technicality of parliamentary law, a two-thirds vote was needed to bring it before the House as an amendment.

Gradually, the long delay in lowering the duties produced a singular effect upon the public mind. The special circumstances under which the duties had originally been levied were forgotten. They ceased to be regarded as a

[29] "It is a mistake of the friends of a sound tariff to insist on the extreme rates imposed during the war. . . . Whatever percentage of duties was imposed on foreign goods to cover internal taxation on home manufactures, should not now be claimed as the lawful prize of protection when such taxes have been repealed."—Speech by Senator Morrill, *Congressional Globe*, p. 3295 (1869-70).

war tax, but were rather viewed by many as an integral and normal part of our financial system.   Moreover, the manufacturers, who were heaping up fortunes through the continuance of the war tariff, exerted all the power which great wealth afforded of creating a sentiment in their behalf.   Liberal gifts to the campaign fund of the Republican party were rewarded by legislative favours.   But the tariff issue was not strictly a party one.   There were high-tariff Democrats as well as low-tariff Republicans.   For instance, Mr. Samuel J. Randall, who was long a Democratic leader in the House and who twice served as Speaker, was as thorough-going a protectionist as " Pig Iron Kelly " himself; and in fact, in some of his canvasses for re-election, the Republicans in his district set up no candidate to oppose him.   Protection sentiment, in a word, was strong in the States where protected manufactures flourished, and weak in the agricultural States, which received nothing from the tariff except an increase in the cost of living. When General Hancock in 1880 said, " The tariff is a local issue," the remark was received with a shout of derision; but in the sense in which he meant it, it was profoundly true.

In the course of time, the agricultural communities of the West began to get an inkling of the truth, and to perceive how preposterous it was to protect industries which had, without protection, successfully maintained themselves against foreign competition before the war.   Various popular movements, such as the Farmers' Alliance, Grangerism, and the like,   made the Republican managers uneasy.   Several revisions of the tariff were undertaken, ostensibly in the direction of lower duties.   The act of 1872 was one of these attempts, but it was so artfully framed as, in fact, to leave things very much as they had been before.   In 1883, a general revision of duties actually raised many of them, as, for example, those on woolen dress goods, iron ore, and steel. Nevertheless, economic causes were at work which were distinctly unfavourable to a perpetuation of high protectionism as a policy. Chief among these causes, as has been seen, was the increasing surplus in the Treasury. Every Republican President, from Grant to Arthur, had called the attention of Congress to this, and had specifically recommended lower rates of duty. It is likely that, had the Republican party remained in power, these recommendations would have been ultimately carried out. It was the election of Mr. Cleveland in 1884 and his attitude toward the tariff, which solidified the Republicans, not merely in support of the old war-rates, but of an extension of these rates to new classes of imported goods.

When Mr. Cleveland made a distinct issue of lowering the tariff, his opponents from sheer necessity were driven to take the other side. They ignored the whole history of protection in the United States. They put aside the utterances of their own leaders in the past. In the end they went even further than they had probably intended, until at last they flatly declared that protection, so far from being a temporary measure, was one to be perpetuated for its own sake, and that duties, instead of being lowered, should be made even higher than they had been under the actual stress of war. The campaign of 1888 had practically been fought out over this issue; and since the Republicans were successful, they felt that the country had given them a mandate to do whatever they saw fit. It was with this conviction that the act of 1890, popularly known as the McKinley Bill, was framed by the Republican members of the House Committee and ultimately reported by the chairman, Mr. McKinley. From this time dates the New

Protectionism, which proclaimed the doctrine that high duties and high prices are a distinct advantage to the country. Its framers intended to reduce the surplus in the Treasury by enacting tariff schedules that were prohibitive.

The McKinley Bill was a very radical measure. It raised the duties on a great number of articles, and it removed from the free list a great many others. Unlike the earlier acts, it laid imposts upon commodities which are used in every household—articles of clothing, carpets, table linen, thread, tools, and also upon many kinds of food. The effect of this was certain to be felt at once throughout the entire country in the shape of a direct rise in prices. Some of the Republicans themselves had an uncomfortable feeling that the measure was eminently unwise. Such was emphatically the view of Mr. Blaine, himself an old-time protectionist and one who remained unconverted to the doctrines of Mr. McKinley. Mr. Blaine saw that the new tariff bill would not only prove unpopular with the country, but that it would shut out American trade from the most desirable foreign markets. " There is not a section or a line in the entire bill," he wrote to Senator Frye, " that will open a market for another bushel of wheat or another barrel of pork." He even appeared before the committees of Congress to urge upon them with all his influence a wiser policy. Mr. Blaine was the shrewdest of politicians. He knew the value of a taking catchword. What he wanted to secure was the admission of foreign goods untaxed from such countries as would admit American products of certain classes free of duty. This was in reality a species of free trade, but he artfully described it as " reciprocity "— a word which would not alarm the timid voter, who had been taught that free trade spelled ruin.   Day after day, the Secretary of State laboured with his party associates to introduce the principle of reciprocity into the pending bill. Every stage of its passage was watched by him with intense interest, and he wrote to Mr. McKinley many pointed notes, of which the following is typical:

WASHINGTON, *April* 10, 1890.

DEAR MR. MCKINLEY: It is a great mistake to take hides from the free list, where they have been for so many years.

It is a slap in the face to the South Americans, with whom we are trying to enlarge our trade.   It will benefit the farmer by adding five to eight per cent. to the price of his children's shoes.

It will yield a profit to the butcher only—the last man that needs it.   The movement is injudicious from beginning to end—in every form and phase.

Pray stop it before it sees light.   Such movements as this for protection will protect the Republican Party into a speedy retirement.   Very hastily,

JAMES G. BLAINE. [31]

Mr. Blaine had small success with the members of the House of Representatives.   The McKinley following had gone mad over high protective duties.   They acted as though, whatever they did, there would be no day of reckoning.   They placed duties upon the sheer necessities of life.   They sought artificially to stimulate the production in this country of commodities, such as tin plate, that had never before been produced in the United States.   They were not forgetful of the fact that the protected manufacturers had furnished the great campaign fund which had carried Indiana for Mr. Harrison.   Remembering that Mr. Cleveland, like his Republican predecessors, had urged the remission of duties on raw materials, Mr. McKinley removed one such duty.   This, however, was the

[31] Hamilton, *Life of Blaine,* p. 683.

duty on raw sugar, and its abolition meant millions of profit to the great Sugar Trust, which was beginning to be extremely powerful in Washington. The folly of such a course was pointed out by Mr. Blaine,[32] who hammered away by argument, exhortation and published letters, in behalf of reciprocity. Before the Senate committee he made a speech so energetic and so full of passion that the reports of it in an imperfect form went all over the country. In his vehemence, Mr. Blaine pounded the desk on which lay a draft of the proposed bill, and in doing so he smashed his tall hat under his descending fist.[33] This appealed to the people's sense of the picturesque. "Blaine has smashed his hat on the McKinley Bill," was the sentence that went from mouth to mouth; and this trivial incident attracted more attention to the measure than whole columns of printed speeches. At last the Senate proved somewhat more open to reason than the House had been, and an element of reciprocity, in a negative form, was introduced into the bill by a Senate amendment, rather ungraciously worded, which authorised the President to impose duties on certain free goods whenever the country from which they came imposed duties that were "reciprocally unequal and unreasonable" upon certain specified American exports.

The McKinley Bill had been passed by the House of Representatives in May. With the reciprocity amendment, it passed the Senate in September; and it became law by receiving the signature of the President on the first day of

[32] "Pass this bill, and in 1892 there will not be a man in all the party so beggared as to accept your nomination for the presidency."—Hamilton, *Life of Blaine*, p. 685.

[33] See Hamilton, *Life of Blaine*, p. 685. Mr. Blaine's latest biographer tells the story in a different way. See Stanwood, *J. G. Blaine*, p. 331 (Boston, 1905).

October, 1890.[34] Even before the measure had been adopted, but when its passage had become a moral certainty, a sharp advance in prices throughout the country was acutely perceptible. Merchants were unwilling to sell their goods at the old rates, when the cost of importation was so soon to be increased. Those who did so made a virtue of the fact by advertising that certain wares would be sold at low figures for the next few weeks, but that after a specified date the prices would be raised because of the McKinley Bill. Although these announcements were only business devices, they helped to imbue the public mind with a belief that the new tariff act was certain to increase the cost of living. Importers hastened to bring in enormous quantities of goods, so as to take advantage of the more favourable rates that still prevailed. Ocean liners sought to break the record for speed in hurrying cargoes across the Atlantic before the new act should take effect. The Cunard steamer *Etruria,* reaching the port of New York a few minutes before the hour set for the enforcement of the McKinley Bill, saved by her speed something like a million dollars for the owners of her cargo.

Everywhere the pinch of higher prices was quickly felt, while no increase in wages was perceptible. For the first time since the war, the nation received an object lesson as to what high protection really meant. Hitherto the average man, and especially the average woman, had turned a deaf ear to tariff talk. What did they care whether steel rails and iron ore cost more or less? They did not clothe themselves in iron, nor did they dine and breakfast upon steel rails. But now every household throughout the land learned that the purchasing power of the family income

[34] For an analysis of the McKinley Bill, see Taussig, *The Tariff History of the United States,* pp. 251-283 (New York, 1899).

had been seriously reduced. The housewife who went to market and suddenly discovered that she must pay much more for supplies than she had ever paid before, began at once to take a very personal interest in the cause of this phenomenon. Butter, eggs, flour, dried apples, lard, potatoes, bacon, corned beef and poultry leaped up in price after a fashion which to persons of limited means was most alarming.[35] It now cost more to clothe the family, to carpet the rooms, to provide table linen, and to keep the domestic utensils properly renewed. An outcry went up from those who usually paid no attention to economic questions. Party hacks tried hard to create enthusiasm for "Bill McKinley and the McKinley Bill," but their efforts were met with sullen silence or open denunciation.

The way in which the measure had been "jammed through" the House of Representatives under the iron rule of Speaker Reed was offensive to the American sense of fairness. Mr. Reed, having got a taste of arbitrary power, apparently became intoxicated by it. At first, the country had applauded the nerve with which he dominated the body over which he presided. So long as he used the new rules only to prevent "filibustering," and to insure the efficient despatch of public business, the sentiment of the people was with him. When he said in his epigrammatic way, "This House is no longer a deliberative body," the remark called forth an approving laugh. But in time, what at first had been a wise autocracy became something very like oppression. It was not permitted to members of the minority to question the accuracy of the Speaker's count. Representatives were recorded by him as present when they were actually hundreds of miles away. Even

[35] See the figures in a report by Senator Aldrich. Senate Report, 968, pt. i. (1891).

the privilege of an appeal from the ruling of the Chair was no longer recognised. Mr. Reed carried his tyranny so far that at last members of his own party were driven to revolt. On one occasion,[36] the Speaker ordered parts of the journal of the House to be omitted in the daily reading. Mr. Mills of Texas objected, and it came out that the Speaker had been guilty of a misstatement and that the parts of the journal which had been omitted contained a record of proceedings which had never taken place. Even then, the arrogant Reed refused to have the necessary correction made. An appeal from his ruling was taken, and enough Republicans united with the Democrats to override the " Czar."

The Congressional elections of 1890 took place at the very moment when public sentiment was most deeply stirred against the record which the Republicans had made. In less than two years the Treasury had been emptied, the odious Force Bill had been introduced, a sort of tyranny had been established in the popular Chamber, the cost of living had been enormously increased, and no one had received any benefit save the multi-millionaires of the protected industries and the Sugar Trust. The election, therefore, proved to be a veritable cataclysm. The Republican majority in the House was swept away. When Congress met in 1891, the Democratic Representatives numbered 235, and the Republicans only 88; while in the Senate the Republican majority was reduced from 14 to 6. A significant fact was the strength which had been shown in the West by a new party which now became known as the " Populists," who elected nine representatives and two senators. In the South, out of 121 members, there were only three Republicans. Even in New England, the Democrats secured a fair majority. In Ohio, Mr. McKinley

[36] June 19, 1890.

was defeated at the polls, and retired for a time to private life. Mr. Blaine's prophecy of disaster had been strikingly fulfilled.[38]

In 1890, great popular interest was aroused by a movement to overthrow the Louisiana Lottery Company. The story of this contest deserves to be repeated here, because the issue presented was not unlike the issue involved in the battle against the Trusts. It was a contest between great wealth and selfish interest on the one hand and an enlightened moral sentiment upon the other. Those who feel a sense of hopelessness when they endeavour to forecast the final outcome of any struggle such as this, may take courage from recalling the defeat of one of the most ably planned conspiracies against the common welfare which this country has ever witnessed. The Louisiana Lottery had been chartered in 1868 by a "carpet-bag" legislature at a time when political conditions in that State were indescribably depraved. The promoters of the lottery were three in number—John A. Morris, Z. E. Simmons and C. H. Murray—men as unscrupulous and as able as any who engineered the later Trusts. At that time, although most States had by law forbidden the sale of lottery tickets within their borders, these laws were

[38] An explanation of this great defeat was given by Speaker Reed in the following words: " In hundreds of cases the 'drummers' were, intentionally or unintentionally, missionaries to preach Democratic doctrine. They went all over the country with their stories of advances in prices that were to be made next week or next month on account of the McKinley Bill. But I am inclined to think that the most important factor in the result of this election was the women of the country. It is the women who do the shopping, who keep the run of prices, who have the keenest scent for increased cost. They heard in every store the clerks behind the counters explain how this article or that could not be sold hereafter at the former price because of the McKinley Bill; they went

practically disregarded. Several enterprises of the sort, nearly all of foreign ownership, reaped a rich harvest by the sale of tickets for their monthly drawings. Among these were the Havana Lottery, the Royal Saxon Lottery, the Hamburg Lottery, and later the Kentucky Lottery.

Morris and his associates, having secured their charter in return for an annual payment of $40,000 to a charity hospital, proceeded to organise their business in a very far-sighted way, taking every precaution to fortify themselves alike against the law and against popular prejudice. They secured the services of General Early and General Beauregard to superintend their monthly drawings. They advertised extensively in leading newspapers throughout the United States, paying for their advertisements several times the ordinary rates. They even established newspapers of their own and maintained them, so that if necessity arose, the Lottery would have staunch defenders in the press. In every great city of the Union the ablest lawyers were employed as counsel for the Company, to watch for and to avert every possible form of danger. In Louisiana, Morris practically controlled the State. Many of the judges were to all intents and purposes appointed by the Lottery. Money was spent lavishly in charity, on behalf of public enterprises, and in private gifts. Vast sugarworks were even opened and operated by the lottery owners, who desired to pose as representative business men engaged in fostering one of the great industries of the State. In 1877, when Louisiana was striving to shake off the last vestige of the carpet-bag régime, the Lottery Company gave the money needed to bribe those legislators whose

home and told their husbands and fathers, and their stories had a tremendous effect at the ballot-box."—Interview in the New York *Sun*, November 15, 1890.

votes were necessary to oust the carpet-bagger, Packard, from the Governor's chair. Public sentiment in Louisiana, therefore, was more than cordial to the Lottery. Its charter was renewed in 1879; and after that, it seemed to be assured of a permanent lease of life. Its revenues were very great. One-third of the entire mail-matter which reached New Orleans was addressed to M. A. Dauphin, the nominal head of the Company. It was said that the postal notes and money orders which it cashed amounted to no less than $30,000 a day.

In 1880, the attention of Mr. Alexander K. McClure, editor of the Philadelphia *Times,* was attracted by the persistency with which the Louisiana Lottery sought to have advertisements inserted in his newspaper. He was startled also by the lavish offers of money made to secure such advertising. An investigation showed him that although the Pennsylvania law imposed a penalty for advertising lotteries, not less than $50,000 a year was paid to the newspapers of the State for the use of their columns. Mr. McClure brought suit in the lower courts to test the law, and it was found to be defective. He then framed a more stringent bill; and after a vigorous canvass he secured its enactment by the Pennsylvania Legislature in 1883. In the course of the discussion which went on in the press, Mr. McClure's own paper spoke out with frank severity of the Lottery managers. These persons, angered by the loss of their Pennsylvania business and wishing to make an example of the man who had opposed them, noted down his name and waited until circumstances should enable them to take revenge.

Two years later (in 1885), Mr. McClure visited the New Orleans Exposition. The Lottery through its spies had learned that he was coming, and at the very moment of his arrival he was served with a writ, sworn out by Dauphin and claiming $100,000 damages for libelling the Lottery. Mr. McClure was in a distinctly hostile community, where the courts were in the hands of Lottery appointees. The lawyers of the city were nearly all in the Lottery's pay; and to defend the suit seemed to be an absolutely hopeless undertaking. Even one of Mr. McClure's personal friends said to him: "We are all in it here, and I hardly know how to advise you." So pleased was Dauphin over his successful *coup,* that he telegraphed an account of it to every city in the land, through the agency of the Associated Press.[39]

This little burst of exultant insolence on the part of Dauphin was perhaps not unnatural, but it cost the Lottery Company dear. It stirred to active indignation a feeling which had lain dormant all over the country, and even in Louisiana itself. Within a few hours after Dauphin's news had been made public, a wealthy Philadelphian telegraphed Mr. McClure that $50,000 had been placed to his credit for use in his defence. The unbought press in every State took up the case with vigour. In New Orleans itself, a committee of lawyers, all strangers to Mr. McClure, called upon him to say that the bar of that city would defend the suit without cost. The Governor of the State, though friendly to the Lottery, deplored its action in this instance, and gave Mr. McClure the benefit of his advice, sending to him as counsel a lawyer whose fidelity and honour were above suspicion. The Lottery managers refused to take warning from this display of enlightened sentiment. They resolved to press the case at once to trial. They felt themselves to be omnipotent. They regarded the judges as their creatures. Even the marshal who drew the names for the jury was in their pay. They

[39] McClure, *Recollections,* pp. 173-183 (Salem, 1900).

had millions of money at their disposal. Why should they not make a conspicuous example of this stranger from the North? They laid their plans in such a way as to prevent (so they thought) all chance of an appeal to the Supreme Court of the United States. Mr. McClure's counsel, however, devised a plea which baffled them. It appeared that a suit instituted against Mr. McClure by the Lottery in Pennsylvania was still before a United States District Court on a question of appeal. The situation was therefore anomalous in that the Company was prosecuting Mr. McClure upon the same charge before two Federal courts at one and the same time. These facts were duly set forth, and a plea of justification was entered, to which was appended a long series of questions which Dauphin would be forced to answer should the case be tried. These questions were most ingeniously framed, and Dauphin could not answer them without giving information which would expose himself and his agents to criminal prosecution in nearly every State and Territory of the Union. This meant not merely fine and imprisonment for the Lottery officials, but the absolute destruction of their business.

So soon as Dauphin's lawyers perceived the gulf which was yawning for their employers, they experienced a genuine panic. When the case was called they actually opposed a motion to have the appeal advanced upon the docket. By this time many leading men in Washington had become interested in the matter. Senator Edmunds and Senator Hawley arranged that the trial, when it took place, should be presided over by Mr. Justice Wood—a judge of unimpeachable integrity. The Attorney-General of the United States appeared in the Supreme Court in opposition to the Lottery Company. An agitation was begun in Congress which seemed full of menace to the lottery interests. Dauphin and his associates, therefore, capitulated on their knees. One of their representatives went to Mr. McClure and begged that the suit might be discontinued, offering to pay all the expenses—counsel fees, the cost of depositions, printing, and the rest. Mr. McClure consented; and within twenty-four hours the Company had settled every bill, and had withdrawn its suit. But they had gone too far, and they had thereafter to deal with the public resentment which they had evoked. Measures were passed in Congress excluding lottery tickets from the mails, and forbidding the transmission of newspapers which contained lottery advertisements. The Anti-Lottery Bill of 1893 even forbade the delivery of registered letters, or the payment of postal orders to the Company. Driven from the mails, the Lottery sought to carry on its business through the express companies; but as these were engaged in interstate traffic, Congress again effectively interfered. At last in Louisiana the question of a renewal of the Company's charter came before the people. A campaign against it was carried on successfully in a burst of moral indignation. The Company offered to pay the State a million and a quarter of dollars every year, but the bribe had no effect; and in 1893, this gigantic structure of lawlessness and corruption was swept out of existence forever.

Public wrath against the Lottery was only one phase of a wider agitation. The Fifty-first Congress enacted two very important legislative measures which reflected a rapidly-growing hostility to Trusts in general, and to the lawlessness of railway corporations. Senator Sherman of Ohio, on December 4, 1889, introduced a bill which, with a few amendments, was subsequently passed, and was approved by President Harrison on July 2, 1890. It is usually spoken of as the Sherman Anti-Trust Law, though its formal title was, " An act to protect trade and commerce against unlawful restraints and monopolies "; and both in its phraseology and in the intention of its framer it was a very drastic measure. Its purpose as described by Senator Sherman himself was

" —to arm the Federal Courts within the limits of their constitutional power that they may co-operate with the State courts in checking, curbing, and controlling the most dangerous combinations that now threaten the business, property, and trade of the people of the United States. It aims only at unlawful combinations. It does not in the least affect combinations in aid of production where there is free and fair competition. It is the right of every man to work, labour, and produce in any lawful vocation, and to transport his products on equal terms and conditions and under like circumstances. This is industrial liberty and lies at the foundation of the equality of all rights and privileges." [40]

The immediate cause of the enactment of this law was an investigation which had been conducted by a committee of the Senate in 1888-1889. Sittings were held in Washington, Chicago, and elsewhere; and in spite of the reluctance of some witnesses and the absence of others, a mass of testimony was taken which proved beyond question that many of the great corporations were crushing out competition and destroying industry by means which were in direct violation of the common law. Some very peculiar facts were brought to light regarding the operations of the Sugar Trust, the Standard Oil Company and the great dressed-beef combination, of which Armour and Company of Chicago were the head. But it was not this investigation alone which made it impossible for Congress

[40] Speech of March 21, 1890 (Senate).

to remain quiescent any longer. Similar inquiries had been conducted by State legislatures, and testimony taken in many civil and criminal cases in the State courts had been made public. Moreover, thousands of business men had felt the crushing weight of monopoly in the destruction of their means of livelihood. Therefore, although certain Senators professed to feel doubts about the constitutionality of the bill, it was passed by a non-partisan vote in both houses.

The essential provisions of this act applied to all contracts and combinations in the form of Trusts or otherwise, and to conspiracies in restraint of either interstate or international commerce. Such contracts or combinations were made illegal, and persons participating in them were declared to be guilty of a misdemeanour, and subject either to a fine not exceeding $5000, or to imprisonment not exceeding one year, or to both these penalties, at the discretion of the court. Furthermore, all goods shipped in violation of the act were to be seized and forfeited by proceedings instituted by the Attorney-General on behalf of the United States. How far this act was to prove effective as a weapon against monopolies will be considered in another chapter. It was in itself a strong measure and did honour to the statesman who framed it and ably advocated it.

Another concession to the widespread sentiment regarding corporate abuses was an act aimed against those railroads which had practically defrauded the Government and the nation in the matter of public lands. The generosity of the national Government to the railways of the West had been remarkable. The case of the Union Pacific Railway Company (after 1880 known as the Union Pacific Railroad Company) is sufficiently illustrative to justify citation. This company had been incorporated in 1862. It received from the Government a grant of five sections of public land for each mile of rail; and two years later, this grant was doubled. In all it received the enormous total of 6,806,497 acres.[42] It is interesting to remember that the contractors of the road, in order to augment the land grants, built their road, not in a straight line across the prairies, as would naturally have been the case, but in an erratic zig-zag, with twists and turns, intended solely to increase the length of line, and thus practically to cheat the Government out of hundreds of thousands of acres. In order to assist the railway still further the Secretary of the Treasury was directed to turn over to it, as a loan, sixteen currency bonds of the United States, each of the denomination of $1000, for every mile of road constructed through the plains, and forty-eight similar currency bonds for each mile of road built through the region of the Rocky Mountains. The total issue of such bonds for the benefit of the railway was $61,000,000. As though all this were not enough, the company was allowed to issue first-mortgage bonds equal in amount to the Government bonds just mentioned. Thus the lien of the Government upon the railway dropped to the position of a second mortgage. The road was actually built by the notorious Crédit Mobilier, which took over all the resources of the original company, both land and cash. Of course, the construction of a railway uniting the Atlantic States with those of the Pacific was a work of immense national importance. On the other hand it became evident in after years that the generosity of the Government had been ill requited. Thus, under the directorship of Jay Gould, and later of Mr. Charles F. Adams, the management diverted a

[42] See Sanborn, *Congressional Grants of Land* (Madison, 1899).

good part of its earnings, above operating expenses and fixed charges, to the building of branch lines, instead of applying a percentage of the profits toward cancelling the obligation to the Government, as provided in the act of 1862. Indeed, the Government received but slight consideration from any of these Western roads for whose construction it had pledged its credit.

In the matter of the public lands, the railroads were peculiarly unscrupulous. In President Cleveland's first message to Congress,[43] attention was sharply called to the whole subject by the declaration that these " princely grants and subsidies " had been " diverted to private gains and corrupt uses. Our great nation does not begrudge its generosity, but it abhors peculation and fraud. A faithful application of the grants to the construction and perfecting of their roads, [and] an honest discharge of their obligations are all the public asks, and it will be contented with no less." But as time went on, it was plain that the railroad magnates had no conception of public duty, and thought simply of their own enrichment. One of them, Mr. C. P. Huntington, who had wrung a great fortune out of his manipulation of Pacific railways, was told that if he did not fulfil his obligations, the Government might step in and take possession. " It's quite welcome to," he cynically answered. " There's nothing left but two streaks of rust and a right of way." In 1890, however, this scandalous state of things came to an end. The Western States were swept by a feeling of anger against the railways, which in impudent disregard of their own obligations, were holding vast tracts of fertile land, and thus barring them against intending settlers under the Homestead Law. An act of Congress which the President approved on September 29th, ordered the

[43] December 8, 1885.

forfeiture of all such lands, of which more than a hundred million acres were thus restored to public uses.

The last two years of Mr. Harrison's administration were marked by great activity in the State Department. This was due not so much to Mr. Blaine's fondness for " a spirited foreign policy " as to circumstances over which he had no initial control.   In March, 1891, a band of Italian criminals in New Orleans reached a climax of sporadic lawlessness by murdering the chief of police.   For a long time they had been extorting money from citizens under threat of death, and had committed other crimes with practical impunity, because the local juries were either afraid to convict them or else had been bribed to disagree in rendering a verdict.   Hennessy, the head of the police, showed immense energy and acuteness in tracking down the members of this band.   They had him watched and followed; and late one evening he was shot almost to pieces at a signal given by an Italian boy.   Against nine Italians strong evidence was gathered, and they were promptly brought to trial.   To the astonishment of the judge himself, the jury acquitted six of the prisoners, and disagreed in the case of the other three.   On the following night a mob, led by some of the most substantial citizens, broke open the prison, seized the prisoners, and either hanged or shot them all.   Within a few hours the Italian Government cabled a strong protest to Mr. Blaine.   Italy's Prime Minister, the Marquis di Rudini, demanded that the lynchers should be immediately punished, and that an indemnity should be immediately paid.   Mr. Blaine answered temperately to the effect that the United States Government had no local jurisdiction in Louisiana, but that to Italian residents the State courts were open precisely as to citizens. He did, however, strongly urge Governor Nicholls of Louisiana to set the legal machinery of the State in motion, and he assured the Italian Premier that the whole affair should receive most careful consideration. The Italian blood was up, however, and Baron Fava, Italy's Minister at Washington, was directed to press Mr. Blaine incessantly. Baron Fava intimated that unless immediate action were taken he must withdraw from Washington. To this hint he received from Mr. Blaine a very sharp reply:

"I do not recognise the right of any Government to tell the United States what it shall do. We have never received orders from any foreign power and shall not begin now. It is a matter of indifference what persons in Italy think of our institutions. I cannot change them, still less violate them."

To this curt note, written much in the same spirit as Webster's famous letter to the Chevalier Hülsemann in 1850, the Italian Minister made no answer, but at once left Washington and took passage for Italy. His action caused great excitement, especially in New Orleans. Many persons expected that Italy would deliver an ultimatum which President Harrison's Government would certainly reject and thus bring war within an appreciable distance. Rumour said that an Italian squadron was being mobilised and might soon appear off the mouth of the Mississippi to menace New Orleans. The situation looked even graver when the American Minister at Rome left Italy. But those who were well informed felt no disquietude, in view of the enormous disparity in fighting strength between Italy and the United States. An English naval officer, who was in New York at the time, made a joking comment which contained a certain element of truth.

" You people," said he, " want more ships for your navy. Just let those Italian fellows send over a fleet. Then you take the fleet, and there you are! "

As a matter of fact, the Italian Government thought better of it before very long; and though many Americans were mobbed and otherwise insulted in Italy, and though the Italian press breathed forth threatenings, amicable relations were soon restored. It turned out that only three of the Italians who had been lynched were subjects of the King of Italy, the rest having been naturalised in this country; and so, when Congress, purely as an act of grace, voted the sum of $25,000 to be given to the relatives of the dead men, King Humbert accepted the award, and diplomatic relations were resumed.

An embroilment between the United States and Chile, which took place at this time, was a much more serious affair. In January, 1891, a furious civil war broke out in Chile. Of all the Spanish-American republics, Chile has been the only one to conduct its foreign and domestic affairs in such a way as to win the respect of other nations. Situated in the temperate zone and ribbed with mountain ranges, its climatic and geographic conditions seem to have developed in its people certain characteristics for which one looks in vain among the other South American States. The government of Chile has been conspicuous for its intelligence, conservatism and integrity. Its finances have been ably administered. Order has been maintained through the strict enforcement of enlightened laws. Its political institutions are modelled upon those of the United States, and throughout the greater part of its history it has been free from turbulence and mercenary insurrection. Its successful war with Bolivia and Peru in 1881 made it plain that henceforth Chile deserved respectful consideration as a naval and military power.

A knowledge of these facts, however, has led the Chilean people to cultivate a self-consciousness which does not always show itself in the most attractive fashion. Educated Chileans are apt to forget that, after all, their nation is a very small one and that, from the nature of things, it cannot figure very conspicuously in the history of the world. They are too fond of comparing it with the wretched little republics which are its immediate neighbours; and they forget that while Chile is an important State when contrasted with Peru or Uruguay or Venezuela, it is only a dwarf beside the United States or the giant nations of Europe. But the typical Chilean has a dream of his own, and one which he has cherished for more than fifty years. He believes that ultimately his country is destined to assert an hegemony over all the Spanish-speaking peoples of South America, and in the end to extend its influence northward, until, at last, having absorbed even Mexico, Chile shall confront the mighty North American Republic upon the borders of the Rio Grande. There are not a few Chileans who even think that by the end, perhaps, of another century the United States may have to do battle with its Southern rival for the mastery of the Western world. There is a touch of Spanish vanity in this magnificent vision; yet, though to Americans it may seem only ludicrous and fantastic, it appeals very strongly not merely to the Chilean imagination but to the Chilean sense of probability. Not unnaturally, therefore, the statesmen of that small republic have always been extremely sensitive concerning the claim of the United States to concern itself with South American affairs; and they resent the assumption that the Monroe Doctrine has any application to their country. It is necessary to remember these facts in order to understand the drift of the events which are now to be narrated.

In 1886, Chile elected as its President one of those extremely able but unscrupulous men who appear from time to time in South American nations, and among whom Francia of Paraguay and Guzman Blanco of Venezuela stand out in history as interesting types. This was Señor Don José Manuel Balmaceda, whose rule up to the end of 1890 was marked by the most enlightened measures. He belonged to the so-called Progressist Party, and as President he did much to promote public education, to foster internal improvements and generally to develop the resources of his country. His political opponents, however, who headed a sort of oligarchy made up of leading members of the Chilean Congress, accused the President of plotting to perpetuate his power by securing the election of a tool of his as his successor. When he dissolved Congress, and raised revenue without the authority of law, the Congressional party proclaimed a civil war[44] and sought to overthrow Balmaceda by force of arms.

In this struggle the United States had no direct interest; but various circumstances soon led to complications of a very serious nature. It had been for thirty years the policy of our Government to give no encouragement to revolts in other countries. Mr. Blaine, therefore, by President Harrison's direction, continued as before to recognise Balmaceda as the lawful head of the Chilean Republic, and to refuse to accord to the Congressionalists the belligerent rights which they claimed. Balmaceda had been legally elected President. He held possession of the capital of the country. He controlled an army which was carrying on operations in the field against the rebels. Therefore,

[44] January 7, 1891.

why should the United States sever its official relations with him and suddenly recognise his enemies?

The case seemed plain enough; yet there were circumstances which made the situation somewhat delicate. Ever since the events of 1882, which have already been narrated, Mr. Blaine had been viewed with a certain rancour by Chileans of all classes. They regarded him as an intermeddler, or even worse, and honestly believed him to be actuated by a feeling of hostility to Chilean interests. Therefore, when he continued to recognise Balmaceda, the Congressional party in Chile claimed that his action was due to an unfriendly spirit; and before long they professed to see what they called his malign influence at work against them. A good part of the Chilean navy had joined the revolutionists. Some engagements took place between these ships and the ships whose officers were Balmacedists. A small American squadron under Rear-Admiral Brown had been ordered to Chilean waters to protect American interests, and the Congressionalists asserted in very bitter language that officers from American vessels had acted as spies; that they had reported to Balmaceda the strength and also the movements of the rebel ships; and that in various other ways the naval force of the United States had violated the requirements of strict neutrality. Admiral Brown indignantly denied this charge, which was made in the most offensive manner. There was, indeed, no evidence at all to justify it. Nevertheless, it was generally believed by the Congressionalists, who presently got possession of the entire seacoast and the great fortified port of Valparaiso. Hatred of the United States became nearly universal in Chile after an incident which occurred in May.

Early in that month, a Chilean ship the *Itata*, chartered

by the Congressional party, put in at the harbour of San Diego, in California. It was reported to the Government at Washington that the *Itata* was taking on a cargo of arms and ammunition for the Chilean rebels, in defiance of the neutrality laws. On May 6th, a United States marshal took possession of the ship, forbidding it to leave the port. On the following day, the *Itata's* commander cut her cable, overpowered the United States officers, and put to sea, carrying them away as prisoners. This high-handed proceeding stirred the Washington Government to instant action. The cruiser *Charleston* was despatched in swift pursuit with orders to take the *Itata,* and to sink her if she resisted. When the Chileans heard of this, the hotheads among them sent their new steel cruiser, the *Esmeralda,* to meet the *Itata* and to protect her against capture. The *Charleston* and the *Esmeralda* were ships of equal size and armament, and the result of a fight between them was awaited with breathless expectancy. It was supposed that the *Itata* would put in at the harbour of Acapulco on the Mexican coast; and to this harbour the *Charleston* hastened. The *Esmeralda* did the same; and both cruisers lay there with steam up, with decks cleared for action, and with the crews ready at their guns. It was an exciting moment, but no shot was fired; for the *Itata* failed to appear, and made her way direct to her destination. By the time of her arrival there, the Congressionalists had thought better of their defiance of the United States; and on June 4th, they delivered up the *Itata* to Rear-Admiral McCann, in command of the American squadron at Iquique.[46]

---

[46] Suit was afterward brought in the United States District Court of California by the owners to test the legality of the Government's action in seizing the *Itata* at San Diego. On appeal the Supreme Court decided in favour of the Government.

The revolt in Chile proved to be successful. On August 7th, Balmaceda's forces were routed by the Congressional army, which marched upon the capital, Santiago, and entered it in triumph. Balmaceda took refuge in the Argentine legation, where, on September 18th, he committed suicide. A new government was proclaimed in Chile under the presidency of Señor Jorge Montt. Everywhere the revolutionists prevailed, and they were now formally recognised by the United States. The most serious part of the whole affair was, however, still to come.

Soon after becoming Secretary of State, Mr. Blaine had secured the appointment, as Minister to Chile, of Mr. Patrick Egan. Mr. Egan was one of the group whom Mr. Blaine's political opponents were accustomed derisively to call "Blaine Irishmen." He had not long been naturalised as an American citizen, having come to the United States somewhat hastily in order to escape arrest and imprisonment at the hands of the British authorities in Ireland, who charged him with political offences in connection with the Irish Land League. Critics of the Harrison administration spoke of Mr. Egan as "an escaped jailbird" and even insinuated that he had been connected with the Phœnix Park murders in 1882. There was not a shadow of truth in all this. Mr. Egan was a man of ability and honour, who had simply made himself disliked by the Castle set in Dublin at a time when the British Government was trying one of its periodical experiments in repression. Nevertheless, his appointment to a diplomatic post was properly open to criticism; and in Chile, especially, where there were so many influential English residents, it was a cause of social embarrassment. Mr. Egan, moreover, in carrying out his early instructions to recognise the Balmaceda Government had perhaps erred through excess of zeal; so that he was peculiarly obnoxious to the Congressionalists, who regarded him as a partisan of their enemy.

When Santiago fell and the troops of the revolution entered that city, intoxicated with their victory, there were enacted fearful scenes of lust and wholesale murder. Many of the Balmacedists, fearing for their lives, took refuge in the American legation, begging the protection of the Minister. By the law of nations, the precincts of an embassy or of a legation are regarded as being the soil of that country whose flag flies over it; but whether the immunity which such a place enjoys should be used to protect citizens of the State to which the embassy is accredited, is a disputed point. Mr. Egan, however, received the Balmacedists—among them the late Minister of Foreign Affairs and the late Governor of Santiago, together with members of their households. The new Chilean Foreign Minister demanded the surrender of the fugitives. Mr. Egan hoisted the American flag and declined to accede to the demand. The Chileans were furious, yet they hesitated to violate the sanctity of the legation. They tried other means, however, hoping to annoy Mr. Egan into compliance. The neighbourhood of his residence swarmed with spies. Drunken soldiers reeled by, yelling out vile epithets and making boisterous threats. It was believed by Mr. Egan that a plot existed to set fire to the legation and thus drive out the fugitives. Meanwhile, the Chilean State Department carried on a correspondence with the American Minister with regard to the rights of the question from the standpoint of international law. Here Mr. Egan neatly scored on his adversary in a series of very able notes, in which he showed that in 1866, during a revolution in Peru, the Chilean Government had directed its Minister in that country to insist upon two principles,—

the right of asylum and the right of safe conduct to a neutral territory for persons taking shelter in a foreign legation. In 1888, at the Congress of American Republics, Chile had again defended the same principles. Mr. Egan, in fact, made out so good a case as to put an end to the design of taking his guests from him by force, though the right of safe conduct was still denied.

All this controversy, following upon the charges against Admiral Brown, and also the affair of the *Itata,* intensified Chilean animosity toward the United States. The newspapers contained violent attacks upon Egan, Blaine, and Americans in general. Every sort of slanderous story was circulated and believed, and day by day popular feeling grew more and more inflamed. At this time the United States cruiser *Baltimore,* commanded by Captain W. S. Schley, was in the harbour of Valparaiso. On October 17th, Captain Schley rather unwisely gave shore-leave to nearly one hundred of his sailors. Within a few hours after they had landed, they were surrounded by a mob of over two thousand Chileans, who separated them into small groups and then attacked them. The sailors were unarmed, but defended themselves manfully until a body of fifty policemen armed with carbines and bayonets took part in the assault upon them. Two of the Americans were killed—one of them being shot by a policeman —and eighteen were badly stabbed, cut, or bruised by stones. The rest were dragged to prison through the streets, some of them by the heels, amid the threats, curses, and uproar of the mob.

The news of this affair naturally caused great indignation in the United States and it led to a long and voluminous diplomatic correspondence, as well as to a sharp interchange of notes between Captain Schley of the *Baltimore* and the Intendente of Valparaiso. Of course, the sailors who had been dragged to prison were speedily released, but the Chilean authorities were unwilling to admit that the United States had a just grievance. An investigation instituted by Captain Schley showed the facts concerning the assault to have been those which have been here set forth—that the police of Valparaiso had taken part with the mob in shooting and otherwise assaulting unarmed bluejackets. The Chileans, on the other hand, asserted that the Americans were drunk, and that they had provoked the attack by their outrageous conduct. The charge of drunkenness was doubtless true, for sailors of whatever nationality are not wont to ask for shore-leave from motives which would commend themselves to total abstinence societies.[47] But it was perfectly evident that the attack had been made upon them because of hatred to the uniform they wore, and that it was directed against them, not as individuals, but as Americans. The conduct of the police, moreover, showed an official animosity which surpassed even that of the rabble. Under the circumstances, Secretary Blaine insisted upon a specific apology from the

---

[47] Commander Evans afterwards summed the matter up with delicious frankness in these words: "He [Captain Schley] was in the midst of a correspondence with the Intendente, conducted in the most perfect Castilian, to show, or prove, that his men were all perfectly sober when they were assaulted on shore. I did not agree with him in this; for in the first place I doubted the fact, and in the second, it was not an issue worth discussing. His men were probably drunk on shore, properly drunk; they went ashore, many of them, for the purpose of getting drunk, which they did on Chilean rum paid for with good United States money. When in this condition they were more entitled to protection than if they had been sober. This was my view of it, at least, and the one I always held about men whom I commanded. Instead of protecting them, the Chileans foully murdered these men, and we believed with the connivance and assistance of armed policemen. That was the issue—not the question of whether they were drunk or sober."

Chilean Government, and upon an indemnity to the wounded men and to the families of those who had been killed. The Chileans put the demand aside pending a further investigation on their part. This investigation was protracted interminably, and on November 25th Mr. Blaine complained of the delay. The Chilean Minister in Washington informed him that Spanish law was " slow in its processes, but exact in its conclusions "; and with this statement Mr. Blaine was for the time forced to be content.

It was plain enough that the Chileans intended to postpone any definite action and to let the affair drag along until it should have been half forgotten. From time to time, vague hints were made looking to arbitration, but nothing definite was suggested. Meanwhile, the newspapers of Santiago and Valparaiso continued their abuse of the " North Americans," and especially of Mr. Egan and Mr. Blaine. It looked as though the final outcome of the incident might be very grave. As a precautionary measure, the United States Government put all its vessels of war into commission. Rear-Admiral Walker with a squadron was ordered to Brazil, and the vessels already stationed off the Pacific Coast were held in readiness for active service. At this time, the opposition press in the United States very intemperately accused Mr. Blaine of seeking to stir up a war with Chile. Reviewing all the evidence, it is impossible now to hold this belief. Mr. Blaine's attitude was a firm one, yet it is certain that all the while he was exerting his influence to hold back the President. Mr. Harrison was, perhaps unconsciously, influenced by the thought that a foreign war would almost certainly re-elect him; but whatever his motives, he seemed anxious to force matters to a point at which war would become inevitable. Mr. Blaine, on the other hand, displayed a commendable patience, and refrained from any action which could be regarded as precipitate.[48] The *Baltimore* was withdrawn from Valparaiso. The *Boston,* which was cruising in Chilean waters, merely touched there and then proceeded northward. During the critical days of December, although the harbour of Valparaiso was dotted with foreign ships of war, the United States was represented only by the little gunboat *Yorktown,* under the orders of Commander Robley D. Evans.

Commander Evans was a Virginian, who had adhered to the Union throughout the Civil War, in which he had fought with great gallantry, receiving several serious wounds. He was popularly known to his comrades in the navy as " Fighting Bob," a name which was always a curious puzzle to the honest commander himself, for in his own estimation he was one of the most peaceful of living men. He thought himself a miracle of patience and forbearance, whereas in fact he was never truly happy unless he could sniff the smell of gunpowder. He resembled that interesting hero of Conan Doyle's who vivaciously announced that he would slash to pieces any man who dared describe him as pugnacious. The position of Commander Evans at Valparaiso was a very trying one. Nearly the whole of the Chilean fleet was distributed about him in the harbour. If he went ashore, he was dogged by spies and scowled at by the rabble. The foreign element, especially the Germans, were still more unfriendly, if such a thing were possible. Finally, the Government at Washington depended upon him for frequent and detailed accounts of the state of

[48] From this time probably dates the estrangement between the President and Mr. Blaine, which was to have important consequences. See p. 286.

public feeling, while Mr. Egan was continually sending to him from Santiago messages of the most alarming character.

Commander Evans, however, kept his head and carried off the situation in admirable form. He treated the Chilean officials with punctilious courtesy, while at the same time resenting hotly any overt acts of enmity. The Chilean torpedo-boats began to engage in what they called practice drill. This drill consisted for the most part in speeding their craft as near to the *Yorktown* as was possible without touching it, often within a distance of a few feet. The object of this was twofold. First of all it was meant to show the American commander how utterly he was at their mercy. In the second place, it was intended as a little diversion at the expense of the *Yorktown* and for the amusement of the German, French and English naval officers whose ships were in the harbour. After a few days of this sort of thing, Commander Evans sent for the officer in charge of the torpedo drill, and protested against his action as discourteous.

" I beg to inform you," said the Chilean, with a veiled sneer, " that the water of this harbour belongs to my government, and that I propose to use it in manœuvering the torpedo-boats under my command."

" Very good," returned Commander Evans. " But I beg to inform you that the *Yorktown* is the property of *my* government, and that if one of your boats so much as scratches its paint I will blow her bottom out." [49]

This put a speedy end to the Chilean torpedo drill. On another occasion, a party of roughs amused themselves by throwing stones at one of the small boats of the *Yorktown* and daring the men in it to come ashore. Commander Evans at once visited the Chilean cruiser *Cochran*,

[49] Evans, *A Sailor's Log,* p. 297 (New York, 1901).

whose captain, Vial, was senior officer, not only of the fleet, but of the city. Evans has described the interview in these words, which suggest that his sobriquet of " Fighting Bob " was not wholly misapplied:

" I could hardly hold myself down while I told him of it; but I did, and then read him the riot act. I demanded of him immediate and efficient protection by the police, and served notice on him, then and there, that a repetition of the offence would be sufficient evidence that they could not control their people; and that I should arm my boats and shoot any and every man who insulted me or my men or my flag in any way. Vial was greatly shocked, turned as white as a sheet—my manner was not very mild, I fancy —swore and damned the discharged soldiers and said they were doing all they could to involve the country in war with the United States. . . . After a few moments Captain Vial hastened on shore to jump on the police, assuring me that I should have an ample apology to-morrow." [50]

In the meantime, the situation of the refugees in the American legation at Santiago was becoming a very serious one. Crowded into a comparatively small house, unable to leave its shelter, their lives threatened at every moment, they were doubtful whether the protection accorded them by the American Minister would prove effectual for very long. The Chileans were now willing to let them slip away secretly to the shore, but refused to grant them formally a safe conduct. As the American Government still refrained from pressing matters to an extremity, the

[50] Evans, p. 287. An entertaining, though inaccurate, narrative of events in Chile at this time may be found in Hervey, *Dark Days in Chile* (London, 1892). See also Hancock, *Short History of Chile*, pp. 365-371 (Chicago, 1896); and for the Chilean view of these occurrences, Matta, *Cuestiones Recientes con la Legacion y el Gobierno de los Estados Unidos* (Santiago, 1892).

arrogance of the Chileans increased from day to day. Most of them believed in all sincerity that their navy was more than a match for that of the United States. Their newspapers boasted that in case of war, San Francisco would be laid in ashes and that the whole Pacific Coast of the United States would be ravaged and laid under contribution. This boast, although it seems preposterous now, was not wholly due to the sort of pride which goes with Spanish blood. There was in Valparaiso a very large German colony composed of merchants and persons engaged in shipping. They, together with the English, had largely monopolised the foreign trade of Chile, thanks to the high protective tariff of the United States. The Chileans, therefore, knew little about Americans. They did not trade with them. They seldom saw them; and they listened eagerly to the German talk about the helplessness and general insignificance of the United States. It came at last to be an article of faith that in the event of war, the German Empire would come to the support of Chile.

One finds it difficult to believe that any such delusion possessed the government officials in Santiago. Yet, perhaps, one member of that Government may have entertained it; since otherwise it is very difficult to understand his action. On December 11, 1891, Señor Don Manuel Matta, formerly a journalist, but now the Minister of Foreign Affairs, addressed a telegram to the Chilean Minister in Washington relating to a message on Chilean affairs sent by President Harrison to Congress. In this telegram, language was used which was insulting not only to Mr. Egan, but to Secretary Tracy and even to President Harrison. Señor Matta spoke of the President's statements as " erroneous or deliberately incorrect " (*deliber-*

adamente inexactos). A note of Mr. Egan's was described as "aggressive in purpose and virulent in language." Matta's telegram ended with an allusion to what he called "the intrigues which proceed from so low a source, and the threats which come from a source so high." This despatch was read by Matta to the Chilean Senate and was telegraphed to all the Chilean legations in Europe, thus publishing the insult to the world.

Mr. Egan at once sent a note to Señor Matta demanding to know whether the text of the telegram as given in the newspapers was correct. Matta replied that it was, intimating at the same time that it did not concern any one save the Government of Chile and its officials. The Chilean Minister at Washington thoroughly appreciated the "blazing indiscretion" of which his chief had been guilty, and he took the responsibility of suppressing the offensive telegram so far as he could do so. It was, however, cabled to the American press and was read by the American people with intense indignation. Even Mr. Blaine no longer sought to hold President Harrison in check. Preparations for war were openly begun. The navy yards at San Francisco and Brooklyn worked night and day. A squadron of eight cruisers was assembled in Pacific waters; blockading ships were ordered to be bought; and an ultimatum was finally sent to the Chilean Government containing three peremptory demands: first, that the Matta telegram should be withdrawn, its language disowned, and an explicit apology offered for it; second, that an indemnity should at once be paid for the outrage upon American sailors; and third, that the refugees in the American legation at Santiago should receive a safe conduct to neutral territory.

For a moment the scales were evenly balanced between

peace and war. Volunteers offered their services to the War Department in Washington. The Chileans boggled over the terms which Mr. Blaine had laid before them. They talked of arbitration. They offered, while refusing to withdraw the Matta telegram, to declare that it was not meant to be offensive. The Chilean Minister argued that it was a purely domestic communication and therefore privileged. Mr. Blaine and the President, however, stood firm, and on January 23d the Chilean Government executed a complete backdown. The terms in which its submission was offered left nothing to be desired on the score of completeness. Wrote Señor Pereira to Mr. Egan:

" The undersigned deplores that in that telegram there were employed through an error of judgment the expressions which are offensive in the judgment of your Government. . . . In fulfilment of a high duty of courtesy and sincerity toward a friendly nation . . . the Government of Chile absolutely withdraws the said expressions . . . —a declaration which is made without reservation in order that it may receive such publicity as your Government may deem suitable."

The sum of $75,000 was paid from the Chilean Treasury to the injured sailors of the *Baltimore;* and the refugees in the American legation received a safe conduct and left Chilean territory unmolested, under the protection of the United States.[51]

This was the second incident during the Harrison administration which showed that the American people were no longer unconcerned with their foreign relations. As in Samoa, so in Chile, a new spirit in American diplomacy had been manifested in a striking manner, and had made

[51] The whole diplomatic and naval correspondence was submitted to Congress by President Harrison as an appendix to his message of January 26, 1892. It makes a volume of some 650 pages.

it plain to all the world that the United States was becoming a force to be reckoned with in international affairs. Mr. Blaine's enemies at home bitterly attacked his conduct of these negotiations. The opposition press accused him of jingoism, of duplicity, and of insincerity. So violent was this opposition in the end, as to find expression in the most unpatriotic sentiments. At the very moment when peace and war were trembling in the balance, a semi-political association in New York, known as the Reform Club, actually invited a Chilean emissary to address it, and listened with applause to his venomous attacks upon the President and Government of the United States.[52] Such incidents as this, however, merely disgusted and repelled all right-thinking people; and Mr. Blaine came out of the Chilean imbroglio with his popularity greater even than it had been before.

Not long after the Chilean affair had reached its climax, events of much interest took place in a distant island of the Pacific. The little kingdom of Hawaii had for forty years been living under a constitutional monarchy which continued the line of native kings. Its independence had been guaranteed by France and England in 1843; and the United States, though not a party to this agreement, had, nevertheless, on more than one occasion, used its armed forces to repress disorder and maintain the reign of law. The white population of the island comprised a large number of persons of American ancestry, and these acted in accord with the resident English, the two together constituting an enlightened and highly prosperous community. In 1881, the Hawaiian king, Kalakaua I., who had not before regarded himself as a particularly im-

[52] One member, Mr. Ellery Anderson, honoured himself by rising at this meeting and protesting against it as unpatriotic.

portant personage, made a tour of the world. Much to
his surprise and delight, he found his kingly dignity recognised by some of the greatest sovereigns of Asia and
Europe, who treated him with every mark of respect as a
member of the royal caste. His flag was saluted by the
fleets of Japan, England, France and Germany; military
reviews were held in his honour; and he was welcomed to
palaces and fêted as cordially as though he were a monarch
of much greater power and pretensions.[53] When he
returned, he brought with him not merely jewelled decorations from the Czar, the Austrian Kaiser, the Queen
of England, and the Pope, but brand-new crowns which
he had purchased in London for himself and for his con-
sort, together with a field battery intended for a standing
army, which, in his imagination, already existed. His
foreign journey, in fact, had turned his head. On a small
scale he reproduced the follies and extravagances of the
Egyptian Khedive, Ismaïl, the greatest spendthrift of
modern times. Kalakaua began to imitate the monarchs
at whose courts he had been so lavishly entertained. In
his private life he gave himself up to the parasites and
panders who swarmed about him and suggested to him
new forms of wastefulness and new refinements of vice.
He instituted an Order with insignia and decorations; he
built himself a palace; he had himself crowned with splendid ceremonial, though he had already been a king for
nine years. Already he saw himself at the head of a
great Polynesian empire; and in 1887 he tried to interfere
in the affairs of Samoa, with some dreamy notion of adding
its islands to his own small kingdom.[54]

[53] For an interesting and often amusing account of this tour, see Arm-
strong, *Round the World with King Kalakaua* (New York, 1904).

[54] The King fitted out a small expedition in 1887 and despatched it to

Worse than this, he tried to ignore or to evade the constitution which had been established and ratified by the Hawaiian people. The royal expenses were now paid, by the personal order of the King, out of the public funds, and without the knowledge or approval of his Ministers. He tried to negotiate a foreign loan of $10,-000,000 in order to maintain a standing army for the enhancement of his royal prestige. He even lent an ear to the native element, who urged him so to modify the constitution, as to exclude from the franchise the white residents of Hawaii. These, however, uniting with the more intelligent of the natives, not only resisted the attempt, but compelled the King to keep more closely within his constitutional limitations.

In 1891, worn out by worry and by unrestrained excesses, Kalakaua died, and was succeeded by his sister, Liliuokalani. The new Hawaiian Queen was a woman of great force of character and of much personal charm. Her bearing was truly regal. She presided over public functions with marked dignity, while all who were received by her in private audience came away charmed by her grace and affability. She had been highly educated, and spoke both French and English with perfect purity and elegance. She was, however, as thoroughly imbued with a sense of her royal prerogative as though she had been an Elizabeth or a Maria Theresa. She was in England when the Constitution of 1887 was established in Hawaii;

Samoa in the steamer *Kaimiloa*. Just what he expected the expedition to accomplish is not very clear; but the drunken crew of the *Kaimiloa* ran the ship aground, and the whole affair ended in an absurd fiasco. See House Exec. Documents, 238, Fiftieth Congress, p. 39 seqq. (1888); and President Cleveland's Message of April 2, 1888, with the appended documents. Further details are given in Foster, *American Diplomacy in the Orient*, pp. 373-374 (Boston, 1903).

and when she learned that under its provisions the white residents were to have an equal share of political power, her indignation passed all bounds. Upon her accession to the throne, she set herself to the task of abrogating that instrument and of restoring the personal government of the Kamehamehas. She had no sooner taken the coronation oath than she declared to one of the Cabinet, " My Ministry shall be responsible to me alone!" She dismissed the existing Cabinet and chose a Ministry of her own selection, which was opposed by a majority in the Hawaiian legislature. To provide the funds needed for her campaign against constitutionalism, she leagued herself with certain interests which sought a lottery franchise and a law licensing the sale of opium. By a series of intrigues which it would be tedious to detail, these measures were legalised, and at once the Legislature was dissolved. On January 14, 1893, the Queen had planned to promulgate by royal decree a new Constitution, which should supersede the old one. Her Ministry informed her that such an act would be revolutionary. She demanded their resignations, but they refused compliance, and issued a proclamation (January 15th) setting forth these facts and declaring the throne vacant. On the following day, a mass meeting of the foreign residents and many of the natives formally decided that in view of the Queen's arbitrary acts, stringent measures were needed " for the preservation of the public credit and to avert the final ruin of a financial condition already overstrained."

A Provisional Government, headed by Mr. Sanford B. Dole, a Justice of the Supreme Court, was organised, with an Advisory Council representing the best elements of the community. This body, in view of the intense excitement prevailing in Honolulu, called upon the United States

Minister, Mr. John L. Stevens of Maine, for assistance in preserving order.   The United States cruiser *Boston* was lying in the harbour; and at the request of Mr. Stevens a battalion of sailors and marines was landed by Captain Wiltse and marched through the streets of the capital, encamping before the Government Building.   Mr. Stevens on his own responsibility recognised the new Government and officially proclaimed Hawaii to be under the protection of the United States (February 1, 1893).   The Queen, seeing that resistance was useless, made a formal protest and then yielded, as she said, only " to the superior forces of the United States of America."

The Provisional Government, doubtful of the effect of these events upon public opinion in the United States, hurriedly despatched a commission to lay their case before President Harrison, and to ask for the annexation of Hawaii to the United States.   The President and Mr. J. W. Foster, who had succeeded Mr. Blaine as Secretary of State, strongly favoured this suggestion, which was, in fact, not a new one, since as early as 1854 annexation had been considered.   A treaty was hurriedly negotiated between the Commissioners and the Secretary of State; and on February 15th a treaty of annexation was signed, providing for the continuance in power of the Dole government, and the retention of the existing Hawaiian laws, subject, however, to the exercise of supreme authority by the United States, which was to appoint a commissioner empowered to veto any or all acts of the local administration.   It was further provided that the United States should assume the Hawaiian debt,[55] that it should allow the deposed Queen an annual grant of $20,000, and that it should give to the Princess Kaiulani, who was next in line of succession, the sum of $150,000 in return for a renuncia-

[55] At this time a little over $2,000,000.

tion of her rights. This treaty, after having been duly signed, was immediately submitted by President Harrison to the Senate for ratification, accompanied by a message in which he said:

" The overthrow of the monarchy was not in any way promoted by this Government, but had its origin in what seemed to have been a reactionary and revolutionary policy on the part of Queen Liliuokalani, which put in serious peril not only the large and preponderating interests of the United States in the Islands, but all foreign interests, and indeed, the decent administration of civil affairs and the peace of the Islands. . . . The restoration of Queen Liliuokalani to her throne is undesirable, if not impossible; and unless actively supported by the United States, would be accompanied by serious disaster and the disorganisation of all business interests. The influence and interest of the United States in the Islands must be increased and not diminished.

" It is essential that none of the great Powers shall secure these Islands. Such a possession would not consist with our safety and with the peace of the world. This view of the situation is so apparent and conclusive that no protest has been heard from any Government against proceedings looking to annexation. Every foreign representative at Honolulu promptly acknowledged the Provisional Government, and I think there is a general concurrence in the opinion that the deposed Queen ought not to be restored." [56]

President Harrison's assertion that the United States had had no part in the revolution in Hawaii was regarded by the opposition as disingenuous. It was said that Mr. Dole and his associates were simply conspirators, who had acted in accordance with a preconceived plan, the details of which had been fully communicated to the American Government. The opportune presence of the *Boston* at Honolulu was viewed as something more than a coincidence. The action of Mr. Stevens was denounced as

[56] Message of February 15th, 1893.

treacherous to the Government to which he had been accredited.   The whole affair was described as an outrage upon a helpless people and as an attempt on the part of Mr. Harrison and his advisers to seize territory in a distant part of the world without any shadow of justification. The white residents of Hawaii were styled " carpet-baggers," and their new Government a barefaced usurpation. Many sneers were directed at these " sons of missionaries," who, though aliens, had deprived the natives of their political birthright.

Reviewing this affair in the light of all that is now known, two facts stand out beyond the possibility of refutation.   In the first place, there can be no doubt that Queen Liliuokalani had justly forfeited her throne.   She had violated the Constitution which she had solemnly sworn to maintain, and was proceeding to action such as would, in the case of an English sovereign, have led at once to the forfeiture of the royal rights.   Furthermore, the sneers aimed at the " sons of missionaries " as aliens, were thoroughly unwarranted.   Mr. Dole, for instance, and his immediate associates were not aliens at all. Though of foreign ancestry, they had been born in Hawaii. Their homes were there.   All their interests were there. They were the ones who had transformed the island into a civilised and prosperous community.   It was they who maintained the system of public education, who paid the greater part of the taxes, and who supported the administration of the laws.   If revolution is ever justifiable—and of this no Anglo-Saxon can feel any doubt— the revolution in Hawaii was surely so, as being the act of men defending their political liberties and personal rights.

On the other hand, it may be regarded as absolutely certain that the American Minister, Mr. Stevens, was not only well aware of what was going on, but that he had fully informed his Government, and that President Harrison and his advisers sympathised with the annexation movement. In February of 1892, Mr. Stevens had written to the State Department a letter in which he said:

"There are increasing indications that the annexation sentiment is gaining among the business men."

On March 8th of the same year, he had asked Mr. Blaine for special instructions, "in case the Government here should be reorganised and overturned by an orderly and peaceful revolutionary movement. I have information which I deem reliable that there is an organised revolutionary party in the Islands. . . . These people are very likely to overthrow the monarchy and establish a republic with the ultimate view of annexation to the United States."

On December 30th, Admiral Skerrett, who was under orders to take command of the Pacific Squadron, had called at the Navy Department in Washington for final instructions. He said to the Secretary:

"Mr. Tracy, I want to ask you about these Hawaiian affairs. When I was out there twenty years ago, I had frequent conversations with the then United States Minister, Mr. Pierce, on the subject of the Islands. I was told then that the United States Government did not wish to annex the islands of Hawaii."

Mr. Tracy answered:

"The wishes of the Government have changed. They will be very glad to annex Hawaii. As a matter of course, none but the ordinary legal means can be used to persuade these people to come into the United States."

" All right, sir," answered Admiral Skerrett, " I only wanted to know how things were going on, as a cue to my action." [57]

Finally, Mr. Stevens, on the day when the American marines were landed in Honolulu, had sent a despatch to Washington saying, " The Hawaiian pear is now fully ripe, and this is the golden hour for the United States to pluck it."

From all these facts, it is quite obvious that the American Government was fully aware of the impending revolution and was in sympathy with it as a means of securing the annexation of the Islands. Whether the revolution would have succeeded had not marines been landed from the *Boston* at the critical moment is a purely hypothetical question. As to the morality of the whole proceeding, opinions will always differ. At the time, the administration received much harsh criticism, and though President Harrison, in his message of February 15th, urged the Senate to ratify the annexation treaty at once, definite action upon it was delayed. The sands of the Harrison administration were fast running out. Its hours were numbered; and the Hawaiian question was soon to assume a new form and to pass through many different phases before it reached a final settlement. A few days more, and another hand had laid a firm grasp upon the helm of State.

[57] Senate Report on Hawaii, p. 10 (1893). See President Cleveland's message of December 18, 1893, with the appended documents.

V

AFTER witnessing President's Harrison's inauguration, Mr. Cleveland had left Washington and presently became a resident of New York City, where he resumed the practice of law, as an associate of the firm of Bangs, Stetson, Tracy and MacVeagh. In the eyes of the professional politicians of both parties, his public career seemed to have ended, and to have ended in utter failure. He was regarded as one who had, by an accident of politics, attained a transitory greatness to which he had proved to be personally unequal. His dogged determination in forcing an apparently unpopular issue, almost on the eve of a presidential election and merely as a matter of conviction, had been quite incomprehensible at the time, and the result appeared to justify the contempt which partisans such as Senator Gorman and Governor Hill confidentially expressed to their intimates. They felt that Mr. Cleveland had now been eliminated from national politics. He had settled down as an every-day lawyer in a great cosmopolitan city, where the complexity of life and the clash of material interests reduce even the most eminent of its citizens to comparative obscurity. Mr. Henry Watterson rather complacently remarked at this time: " Cleveland in New York reminds one of a stone thrown into a river. There is a ' plunk,' a splash, and then silence."

The ex-President accepted this verdict with philosophical good humour. He had nothing to regret. He had acted in accordance with his sense of right, and had done

what he believed to be the best both for his country and
for his party.   As he said a little later, at a banquet given
in his honour: [1]   " We know that we have not deceived
the people with false promises and pretences.   And we
know that we have not corrupted and betrayed the poor
with the money of the rich."

By his savings and by judicious investments in real es-
tate, Mr. Cleveland had already secured a modest competence.   As a lawyer, his professional labours yielded
him a generous income.   He practised little in the courts;
but important cases were often referred to him by the
sitting justices, while his unquestioned integrity and conscientiousness led many prospective litigants to submit their
interests to his arbitration.   There was one kind of legal
practice which he persistently refused to undertake.   No
persuasion could induce him to accept retainers from the
great corporations. [2]   Mr. Cleveland was convinced that
the moneyed interests had already become a menace to the
welfare of the nation; and with them he was unwilling to
associate himself in any fashion whatsoever.   In the
message which he sent to Congress soon after his defeat
for re-election, he had pointed out the perils which he saw
in vast and irresponsible aggregations of wealth, whose
possessors felt themselves to be above the law.

" The fortunes realised by our manufacturers are no longer
solely the reward of sturdy industry and enlightened foresight, but
they result from the discriminating favour of the Government and
are largely built upon undue exactions from the masses of our
people.   The gulf between employers and the employed is constantly widening, and classes are rapidly forming, one comprising

1 By the Democratic Club of New York, April 27, 1889 (Parker, p. 248).
2 Hensel and Parker, *Life and Public Services of Grover Cleveland*, pp.
319, 320 (Philadelphia, 1892).

the very rich and powerful, while in another are found the toiling poor.

"As we view the achievements of aggregated capital, we discover the existence of trusts, combinations, and monopolies, while the citizen is struggling far in the rear or is trampled to death beneath an iron heel. Corporations, which should be carefully restrained creatures of the law and the servants of the people, are fast becoming the people's masters.

"The existing situation is injurious to the health of our entire body-politic. It stifles in those for whose benefit it is permitted, all patriotic love of country, and substitutes in its place selfish greed and grasping avarice. Devotion to American citizenship for its own sake and for what it should accomplish as a motive to our nation's advancement and the happiness of all our people is displaced by the assumption that the Government, instead of being the embodiment of equality, is but an instrumentality through which especial and individual advantages are to be gained.

"Communism is a hateful thing and a menace to peace and organised government; but the communism of combined wealth and capital, the outgrowth of overweening cupidity and selfishness, which insidiously undermine the justice and integrity of free institutions, is not less dangerous than the communism of oppressed poverty and toil, which, exasperated by injustice and discontent, attacks with wild disorder the citadel of rule." [3]

But although Mr. Cleveland was no longer an object of interest to the politicians, there were many quiet indications that the great mass of his countrymen had not forgotten him. Invitations came to him continually from professional, commercial, religious, educational, and civic organisations, which sought the honour of his presence at commemorative banquets and other public gatherings.[4]

[3] Message of December 3, 1888.

[4] For instance, at the laying of the corner-stone of the New York Academy of Medicine; at the banquet of the Hibernian Society of Philadelphia;

When his engagements permitted, he acceded to these requests; for, as he said on one occasion, he had no sympathy with those good souls who " are greatly disturbed every time an ex-President ventures to express an opinion on any subject." Not infrequently he spoke at length to interested listeners; and what he said was always sensible and wise, and sometimes pregnant with suggestion. As a public speaker, Mr. Cleveland was far from attaining brilliancy. Even his warmest friends could scarcely claim that he was an orator. His manner and his style alike were heavy. He had a strong preference for polysyllabic words, and for sentences so involved as to be Johnsonian in their ponderosity. He had probably never heard the dictum of the French stylist who said: *L'adjectif, c'est le plus grand ennemi du substantif;* for almost every noun was coupled with an adjective, and these adjectives were frequently applied in pairs. Moreover, like many another statesman, he often took refuge in the baldest truisms, which were seldom freshened up by originality of phrasing. Mr. Abram S. Hewitt once said of him, in a tartly cryptic epigram, which may be interpreted as conveying either praise or censure: " Cleveland is the greatest master of platitude since Washington."

It is likely, however, that Mr. Cleveland's oratorical deficiencies were, on the whole, a distinct advantage to him. The American people at that period still held to the conservative tradition which viewed exceptional accomplishments in public men, if not with suspicion, at least with a certain amount of caution. Brilliancy might rouse admiration, but it could not inspire confidence. In the

at the Cornell Alumni Society meeting; at the Thurman birthday banquet in Columbus, Ohio; at the banquet of the New York Chamber of Commerce; and before the Young Men's Democratic Association, Philadelphia.

long run it was the safe man rather than the showy man who secured the highest honours from the electorate. Clay and Webster and Blaine had won the frantic applause of millions; yet they had all failed to achieve the one great prize on which their hearts were set. No President had ever been an orator of the first rank, save only Lincoln; and Lincoln's great political addresses represented the oratory of reason rather than the oratory of emotion. And hence, in Mr. Cleveland's case, even when his utterances were very tame and his sentences quite commonplace, they appealed to the multitude as embodying sound morality, conservative opinion, and what General Grant was fond of calling " good horse sense."

Mr. Cleveland's lines, therefore, at this time were cast in pleasant places. Successful in his profession, and respected by those whose personal esteem was worth the having, he enjoyed a period of tranquillity that must have been most grateful after his stormy years of public office. He spent his summers at a charming country-seat upon the Massachusetts coast, to which he gave the name " Grey Gables." There he entertained his intimate friends with a genial, friendly hospitality; and there, as an angler, he won a reputation which he was said to value quite as much as any public honours that he had ever gained. It was an ideal life for a retired statesman, a life that he would gladly have continued to enjoy, unvexed by the strife and din of party politics. But the fates had decreed it otherwise.

The discussion of the McKinley Bill in 1890, and the overwhelming Republican defeat in the congressional elections which followed close upon the passage of that measure, brought Mr. Cleveland once again into a prominence such as he was far from seeking. It was he who in

his bold message of 1887 had first raised the tariff issue.
It was he who had forced the Republicans to adopt a
policy which had ended in their utter rout.   Though he
had, at the time, failed of re-election, he had, nevertheless,
inspired his party with aggressiveness and confidence.
Many Democrats now began to ask whether any one was
so well fitted as he to lead the party back again to power.
The campaign of education, begun in 1888, was commencing to bear fruit.   Looking forward to the coming
struggle for the presidency, popular feeling instinctively
went out to Mr. Cleveland as the logical candidate for
1892.   Yet, although this sentiment was beginning to per-
vade the rank and file of the Democracy, it was most distasteful to the party managers.   In a phrase of their own
choosing, they " had no use " for Mr. Cleveland. To them
he had always shown himself intractable, and they had
been pleased at what appeared to be his permanent elimina-
tion from politics.   It was not agreeable to think of him as
likely to become again a candidate.   Therefore they took
no notice of the popular feeling in his favour, but endeavoured to ignore him and to speak of him in public with
a studied indifference, as of one whose day was over and
who had become politically " a back number."   Most of
the party organs refrained from mentioning him in connection with the presidency.   Some of them endeavoured
to discredit him by a systematic press campaign of defamation.   Conspicuous in this was the New York *Sun,* at that
time under the editorship of Mr. Charles A. Dana.

Charles Anderson Dana was undoubtedly the most remarkable figure that had yet arisen in the history of American journalism.   Born in 1819, and educated at Harvard,
he was a careful student and omnivorous reader, with a
memory so tenacious as to place at his command a vast

array of facts, which his quick wit and literary skill enabled him to use with singular effectiveness. As a very young man he had joined the Fourierites for a time, in the erratic though memorable experiment at Brook Farm. A little later, he was engaged in miscellaneous writing for the Boston newspapers. In 1847, he joined the staff of the New York *Tribune,* in whose office he developed a pungent style, which was afterward to make him feared and famous. Here, too, he came into contact with all the most important public men of the ante-bellum period. A violent dispute with Horace Greeley over the latter's unfortunate " On to Richmond " editorial led to Dana's retirement from the *Tribune* in 1862; [5] and in the following year he was made Assistant Secretary of War. In this capacity he rendered highly important service to his chief, Stanton, who sent him upon confidential missions to the headquarters of the army, with instructions to report upon the character and conduct of the leading generals. Dana's knowledge of human nature, his grasp upon essentials, and his power of going to the very heart of things, made his reports invaluable both to the Secretary and to Mr. Lincoln. It was due to Dana's favourable judgment that General Grant was not relieved of his command in 1863, but was upheld by the administration in the teeth of the fiercest criticisms. In 1864, however, Dana left the War Department and returned to journalism, editing for a while the Chicago *Republican.* In this he failed completely. Discouraged and uncertain of his future, he came to New York, where he established himself, in 1868, as editor of the New York *Sun.*

It was the year of Grant's first election to the presi-

[5] An interesting account of the relations between Greeley and Dana is given in Benton, *Greeley on Lincoln* (New York, 1893).

dency. Dana, remembering the service which he had done the General, and having, besides, a real liking for the man, wrote a life of Grant, which he intended to be a sort of campaign biography; for it was highly eulogistic and was written with an intimate knowledge of its subject. Political usage and personal gratitude might have suggested to the new President the bestowal of some reward on one whose ability was so exceptional as Mr. Dana's. Yet for some reason which has never been satisfactorily explained, Grant absolutely ignored the claim. It was Dana's desire to be made Collector of the Port of New York, but the office was given to another; and by this act Grant made an enemy whose unrelenting hatred pursued him to the grave. With an almost frantic eagerness, Dana set about destroying every copy of the *Life* upon which he could lay his hands; so that to-day the book is practically unattainable outside of a few libraries. Then, in the columns of the *Sun,* he waged upon Grant a war of slander which for sheer malignity has never been surpassed. Dana knew quite well that Grant was honest, clean-living, patriotic and sincere; [6] yet now, with a perversion of facts that was infernal in its ingenuity, he painted him as a corrupt and brutal scoundrel, one who used his office for his personal enrichment, a tyrant, a vulgar ruffian, and a common drunkard. Every one connected with the President, even his wife and family, came in for a share of Dana's wrath or ridicule. At one time the editor was indicted in the District of Columbia, and an attempt was

[6] Dana had written in his life of Grant: "The unimpeachable and enduring record of his acts bears testimony to the zeal, urbanity, patience and ability with which he has executed his responsible trusts. . . . He possesses abilities and attainments that entitle him to a place among the wise and prudent statesmen of the country."—Dana, *Life of Ulysses S. Grant,* pp. 422-424 (Springfield, 1868).

made to have him removed to Washington for trial.
Over such a prospect, Dana was almost beside himself
with fear. His hysterical editorials made it plain that
had his case been actually tried in Washington he must
have gone to prison; but Judge Blatchford, sitting in New
York, refused the change of venue. In consequence, the
case was dropped, and Dana continued to lash the President with even greater fury than before. After Grant's
retirement to private life, the attitude of the *Sun* remained the same. Even when the hero of the great war
was awaiting burial, and when all other criticism was
stilled in the presence of death, Dana launched a poisoned
shaft at those who loved Grant best. The *Sun* published
an account of an undertaker's bill which the General's
family had very properly refused to pay, but which Dana
himself had settled with an ostentatious show of hypo-
critical benevolence that was absolutely devilish.

The change in Dana's attitude toward Grant in 1868
was, however, only a single aspect of a change which had
altered his entire nature. Until then he had been genial
and fair-minded, with a touch of something like idealism
in his view of things. He had associated with honourable men, and his life had been a useful one. But as he
now looked back upon it, that life appeared to him a failure. Uprightness, optimism, and a regard for others had
not " paid." Both in journalism and in public life he had
somehow missed success, and he was now in his fiftieth
year. And so he seems to have said to himself that henceforth in his career as journalist he would take no heed of
right or wrong, but would gain a certain sort of fame and
a sure material reward by throwing overboard all principle. From that time he was thoroughly a cynic and a
pessimist. In his charming home at Roslyn and to a very

few intimate friends, he still showed himself to be a genial, cultivated gentleman, interested in his books and flower-gardens, and with a genuine enthusiasm for rare pottery, of which he was a connoisseur. But as editor of the *Sun,* he played consistently the part of devil's advocate. He set himself to jeer at whatever was best and noblest, to degrade and burlesque whatever decent men respected, to defend or palliate the base, and to treat corruption as an admirable joke. Thus, he supported Tammany in the days of its worst offences. He was the apologist of Tweed. He warmly commended the proposal to erect a public monument to that notorious malefactor. On the other hand, every attempt to improve political conditions—such as the reform of the civil service and the movement for an honest ballot—was greeted by Dana with an outburst of derision. He used his newspaper also as a weapon to avenge his personal dislikes; and whoever incurred his enmity or roused his prejudice was pilloried in the columns of the *Sun.*

Had Mr. Dana been a journalist of the usual type, his hatreds and his expression of them would soon have ceased to be of any interest, and would most probably have proved the ruin of the *Sun.* But the man was a genius in his way. His rhetoric was superb, and even those who most disliked him were reluctantly compelled to own the power of his invective. He had an unerring instinct for touching his victim on the raw; and his ingenuity in giving pain was marvellous. Furthermore, there was something tricksy, something impish, even, in his malevolence; so that, outrageous though he was, his outrageousness had an indefinable quality which raised it far above the level of vulgarity. To him might well have been applied the description which Disraeli once gave of Lord Salisbury—" a

master of gibes and flouts and jeers." A careful student
of his editorial work once wrote of him: "He had a gift
for making men seem hateful or contemptible or ridiculous, and he used this talent most unsparingly. His
nicknames and epithets stuck like burrs to those at whom
he hurled them. Who cannot recall a score of these
appellations,[7] every one of which conveyed to the mind
the suggestion of something ludicrous?" And, quite
apart from its editorial page, the *Sun* was managed with
great ability. It was then, perhaps, the most readable
newspaper in the United States. Its news was collected
with the utmost accuracy. Its reporting was often done
with a skill and cleverness that gave it a distinctly literary
quality. Its editor was regarded with intense admiration
by journalists throughout the country, and he became the
founder of a journalistic cult.

Dana was ostensibly a Democratic partisan. His
friends asserted that at election time he always voted the
Republican ticket. If so, this was a characteristic example of his cynicism; for in his editorial columns everything Republican was anathema. Most probably he preferred to be in opposition, because such a rôle gave fuller
scope to his peculiar gifts. Indeed, in 1880, when the
September elections seemed to indicate that the Democratic candidate, General Hancock, was likely to be chosen
President in November, Dana deliberately wrote a double-
leaded editorial, in which he sneered at Hancock as "a
good man, weighing 250 pounds"—a gibe which greatly
delighted the Republicans. The only note of sincerity in
Dana's writings was found in his support of Mr. Tilden,

[7] *E. g.,* "Seven Mule Barnum," "Pinkpank Wheeler," "Coffee-Pot
Wallace," "Fire-Alarm Foraker," "Sambo Bowles," "Aliunde Joe,"
"His Fraudulency."

who was his personal friend.   When Mr. Cleveland was elected Governor of New York, Dana at first was favourable to him, but presently he became inimical for reasons that are variously given.   Some say that as Mr. Tilden's liking for Governor Cleveland cooled, Dana took his own cue from Tilden.   Others assert that Mr. Cleveland rejected certain overtures that were made to him by Dana, and declined to invite the editor to Albany in answer to a hint.[8]   However this may be, the *Sun* soon ranged itself

[8] See the detailed statement in McClure, *Our Presidents*, pp. 312-315 (New York, 1905), of which the following quotation contains the essential points:

" Dana had very earnestly supported Cleveland's nomination and election for Governor in 1882, and after the election he wrote a personal letter to Cleveland asking the appointment of a friend to the position of Adjutant-General. His chief purpose was to give a position on the staff to his son, Paul Dana, who is now his successor in the editorial chair. Cleveland received that letter as he received thousands of other letters recommending appointments, instead of recognising the claim Mr. Dana had upon him for the courtesy of an answer. Beecher had a candidate for the same position, and Cleveland gave it to Beecher's man without any explanation whatever to Dana, who felt that he had been discourteously treated by Cleveland. Mr. Dana gave no open sign of disappointment; but some time after Cleveland's inauguration, when it became known that Dana felt aggrieved at the Governor, some mutual friends intervened and proposed to Cleveland that he should invite Dana to dine with some acquaintances at the Executive Mansion. To this Cleveland readily assented. Dana was informed that Cleveland would tender such an invitation if it would be accepted, and he promptly assented. Cleveland then became involved in the pressing duties of the Legislature and allowed the session to close without extending the promised and expected invitation to Dana. Mr. Cleveland told me that he was entirely to blame for neglect in both instances, as Dana would doubtless have been satisfied if he had courteously informed him of his conviction which required him to appoint another for Adjutant-General; and he had no excuse to offer but that of neglect for not inviting Dana to dinner.

" Dana naturally assumed that Cleveland had given him deliberate affront, and Cleveland could make no satisfactory explanation. As Governor and as President he was first of all devoted to his official duties,

among the anti-Cleveland journals; and in 1884, it supported the Greenback nominee, General B. F. Butler. It was exceedingly like Dana to advocate the election of this brazen charlatan, who holds in history the bad eminence of having been the only conspicuous Northern commander in the Civil War against whom charges of personal corruption were practically proven.[9] Throughout Mr. Cleveland's Presidency, Dana maintained a sort of malevolent neutrality, giving many a satirical thrust at the man whose reforming spirit was obnoxious to the presiding genius of the *Sun*. On the day after Cleveland's defeat in the election of 1888, Dana printed without comment an entire column of quotations from medical and physiological works on the subject of obesity. Thereafter, the *Sun* ignored the ex-President until once more he loomed up as a possible candidate. Now, dipping his pen in vitriol, Dana outdid himself in running the entire gamut of abuse, from ridicule to excoriation. To him Mr. Cleveland became "the Perpetual Candidate," and later "the Stuffed Prophet." Some of these editorials were masterpieces of malignity, and as such they are almost worthy of permanent preservation. They served no end, however, save to draw increased attention to his enemy's political availability. It was Mr. Cleveland himself who, in the judgment of many persons, deliberately ruined his own prospects by an utterance which he made at this time upon

which he discharged with rare fidelity, and he gave little time even to the common courtesies which most Governors and Presidents would recognise as justly belonging to their friends. Efforts were made to conciliate Dana, but he never would discuss the question, and he sacrificed half the circulation of his paper in the campaign of 1884 in his battle against Cleveland."

[9] Official Records of the War, series iii., vol. ii., p. 173; Rhodes, *History of the United States from the Compromise of 1850*, vol v., pp. 303-308, 312, 313 (New York, 1904).

a question which had been violently injected into national politics. Before narrating the occurrence, it is necessary to give a brief account of the growth of the silver movement in the Western States.

In the early years of its existence, the Republican party had been dominated by one controlling purpose—the destruction of slavery. The issue which gave it birth was distinctly a moral issue, and the enthusiasm which inspired it was a moral enthusiasm. Its first declaration, made at Jackson, Michigan, on July 6, 1854, declared that the Republican party was "battling for the first principles of Republican government and against the schemes of an aristocracy." All Republicans were pledged in this declaration to "act cordially and faithfully in unison, postponing and suspending all difference with regard to political economy or administrative policy." [10] The Republican party, therefore, was distinctly not a party of caste or of class but preëminently a party of the people, devoted to the cause of human freedom. In those days the power of wealth and the pride of birth were equally arrayed against it. The rich merchants and bankers of Boston, New York, and Philadelphia viewed this new party as a menace to political tranquillity and vested interests. They joined hands gladly with the aristocratic planters of the South in seeking to stamp out so strange and disquieting a fanaticism. It was the most respectable citizens of Massachusetts who ostracised Charles Sumner, who broke up anti-slavery meetings, who mobbed Garrison and threatened to lynch Whittier. The Republican leaders boasted that their party was not one of wealth and privilege, but of intelligence and moral worth. Clergymen, teachers, writers and small professional men joined its ranks, which

[10] Curtis, *The Republican Party*, i., p. 1 (New York, 1904).

were still further recruited from the agricultural portions of the country. The great strength of the Republican party lay, not in the Eastern States, but in the young commonwealths of the West—in Ohio, Illinois, Iowa, Michigan, Wisconsin, and Minnesota. The first Republican President was the very incarnation of democracy, so plain in manner, so simple in life, and so ruggedly sincere, as to seem to the fastidious denizens of the East a mere barbarian.

It was, therefore, as a party of the people that Republicanism first won its way to political power. When the Civil War ended, the great purpose of the primitive Republicans had been achieved. Slavery was abolished forever. The feudalism based upon it was annihilated. Every inch of American territory had become free soil. As we now look back upon that period, with a sense of true political perspective, it is plain that the old Republican party really died in the year 1866. The party which afterwards continued to bear its name was altogether different from that which had rallied around Frémont in 1856, and which had twice elected Lincoln. It was different in its aims and aspirations, different in the character of its leaders, and different in the influences which shaped its policy. Its years of almost irresponsible power had utterly transformed it. Controlling the national finances, with an overwhelming majority in Congress, and having in its gift not merely office and opportunity, but every sort of legislative favour, it drew to itself the support of every interest which ten years before had been arrayed against it. It was now the party of the bankers, the manufacturers, the lords of commerce, and all those active, restless, scheming spirits who had learned that great fortunes were to be made in other ways than by legitimate industry. The true citadels of the Republican party were now the crowded centres of the East, while the agricultural States received but slight consideration. The continuance of the war tariff, which enriched a comparatively few interests at the expense of the entire population, was the most striking factor in the development of this new Republicanism. The farmer was compelled to pay tribute to the manufacturer; and so the Republican party in this second phase of its existence became a party of class, as truly as the Democratic party had ever been in the days before the war.

The West was slow in recognising the significance of this change; but as time went on, financial conditions operated to cause serious distress. In the first place, the gradual appreciation in the value of the paper dollar pinched the debtor class severely. The farmer, for example, who in 1863 had mortgaged his farm for five thousand paper dollars, worth, perhaps, not more than half that sum in gold, found that he must repay the loan in dollars worth nearly twice as much, and therefore representing twice as much economy and diligence and labour. The resumption of specie payments in 1879, though a triumph of financial management, did, nevertheless, inflict a serious hardship upon all men who had borrowed money at a time when the paper currency of the United States was worth much less than its face value. This hardship was of course inevitable; but it was none the less a hardship, and it is not surprising that those who suffered from it should have tried to seek a remedy. Hence arose the so-called Greenback party, which as early as 1876 nominated candidates for the presidency and vice-presidency on a platform which demanded the repeal of the act for resuming specie payments and which advocated the issue of United States notes as the sole currency of the nation.   Upon this platform, Peter Cooper of New York received in that year a popular vote of 81,000; while in 1880, another "Greenback" candidate, James B. Weaver of Iowa, polled a vote of over 300,000.

This movement, however, represented only one form of popular discontent.   There were other grievances more irritating and apparently more easily remediable.   One was the manner in which the railways of the country had monopolised the public lands,   barring great tracts to settlers, while refusing to comply with the conditions under which the grants of land had been bestowed.   Another grievance was the discrimination in railroad rates, by which the small shipper was forced out of business by powerful corporations.   Still another was the working of the tariff laws, which had steadily discriminated against the most widespread of all American industries—agriculture—while forcing it to bear the greater burden of taxation.   It came at last to be widely asserted and believed that the Government of the United States was becoming a creature of the corporations, that Congress was filled with corporation agents—"railway Senators" and Trust representatives—and that even the judges on the bench were often men whose antecedents as corporation lawyers discredited their judicial decisions.

All these and still other reasons for public discontent first found expression in isolated political movements throughout the West.   Besides the "Greenback" or National party, there arose the so-called Anti-Monopoly party, which held its first convention at Chicago in 1884. In 1888, two Labour parties appeared, each with a different set of grievances.   The so-called Granger movement was another evidence of the popular discontent.   The Grangers, or, as they were officially styled, the "Patrons

of Husbandry," were an organisation of which the founder
was one O. H. Kelly, a clerk in the Bureau of Agriculture.
Their general aim was to unite for self-protection all who
were actually engaged in agricultural pursuits. By 1875,
the Grangers, who then numbered more than 1,500,000
men and women, had definitely formulated certain measures which they hoped to have embodied in both State and
national legislation. Like the Knights of Labour, they
advocated woman's suffrage and the regulation of railway
rates.

This organisation afterwards grew into the Farmers'
Alliance, just as the Knights of Labour grew into the
American Federation of Labour; and as both of them had
many aims in common, they effected a coalition in 1889,
when they agreed upon a common platform of principles,
demanding the abolition of national banks, an increased
issue of Government paper, and the Government ownership of all means of transportation and public intercourse.

By this time, the Western States were in a condition of
political ferment. As yet there was no general cohesion
or agreement between the different factions and parties.
They lacked a leader. They had not as yet developed any
political machinery. In the East, little notice was taken
of them. The newspapers treated them with easy ridicule
and described the intensely earnest men and women who
composed them as " cranks " and " calamity howlers."
Many of them were, indeed, unintelligent fanatics. Many
of their wrongs were fanciful. Many of their remedies
were quite impossible. Yet there did remain a very solid
substratum of reason for these various movements, and
the discontent was not without substantial justification.
The epithets so sneeringly applied to the rank and file of
the new parties recalled the no less sneering epithets that

had been hurled at the Republicans in the days of their anti-slavery crusade. They, too, had been described as wild men and fanatics and enemies of public order.

It may be asked why the discontented did not flock to the Democratic party and use it as an instrument for turning out the Republicans, who were held to be primarily responsible for existing conditions. The reason was that both of the old parties were now almost equally distrusted. Both were regarded as being under the control of the "money power." During Mr. Cleveland's administration, from 1885 to 1889, it had been made clear that the Trusts were quite as influential in Democratic as in Republican politics. Mr. H. B. Payne, for whom the Standard Oil Company had bought the Ohio legislature, was ostensibly a Democrat. It was charged also that Secretary Whitney, Mr. Cleveland's closest adviser, was dominated by the same sinister influence. Senator Hoar had asked, "Is it [the Standard Oil Company] represented in the Cabinet at this moment?"[13]—and the question had rasped the nerves of the entire nation. Therefore, these new factions that were springing up in the West and in the South felt that a clean sweep must be made, and that both of the old parties must be driven out. Seceding Republicans in the West declared themselves to be reverting to the earlier Republicanism of Lincoln, while in the South those who had once been Democrats professed to be reviving the Democracy of Jefferson. All of them "wished to get back to simplicity, honesty, and economy in government; to secure a fair field for all; to resist commercialism, to oppose the money power and the general corruption and cowardice of the old parties."

[13] *Congressional Record* (September, 1886), pp. 8520-8604. Mr. Whitney in an open letter afterwards denied the implied accusation.

" Party conventions and organisations were now mere machines for winning elections and keeping control of the offices. They were unscrupulous oligarchies, controlled by the rich. A few astute and wealthy managers and magnates, called ' business men,' controlling the party managers as their henchmen, set things up in private conferences, while the masses were being fooled and manipulated like voting herds. Then the business magnates, who dictated the nomination of the candidates and furnished the sinews of war for the campaign, were, of course, to conduct the Government; and, equally, of course, the laws were to be made and administered in such a way as to take good care of these managers' business interests. It was felt that if any President or Senator or Congressman began to urge, honestly and effectively, that the great mineowners, or railroads, or trust combinations,—the moneyed forces that controlled the money, land, and transportation of the people,— should be actually brought face to face with the enforcement of just and equal laws, then some silent but powerful influence within the parties would retire such public servants to private life." [14]

The storm-centre of this third-party agitation was the State of Kansas. In September, the Farmers' Alliance and the Knights of Labour assembled in convention there and nominated a full State ticket and also candidates for Congress. In the October elections, this ticket was elected, and out of the seven Congressmen allotted to Kansas, the new party elected five, while the State Legislature sent to the Senate a country editor, Mr. William Alfred Peffer, who had been a leader in the movement. In the following year, a general fusion took place of the different factions representing both the industrial and agricultural interests, now uniting for the first time as a definite political party under the name of " People's Party," or " Populists." Their first national convention was held

[14] Woodburn, *Political Parties and Party Problems in the United States*, pp. 114, 115 (New York, 1903).

at Cincinnati, in May, 1891, and it drew up a platform which demanded the free and unlimited coinage of silver; the issue of paper money which should be loaned to the people at not more than two per cent. per annum on the security of non-perishable agricultural products; the national ownership of railroads, telegraphs, telephones, and steamship lines; a graduated income tax; and the election of United States Senators by popular vote.[15]

It was the financial part of this platform that was most immediately important. The demand for the free coinage of silver represented a general belief which had permeated the minds of the Western people. They had come to entertain what is known as the quantitative theory of money, believing that an increased supply of money would raise the prices of farm products. It was a matter of indifference to them how this increase of money was to be effected, whether by the issue of irredeemable " greenbacks " or by the unlimited coinage of silver. They would have preferred, if left to themselves, to substitute paper money for a metallic currency of any sort. But here came in another influence which for some time past had been at work. The price of silver, as compared with that of gold, had for a long while been steadily falling. In consequence, the great mine-owners of Nevada, Colorado and other Western States found the production of silver ceasing to be profitable. They had, therefore, as early as 1877, secured the passage of the Bland Silver Law, directing the Government to purchase silver bullion and to coin each month not less than 2,000,000 or more than 4,000,000 silver dollars. In 1890, this act had been repealed, and in

[15] Hopkins, *Political Parties in the United States,* pp. 187, 188 (New York, 1900) ; see also Reynolds, *National Platforms and Political History* (Chicago, 1898).

place of it the so-called Sherman Silver Law had been enacted, directing the Government to purchase every month 4,500,000 ounces of silver, and to issue against it legal tender notes redeemable on demand in " coin "— either gold or silver, at the discretion of the Secretary of the Treasury.[17] These two laws, although afterwards attacked by the Republicans, involved a logical application of the doctrine of protection. Silver was an American product; and the mine-owners, as representing an American industry, demanded legislation which should make their industry a profitable one. As the tariff could not effect this, it was accomplished by forcing the Government to provide an artificial market for the product of the silver mines. The Sherman Law was passed in the hope of propitiating the adherents of silver in the West, but it failed entirely of its object. It did not go far enough to please the silver men, while it alarmed conservative financiers. What the Populists now desired was to make the coinage of silver an unlimited one, so as to render money plentiful and " cheap," to drive gold out of circulation, and thus to secure artificially a general increase in the values of agricultural products. The silver propaganda was received with great enthusiasm in the West. Meetings were held in thousands of country schoolhouses to hear this new gospel of prosperity proclaimed by perfervid orators. The movement threatened to demoralise both of the old parties; for it was felt that the silver vote would be able at the next election to turn the scale in favour of whatsoever candidate should show himself to be most truly " a friend of silver."

It was while this agitation was at its height that the

[17] Under the Bland Act and the Sherman Act, the currency had been expanded by some $450,000,000.

Reform Club in New York City [18] held a meeting to voice the opposition of New York business men to the free coinage of silver. An invitation to be present was sent to Mr. Cleveland. When this fact became known, many of his friends urged him to stay away and to keep to himself his opinions on the silver question. They knew that he was inflexibly opposed to an increased silver coinage. His messages to Congress had shown this very plainly. But they pointed out to him that by keeping silence he might let it be supposed that he had changed his mind, or that at least he was willing to approve a compromise. To offend the silver men was, they said, to throw away his chances for the presidency. He could not possibly receive a nomination if it were known that he was not a " friend of silver." The West would be solidly against him. It was a time to temporise and to exercise a little diplomacy both for his own sake and for the welfare of his party. Mr. Cleveland listened to this talk without saying very much. His engagements made it impossible for him to attend the Reform Club meeting. But he wrote a letter to the chairman, which on the following morning appeared in every newspaper throughout the United States. In it he said :

" It surely cannot be necessary for me to make a formal expression of my agreement with those who believe that the greatest peril would be invited by the adoption of the scheme for the unlimited coinage of silver at our mints."

And in the last sentence of his letter he spoke of " the dangerous and reckless experiment of free, unlimited, and independent silver coinage."[19]

[18] February 11, 1891.

[19] Parker, *Writings and Speeches of Grover Cleveland*, p. 374 (New York, 1892).

These bold, uncompromising words created an immense sensation. Mr. Cleveland's enemies read them with exultation. Cleveland was out of the race at last! He had once more played the fool and made himself a political impossibility out of sheer pig-headedness. At last he was in reality "a dead one." So thought the cynical Mr. Dana of the *Sun,* and so thought all the leading Democrats who had been nourishing presidential ambitions of their own. Admirers of the ex-President admired him more than ever; yet they could not repress a feeling of regret that he had spoken out so freely and, as it seemed to them, so unnecessarily. For they, too, viewed this Reform Club letter as putting an end to the movement for his re-election. Such was, in fact, Mr. Cleveland's own belief; yet in his heart there lurked no shadow of regret. An intimate friend who met him on the day after the letter had been published, spoke to him ruefully about the matter. Mr. Cleveland's only answer was to throw out both his arms with the gesture of one who casts away a heavy burden.

"Ouf!" said he.

And then, with a gleeful look at his friend's troubled face, he went on to talk about his summer plans.

Yet neither his enemies, nor his friends, nor he himself, had accurately gauged the effect of this act of defiant frankness. Beyond the haunts of the scheming politicians who manage caucuses and pack conventions, the pregnant sentences of that letter were read with an electric thrill of joyful recognition. Here at last was a Man—one who knew his own mind and was not afraid to speak it; one who would not trim and shuffle to win votes; one who would kick aside a nomination for the presidency rather than wear a muzzle even for a moment. A shrewd English observer was once asked to explain the secret of Lord Palmerston's unbounded popularity. " Why," said he " what the nation likes in Palmerston is his you-be-damnedness! " It was something of the same quality in Mr. Cleveland that caused the American people at this moment to let their hearts go out to him; for the American people admire courage in their public men in exact proportion to the infrequency with which they have a chance to see it. Instantly, from having been merely a logical candidate for the presidency, Mr. Cleveland became the inevitable candidate. The stampede of Democrats to the ranks of the Populists was checked at once. All through the West, the party lines were closed up solidly once more; while in the East, conservative men, Republicans and Democrats alike, rejoiced over the growing influence of this dominant personality. It was only among a small coterie of professional politicians that the new aspect of affairs produced a feeling of anger and consternation.

Before the appearance of the Reform Club letter, there had been several aspirants whose chances for the next Democratic nomination were seriously considered. One was Mr. Horace Boies of Iowa, an earnest, able leader with convictions and a reputation for intelligence and integrity. He had fought a hard fight on the tariff issue ever since Mr. Cleveland's message of 1887 had brought that question to the forefront; and in the campaign which followed the passage of the McKinley Bill, he had wiped out the vast Republican majority in Iowa and had been elected Governor. He was a man of the people, in the best sense of the term, representing new issues and new blood; and he had always been consistently a Cleveland Democrat. Mr. Isaac Pusey Gray of Indiana was an old-school party leader, not conspicuous for his mental attain-

ments, but popular in his own State, of which he had been
Governor. It was thought that he could carry Indiana,
and he had the negative qualification of having made no
important enemies in the party. Still another receptive
candidate was Mr. Adlai E. Stevenson of Illinois, who
had been Assistant Postmaster-General in Mr. Cleveland's
administration. His partisanship while holding that
office had highly commended him to the petty spoilsmen
of the Democracy, and they pictured to themselves, with
rare enthusiasm, the liberal fashion in which, if elected
President, he would deal out offices to faithful henchmen.
In the background, alertly watching every opportunity,
was Senator Arthur P. Gorman of Maryland. Senator
Gorman was one of the most astute and subtle of all the
Democratic leaders. Of Irish descent and humble origin,
he had, as a boy, been a page in the Senate Chamber. In
after years, with a truly Celtic genius for political intrigue,
he had made himself master of the party organisation in
his own State, and an important personage in the national
councils. Smooth, bland and insinuating, he resembled
both in appearance and in manner a typical Italian ecclesiastic; and his adroitness and inscrutability fully carried out
the same resemblance. Mr. Gorman had kept on good
terms with Mr. Cleveland during the latter's presidency.
For his sake the administration had incurred the odium
of retaining Mr. Eugene Higgins in office against the
protest of the Maryland civil service reformers, and had
given aid and comfort to Mr. Gorman in his local party
fights. Senator Gorman, however, was always at heart
absorbed in his own ambitions. He had many private
interests and personal associations not known to the world
at large; he spun webs of exceeding fineness that were in-
visible even to his nearest friends; and, while he was all

things to all men, oily of speech and propitiatory in manner, he nourished ambitions for which he would sacrifice unsparingly whatsoever person interfered with them.

The effect of Mr. Cleveland's outspoken letter on the silver question had been to eliminate these four would-be rivals from immediate consideration. There still remained, however, one who was rightly regarded by the Cleveland Democrats as a very formidable obstacle in the way of their candidate's success. This was Mr. David B. Hill, who had been chosen Democratic Governor of New York in 1888, receiving for that office some 18,000 votes more than were given to Mr. Cleveland at the same election. Governor Hill now stood forth conspicuously as the only person who could possibly wrest the next Democratic nomination from Mr. Cleveland; and therefore around him there rallied all who represented machine politics, hatred of reform, and the worship of the great god Expediency, together with such as entertained a personal dislike for the only Democrat who had been inaugurated President since 1857.

Mr. Hill was a lawyer who had attained to his prominent position by the most meticulous attention to the minutiæ of New York politics. His private life was as blameless as his public record was vulnerable. He had no personal vices even of the minor sort. He neither smoked nor drank. To the society of women he was utterly indifferent. He cared nothing for money, and earned a moderate income by hard professional labour. His one joy in life was found in political strategy and intrigue, to which his heart and mind and soul were unstintedly and absolutely given. Over great questions of public policy he wasted no reflection. He seems to have had at this time no serious convictions on such national issues as the tariff, finance, or foreign relations. It was the machinery of politics that absorbed his whole attention—the manipulation of primaries, the arrangement of " slates," the elaboration of " deals," the word-juggling of party platforms, the carrying of elections. He knew the pettiest details of New York State politics by heart. Nothing was minute enough to escape his microscopic eye. He mistook, in fact, political myopia for statesmanship, and the march of great events bewildered him. But in his own sphere he was unsurpassed as a wily, patient, and hitherto successful plotter—a consummate artist in intrigue.

During his two terms as Governor, Mr. Hill had devoted all his powers to building up an organisation in New York State which should have the efficiency of an absolutely flawless machine, and he had succeeded to a marvellous degree. Every local leader was a partisan of Mr. Hill, taking orders from him alone, and executing them implicitly. An alliance with Tammany Hall gave him the support of that well-drilled and disciplined organisation. In short, Mr. Hill was now absolute master of the New York political engine, and this fact gave him an undoubted claim upon the attention of the Democratic party throughout the nation. Mr. Hill's friends said with an air of finality: " Hill carried New York State in 1888. Cleveland lost it. You can't win without New York. Hill is the man who can surely give you New York's thirty-six electoral votes."

This boast, however, was heard by many Democrats with the deepest anger and resentment. They said: " Yes, Cleveland lost New York and Hill carried it. But why? Because Hill sold out Cleveland, and made us lose the presidency in order that he might gain the governorship. Do you think that we have forgotten this, and that we are going to give the highest honours of the party to the man who openly betrayed it?"

But Mr. Hill cared little for mere talk. He set about giving the party and the country an object lesson of his grip upon New York. He remarked to a friend of his: "Presidential nominations are not handed out on silver salvers in these days!" In January, 1892, the Democratic National Committee issued a call for the Convention of the party, to be held in Chicago on June 21st. Within a few days (on January 25th) after this call had been promulgated, the New York State Committee, at Mr. Hill's dictation, summoned a State Convention to meet in Albany on February 22d, for the purpose of choosing New York's delegates to Chicago. The Democrats of New York were startled. Never had a State Convention been called so early—four full months before the National Convention. It was clear that Mr. Hill intended to steal a march upon the Cleveland men, to pack the State Convention, and to secure for himself the delegates from New York. A burst of indignation and of angry protest came from every quarter against the attempt to force a snap judgment from a "snap" convention. But the Hill machine worked smoothly, and began at once to grind out delegates to Albany. Democrats friendly to Mr. Cleveland refused to take any part in the district caucuses; and so a solid body of "Snappers," as they were called, poured into Albany on the 22d, to do the bidding of their master. The Convention met, organised, and finished its entire business in two hours and a half. Only three speeches were made, all carefully revised beforehand. Mr. Cleveland's name was not so much as mentioned. A delegation to Chicago was selected, pledged to Mr. Hill, who was then summoned from the Delavan House, where, in

Tweed's old headquarters, he had been waiting for his followers to do their work. He spoke briefly and in a perfunctory sort of way, and the gathering then adjourned. The only spontaneous applause which had been heard there on that day was given to Mr. Richard Croker, the new head of Tammany Hall.

Once more, then, Mr. Cleveland was thought to be out of the running. His own State had apparently declared against him; and no candidate had ever received a nomination for the presidency without the support of his home delegation. Whether Mr. Hill should win or not, he seemed to have it in his power to defeat his quiescent rival, or, failing that, to give the nomination to any one with whom he could make the best political bargain. The Cleveland men in New York called a convention of their own, alleging that the gathering at Albany had not been truly representative. These "Anti-Snappers" chose a Cleveland delegation for Chicago, though there was practically no chance of its securing recognition there.[23] For the moment, the star of Mr. Hill was undoubtedly in the ascendant.

The Republicans entered dispiritedly into the campaign of 1892. Harrison's colorlessness, the professional party politicians' lack of unity, the confusion that attended Blaine's possible candidacy all helped to depress Republican hopes. On the Democratic side, professional disdain

[23] See Breen, *Thirty Years of New York Politics,* pp. 717-719 (New York, 1899).

for Cleveland was overcome by popular enthusiasm for the plain-speaking ex-President. The Democratic Party program of that year rang with denunciations of the McKinley Tariff. The Democrats pledged free raw materials and cheaper manufactured goods. They went into the election campaign with Cleveland and, for Vice-President, Adlai E. Stevenson of Illinois, and chanting:

> Grover! Grover!
> Four more years of Grover!
> In he comes,
> Out they go,
> Then we'll be in clover!

The Populists nominated General James B. Weaver, who stood on their famous Omaha platform of free and unlimited coinage of silver and gold at the rate of sixteen to one. The Iowa statesman also demanded a graduated income tax, establishment of postal savings banks, and the public ownership of railroads, telegraphs, and telephones, among other notable reforms.—L. F.

Few political campaigns in American history have been conducted upon so high a plane as that which followed in the summer and autumn of 1892. President Harrison said, in a spirit that did him honour, " I desire this campaign to be one of Republicanism and not one of personalities." A very dignified campaign it was. Even the speakers upon the stump alluded to their opponents in terms of personal respect. No scandals were unearthed, and no sensational episodes occurred, like that of the Murchison Letter. The main fight between the two great parties was fought out upon the issue of the tariff. For the first time in its history the Republican party was on the defensive. In 1884, it had been obliged to defend the record of Mr. Blaine, but its own past was held to be unassailable. Now the inequalities of the McKinley tariff were vigorously attacked by every Democratic speaker, and the explanation and defence of them taxed the ingenuity of the Republicans. Higher prices and lower wages were, indeed, strong Democratic arguments. President Harrison's own contribution to political discussion consisted of the sapient remark, " A cheap coat means a cheap man under the coat "—an epigram which was about as convincing as Dr. Johnson's burlesque line:

" Who drives fat oxen must himself be fat."

By tacit consent, both Republicans and Democrats said very little about the silver question. The Populists, on the other hand, preached the doctrine of free silver with great vigour and enthusiasm. In some States of the West and South, coalitions were made with the Populist party. Thus, in Louisiana, the Republicans divided their electoral ticket evenly with the Populists. In Oregon, one Populist elector was placed upon the Democratic ticket; and in Minnesota both Democrats and Populists united upon four electors. In five States—Colorado, Idaho, Kansas, North Dakota and Wyoming—the Democrats nominated no electoral ticket at all, but voted for the Populistic candidates. The object of this was not merely to defeat the

Republicans at the polls. It was thought possible that enough Populist electors might be elected to prevent any party from having a clear majority in the Electoral College. In that event, the election would be thrown into the House of Representatives,[30] voting by States, in which case the Democrats would have a clear majority.

As the summer drew near its end, both parties were hopeful, yet both believed that the result would be very close. One feature of the election would be novel. For the first time it was recognised that money could no more be used in directly bribing voters. Of the forty-four States of the Union, thirty-five had adopted some form of the Australian ballot, thus enabling the voter to cast his vote in secrecy. As was written at the time :

" No ' blocks of five ' can be marched to the polls on election day with their ballots held in sight of the man who has bought them till they are dropped into the ballot boxes. What the same isolation will accomplish in great manufacturing centres is equally obvious. . . . No working man need fear loss of employment if he votes in accordance with his own beliefs and against the ' interests of his employer '; for his employer cannot see how he votes. In the list of the thirty-five States which have the new systems are to be found all the so-called ' doubtful States,' and all those States in the Northwest in which the tariff reform sentiment has made such havoc with old-time Republican majorities. . . . In the great cities of the land there is another gain from the new system which is as important as that of the secret ballot. Trading and deals will be practically impossible, because of the difficulties which are thrown in the way. . . . Other agencies for securing votes must be sought, and other managers than professional corruptionists and traders must be put at the head of the party organisations to conduct the campaign." [31]

[30] As provided by the Twelfth Amendment to the Constitution.

[31] The Nation, June 16, 1892 (pp. 442, 443).

Something which occurred in Pennsylvania during this year did much to endanger the prospects of Republican success. In June, the Carnegie Steel Company at Homestead, reduced the wages of its employés. A trade organisation known as the Amalgamated Steel and Iron Workers sought to intercede; but the Carnegie Company refused to recognise it, and soon afterwards ordered a shutdown, and closed its works, throwing thousands of men out of employment. These men, a majority of whom had served the Company long and faithfully, were not strikers. They were summarily deprived of their employment, for the sole reason that they were members of a union. The intention of the Company was to reopen the mills with non-union men. Anticipating trouble, the Carnegie managers, instead of appealing to the authorities for legal protection, employed a force of armed men to act as a garrison for the mills. This small army was placed in armoured barges and brought to Homestead by the river. As they neared their destination, the men who had been locked out fired upon them and were met by a counter-fire. A sort of battle took place, lasting for nearly two days and involving the use of cannon and of burning oil, with which the river was flooded. Seven of the Carnegie " army " were killed and a much larger number wounded. The loss of their assailants was even greater. In the end the men in the barges surrendered and were badly treated by a mob; and finally State troops were sent to Homestead and restored order by the establishment of martial law.

In various ways this incident was unfortunate for the Republicans. In the first place, here was a highly protected industry cutting down the wages of its workmen at the very time when Republican orators were proclaiming the blessings of the McKinley Bill. In the second place, the country beheld a very striking instance of the lawlessness of corporations. These great steel magnates, so said the Democrats, were acting precisely after the fashion of feudal barons, maintaining private armies, disdaining the protection of the law, and shooting down citizens without any legal warrant. The employment of armed men by corporations had already attracted the attention of Congress, and the bloody affair at Homestead made the private militia system exceedingly unpopular. Another cause of concern to the party in power was the condition of the national treasury. The " Billion Dollar Congress " had not only wiped out the surplus, but had authorised expenses which it was practically impossible to meet. For the six months ending December 31, 1891, the Treasury had paid out $86,000,000 less than was called for by the existing laws. This sum had not been paid, for the excellent reason that the funds were lacking. The customs revenue had fallen off; expenses had increased; and now the Government of the richest nation in the world was in the position of a hard-up debtor, postponing from day to day the payment of its bills, and living, as it were, from hand to mouth.

On the whole, then, the Democratic chances seemed very good. Only in one State, but that a most important one, could danger be detected. This was in New York. Mr. Hill and his followers had returned from the National Convention in a sullen mood. They had been soundly beaten by the Cleveland element. Would they take their revenge upon election day? This was a question which perplexed the Democratic managers, and most of all, Mr. W. C. Whitney, who felt himself responsible for the result in his own State. The most dangerous element of opposition, as in 1884, was to be found in Tammany Hall. John Kelly had died, and had been succeeded by Mr. Richard Croker, who now wielded a power far greater even than that of Kelly. Croker was an Irishman by birth, who had been brought to the United States when he was two years old. He had been a machinist and then a fireman, and had gradually worked his way into local politics, advancing from one position to another, until in 1886 he became the head of one of the most formidable political organisations in the world. He was a man of immense force of character, illiterate, but shrewd. In many of his personal traits, as in his physical appearance, he reminded one of General Grant—having the same taciturnity, the same grim doggedness of purpose, the same iron strength of will. The vote of New York City was in his gift, and he had been consistently opposed to Mr. Cleveland. Nevertheless, it was known that Tammany Hall was anxious not to be regarded as disloyal to the party.

Years before, Croker had been accused of murder, and among his counsel had been Mr. Whitney. For him, ever since that time, Croker had entertained a kindly feeling. Upon this feeling Mr. Whitney diplomatically worked, until Croker agreed to meet his party's candidate and come, if possible, to an understanding. He not unnaturally supposed that Mr. Cleveland would give promises in exchange for Croker's own promise to make his men "vote straight." Mr. Cleveland, however, showed no inclination for an interview with Croker. It was only as a personal favour to Mr. Whitney that he at last consented; and the three men, with a second Tammany chief, dined together in a private room at Mr. Whitney's house. When the political conversation began, Mr.

Cleveland took a line that was most unexpected. Instead of suggesting conciliation and speaking smoothly, he squared his shoulders and gave Croker such a talk as he had never listened to before. He told him what he thought of Tammany Hall, of Tammany politics, and of Tammany men. As he towered above Croker, punctuating his remarks with heavy blows of his fist upon the table, he completely dominated the great " boss," who in reply could merely iterate his hope that matters might be arranged between them. In the end, Mr. Cleveland said that what had happened in the past would not influence him in his future actions; and with this very meagre concession Croker had to go away content.

Mr. Cleveland, in fact, meant to win the Presidency, if he won it at all, without giving pledges to any human being. Among the many interesting anecdotes then current regarding him, one of the most characteristic was told by a distinguished man of letters who had long been his intimate personal friend. There was a certain rich contractor, a " Blaine Irishman," a liberal employer of labour, who, because of his own ancestry, was thought to have great influence with the Irish voters in New York. Just at that time, the " Irish vote " in New York was a very uncertain element in Democratic calculations. Therefore, it occurred to the literary gentleman, who happened to know the contractor very well, that he might perhaps do his favorite candidate a good turn by bringing the two men into personal relations. So it came to pass that one evening they met in the poet's library, without the least suspicion on their part that the interview had been pre-arranged. After a few moments, their host made some excuse for slipping out of the room. Returning at the end of half an hour, he found Mr. Cleveland and the contractor chatting very amicably together. A little later, the ex-President, having finished his call, departed.

"Well," said the host, "what do you think of him?"

The contractor's face fairly glowed.

"Ah, sure," said he, slipping into his native brogue, "he's the greatest man I ever saw. He's a fine man—a grand man. *He wouldn't promise to do wan d——d thing I asked him!*"

And from that time until election day, no one worked harder for Mr. Cleveland than the man who had failed to extort a single promise from him.

The November election astonished Democrats, Republicans, and Populists alike. Mr. Cleveland swept the country. Of course, the Southern States were solidly for him; but in addition he carried all the "doubtful" States —Connecticut, Indiana, New Jersey, and New York— while to the amazement of the political prophets, California, Illinois, and Wisconsin gave him their electoral votes. Michigan cast five of its nine votes for him, and even Ohio, the home of Mr. McKinley, returned one Democratic elector. In the Electoral College, Cleveland and Stevenson had 277 votes against 145 for Harrison and Reid.[32] Even had Mr. Cleveland lost New York, the presidency would still have been his own.

A very startling result of the election was the enormous strength displayed by the Populists throughout the West. Not only did their candidate, General Weaver, poll more than a million votes, but he actually carried four States— Colorado, Idaho, Kansas, and Nevada—receiving also one electoral vote in Oregon and one in North Dakota. For the first time since the birth of the Republican party,

[32] Cleveland's majority over Harrison in the popular vote was 380,000.

a third political organisation was represented among the presidential electors.[33] It is true that the vote given to the Populists was an exaggeration of their actual numbers, because in all but one of the States which they carried, the Democrats had made no nominations; but none the less, the election figures were indicative of an immense popular upheaval that was ominous for the future of the older parties.

Meanwhile, Mr. Cleveland had won an extraordinary personal triumph. Disliked by all the politicians, nominated against the protest of his own State, and opposed by the powerful corporate interests throughout the country, he had, nevertheless, been carried into the presidency by a great spontaneous movement of the people themselves, who gave him their implicit confidence because they felt that in him they had found a leader courageous enough to defy coercion, and of moral fibre strong enough to resist those other influences which are only the more dangerous because insidious. He received the presidency for the second time, bound by no pledge save that contained in the declaration of his party to govern honestly, to reduce the tariff, and to curb the Trusts.

[33] Weaver's strength in the Electoral College was 22.

VI

WHEN Mr. Cleveland, as President-elect, proceeded to the Capitol to take the oath of office for the second time, it seemed almost as though the earlier ceremony of 1889 were being faithfully repeated. Now as then, he was accompanied by Mr. Harrison, and only the relations of the two were changed. Then, Mr. Cleveland was a defeated candidate giving place to his victorious successor. Now, it was Mr. Harrison who was gracefully sustaining the same rôle, and in his turn making way for an opponent. In externals, however, the scene was essentially the same, even to the aspect of the weather; for a storm of mingled sleet and rain was raging, and Washington had awakened on that raw March morning to find the streets all whitened by a swirl of snow.

Amid a driving gale, and standing in what an observer graphically described as " a blizzard-riddled wooden pen," the new President, bareheaded, delivered without notes of any kind, a brief inaugural address; and then for five hours he reviewed the long procession which marched past the presidential stand. Its most conspicuous feature was the entire National Guard of Pennsylvania, headed by the Democratic Governor of that State. For the first time also in the history of inaugural parades, women participated in the pageant. A cavalcade of them from Maryland, superbly mounted, rode past the President, adding a new element of the picturesque. More interesting, however, in view of recent political events, was the presence of three thousand Tammany men, of whom several hundred were arrayed in Indian garb, and with whom were leaders such as Croker, Grady and others, who for nine years had waged relentless war on Mr. Cleveland. Assuredly it was for him a day of genuine triumph when even such consistent enemies as these had been brought to heel. On the day following the inauguration, Senator Hill called upon the President, and the two were closeted for hours. Just what passed between them no one ever learned; but it seems quite certain that Mr. Hill accepted frankly the inevitable. From that day he never seriously opposed the policy of his successful rival, and more than once in the tempestuous times which followed, he did staunch service in its defence.

And thus began the years of President Cleveland's second term of office, which a philosophical writer has truly characterised as " the most momentous period in a time of peace in the history of the country, and the most interesting, from a political point of view, in either war or peace."[1] The fury of the elements, that raged throughout the day of its inception symbolised, as it were, the storm and stress which marked the years of its continuance, and which reached a climax at its close.

The composition of the new Cabinet had become known to the people before the nominations were laid before the Senate. The Secretary of State was Mr. Walter Q. Gresham of Illinois, lately a judge in one of the Federal courts. Mr. Gresham had been a lifelong Republican until a few months prior to President Cleveland's election. He had even been regarded as a possible Republican candidate for the Presidency. At the Republican National Convention of 1888, he had received on the first ballot 111 votes, standing second only to Senator Sherman, who led the

[1] Stanwood, *A History of the Presidency*, p. 519 (Boston, 1898).

poll until the combination in favour of Harrison was effected. Mr. Gresham had always been a conservative, a " Lincoln Republican," wholly out of sympathy with the later tendencies of his party; and when the tariff was made a direct issue in 1892, he turned his back upon high protection as a policy, and publicly announced his purpose of voting for Mr. Cleveland. Mr. Gresham was popular with the labour element in the Middle West, and as a judge had given from the bench decisions accompanied by *obiter dicta* that greatly pleased the opponents of privilege. He was a man of the Cleveland type, sternly honest, inflexible of purpose, and vigorous in mind. In some respects he fell short of the ideal requirements in a Secretary of State. His training had not sufficiently familiarised him with the minutiæ of diplomatic relations. He failed, perhaps, to appreciate the importance of these relations as compared with concerns of domestic interest. Moreover, on the personal side, he lacked something of that regard for the fitness of things which ought to characterise one who has to do with the representatives of foreign countries. It was Mr. Gresham's wont to receive ambassadors and ministers—men bred to the most punctilious etiquette—sitting in his shirt-sleeves at his desk, and chewing on the stump of a cigar; while he was overfond of lounging about the corridors of Willard's Hotel and mingling with the very motley mob which sprawled there at all hours of the day and night. Naturally, Mr. Gresham's appointment was rather sharply criticised. Republicans regarded him as a renegade from their ranks, while many Democrats thought it hard that the chief Cabinet position should go to so very recent a convert to Democracy.

Mr. John G. Carlisle of Kentucky was made Secretary

of the Treasury, and offered a brilliant contrast to his two immediate predecessors. He was an experienced legislator, who had been three times Speaker of the House and a member of seven different Congresses, in all of which he had concerned himself with questions of theoretical and practical finance. Mr. Carlisle was of a calm, reflective, and judicial cast of mind, and he had to an exceptional degree the gift of lucid and convincing exposition. While acting as Speaker, Mr. Carlisle once received an unusual compliment from a political opponent. Mr. (afterwards Senator) Hiscock of New York, said of Mr. Carlisle: " He is one of the strongest of Democrats and I am one of the strongest of Republicans; yet my imagination is not strong enough to conceive of his making an unfair ruling or doing an unfair thing against the party opposed to him in this House." [3]

The President appointed as Secretary of War, Colonel Daniel S. Lamont of New York, who had been private secretary to Mr. Cleveland while the latter was Governor of New York, and also during his first administration as President. It was essentially a personal appointment, well justified both by Colonel Lamont's devotion to Mr. Cleveland and also by his ability, his sound judgment and his admirable tact. Another personal appointment was that of Mr. Wilson S. Bissell of New York, an old and intimate friend, to be Postmaster-General. The new Secretary of the Navy was Mr. Hilary A. Herbert of Alabama—the first ex-Confederate to be placed in charge of one of the military departments of the Government. Mr. Herbert was an accomplished gentleman and a skilful administrator. He had served as chairman of the House Committee on Naval Affairs in three Congresses and was intimately familiar with the duties of his new office.

[3] A. D. White, *Autobiography,* ii. p. 126 (New York, 1905).

Under him, the navy of the United States, which a few years before had ranked as only twelfth among the navies of the world, advanced to the fifth place, being surpassed only by the armaments of Great Britain, France, Russia and Germany. Mr. Hoke Smith of Georgia became Secretary of the Interior and Mr. Julius S. Morton of Nebraska, Secretary of Agriculture. The Cabinet was completed by the appointment to the Attorney-Generalship of Mr. Richard Olney of Massachusetts, whose name was destined to be honourably associated with some of the most stirring events of President Cleveland's administration. When he became Attorney-General he was almost unknown outside of his native State. Educated at Brown and Harvard, he was a successful lawyer who had mingled but little in public life, beyond serving in the Massachusetts Legislature. He had, however, a very forceful personality, combining the keenness and prompt decisiveness of a trained reasoner with a certain aggressive quality which suggested, under all the suave amenities of a polished gentleman, the pugnacity, and also the tenacity, of a bulldog.

President Cleveland entered upon his duties under no illusions as to the difficulty of the problems which confronted him. There was a seriousness, amounting almost to solemnity, in some of the sentences of his inaugural address, which may have been regarded lightly by those who then heard or read them, but which afterwards were seen to have been full of meaning. Toward the close, he said with something like the spirit of prophecy:

"Anxiety for the pledges which my party has made . . . constrains me to remind those with whom I am to co-operate, that we can succeed in doing the work which has been especially set before us, only by the most sincere, harmonious, and disinterested effort. Even if insuperable obstacles and opposition prevent the consummation of our task, we shall hardly be excused; and if failure can be traced to our fault or neglect, we may be sure the people will hold us to a swift and exacting accountability."

And then he added:

"I shall, to the best of my ability and within my sphere of duty, preserve the Constitution by loyally protecting every grant of Federal power it contains, by defending all its restraints when attacked by impatience and restlessness, and by enforcing its limitations and reservations in favour of the States and the people.

"Fully impressed with the gravity of the duties that confront me . . . I should be appalled if it were my lot to bear unaided the responsibilities which await me. I am, however, saved from discouragement when I remember that I shall have the support and the counsel and co-operation of wise and patriotic men, who will stand at my side in Cabinet places or will represent the people in their legislative halls."

In a letter to Mr. Justice Lamar, which was written at this time, but of which the full text still remains unpublished, the President spoke of his own misgivings and of his doubt as to whether his administration were not destined to disaster. It may, however, be questioned whether even he had yet become aware how formidable were the dangers which beset him. There were three elements in the political situation so closely interrelated as to make action in regard to any one of them involve an instant complication with the other two. These three factors were (1) the relation of the great moneyed interests to national legislation; (2) the spread of Populism in the West and South; and (3) the condition of the Government's finances.

The rapid growth of great fortunes which accompanied and succeeded the Civil War had long been a subject of comment and, very properly, of pride among Americans of every class. Never, perhaps, in the history of the world was there witnessed a parallel to the extraordinary outburst of energy and genius devoted to material success, which marked the years from 1864 to 1890. All at once the untouched resources of the United States seemed to be revealed to its inhabitants; and thousands upon thousands of keen-witted, inventive, far-seeing men had grasped the vast possibilities which the development of these resources inherently contained. What had been accomplished in the whole of the preceding century was now surpassed by the railway builders, miners, traders, promoters, manufacturers and financiers of this new era. The United States was like a freshly opened gold field into which prospectors flung themselves in a frantic rush for wealth. And from one point of view the results were admirable. Here were rich rewards for brain and muscle, for courage and capacity. America, far more than ever, was for a time a land of opportunity. Yet there was another and a darker side, which more and more became apparent as the years went by. This was seen first of all in the growing tendency of many who had become extremely rich to monopolise the sources of their wealth and thereby to bar the door of opportunity to others; and furthermore, in the effort, too often successful, to render subservient or worthless the machinery of the law, to which alone those who were wronged must look for swift redress. The most signal instance of corporate power was to be found in the railways. These companies, the creatures of the State, deriving their charters from the people, and often aided by generous public grants, went far beyond the rights that were conceded to them.   From being simply common carriers, they began to get possession of those natural products which are included among the necessities of life.   First in order, they secured the three great coal fields in which 95 per cent. of the anthracite coal of the United States is mined—and they secured them, not by legitimate purchase, but by forcing private owners to sell at prices fixed by the railway managers.   Those who refused, found that the railways would no longer furnish cars for the shipment of " private " coal, thereby shutting off the individual miner from his market.   When the State of Pennsylvania in 1873 forbade, by a constitutional provision, its railways to engage in mining coal, the prohibition was at once evaded.   Railway officials formed mining companies, of which the directors were the same men as those who made up the railway directorates; and the old abuses were continued, with the added zest of defying the fundamental law.   This arrangement even augmented the extortion; for now the railways, acting as common carriers, could charge exorbitant freight rates, thus justifying the mine owners (*i. e.,* the railway owners) in selling the coal they shipped at whatsoever prices they pleased. It was found by a Congressional committee in 1893 that the railway charge for carrying coal was far greater than the charge for carrying wheat or other similar freight; and that while the means of transportation had been continually improved and the cost of handling cheapened, the railway rates were higher than they had been fifteen years before.[4]

What was true of coal was also true of timber, cop-

[4] Report of the Interstate Commerce Commission, pp. 183 foll. and 242 foll. (1893.) See also House Report, 2278; Fifty-second Congress (2d session) ; and Parsons, *The Heart of the Railroad Problem* (Boston, 1906).

per, iron and other minerals. In the West, great tracts of arable land were held by the railways and barred to settlers; while there, too, by an unfair discrimination in freight charges, one locality was favoured at the expense of another, just as one merchant or manufacturer might be ruined because of the more favourable terms that were secretly given to his competitors. Thus the railways were, in a sense, the masters of the State rather than its servants, arbitrarily bestowing or withholding prosperity, getting a firm grip on small communities, fixing at will the cost of articles of prime necessity, choking competition, and thus earning for the companies the great sums necessary to enable them to pay extravagant salaries and to keep up dividends on " watered " stock.[6]

But the railway owners offered merely the most conspicuous and worst, and not by any means the sole, example of a gross abuse of power. They had bred a score of other organised and equally rapacious corporations, of which the Standard Oil Company and the so-called Sugar Trust were especially obnoxious to public sentiment and most successful in their defiance of the processes of law. The continuance of a high protective tariff had added to the number of these monopolies; for while the tariff did not invariably or necessarily create an actual monopoly, its tendency was distinctly to limit competition; and in 1892, Mr. John De Witt Warner, a careful student of politico-economic questions, published a list of one hundred corporations of this sort which had, by one means or another,

---

[6] " The excess over just and reasonable rates of transportation constitutes an available fund by which they [the railways] are enabled to crush out the competition of independent coal-producers."— Interstate Commerce Commission Report, p. 4 (1893).

secured tariff legislation in their own favour. The tariff, however, had nothing to do with the absorption by private corporations of valuable franchises all over the country, for which they paid little or nothing, while they usually exploited them in a spirit of insolent rapacity. Gas companies, having a monopoly in many cities, used fraudulent meters, supplied inferior gas and collected excessive rates from the consumers, who were absolutely helpless and without redress against what every one well knew to be sheer robbery. It was the same with electric lighting. The street railways were in the hands of another set of owners, who treated the travelling public like mere cattle —crowding them into insufficient cars in defiance of either comfort or decency, charging excessive fares for an inadequate service, and caring nothing for remonstrance or complaint. The telegraph was still another instance of an almost complete monopoly; the telephone of another; the business of the express companies of another.

The mere enumeration of these facts, however, is less significant than another circumstance connected with them. Every country has witnessed phenomena not unlike these. Unscrupulous and able men are always ready to enrich themselves and to wring great fortunes from the people. In the United States, even at the time of its birth as a nation, the records were smirched by the story of stockjobbing, dishonest contracts, and the sale of influence and by a vicious eagerness to exploit every public source of private gain.[8] Some decades later, the nation had a further experience of the political power of wealth, at the time when Nicholas Biddle and his associates of the United States Bank waged a long war against the national admin-

[8] See, for instance, McMaster, *With the Fathers*, pp. 71-86 (New York, 1896).

istration, until they were routed by the fiery Jackson. Later still, the period of the Civil War, which may be extended to cover the years from 1860 to 1875, saw men wielding the weapon of wealth with an unscrupulousness that has never been surpassed. But in business and in public life, this period is one to be recalled with shame by every American. Senator Hoar, in a memorable speech, once gave, as by a sudden glare of lightning, a glimpse of those appalling years.

" My own public life," said he, " has been a very brief and insignificant one, extending little beyond the duration of a single term of senatorial office. But in that brief period I have seen five judges of a high court of the United States driven from office by threats of impeachment for corruption or maladministration. I have seen the Chairman of the Committee on Military Affairs in the House rise in his place and demand the expulsion of four of his associates for making sale of their official privilege of selecting the youths to be educated at our great military school. When the greatest railroad of the world, binding together the Continent and uniting the two great seas which wash our shores, was finished, I have seen our national triumph and exultation turned to bitterness and shame by the unanimous reports of three committees of Congress—two of the House and one here—that every step of that mighty enterprise had been taken in fraud.

" I have heard in the highest places the shameless doctrine avowed by men grown old in public office, that the true way by which power should be gained in the Republic is to bribe the people with offices created for their service; and that the true end for which it should be used when gained is the promotion of selfish ambition and the gratification of personal revenge. I have heard that suspicion haunts the footsteps of the trusted companions of the President himself." [9]

[9] Speech on the impeachment of Secretary Belknap, May 6, 1876 (Senate).

Yet the things done in those years gave in their direct results no reason for despair. Those who did them were acting almost in isolation, and in most instances professedly outside the pale of honesty and decency. Fisk and Gould and Huntington, Belknap, Babcock, Brady, the chiefs of the Whiskey Ring, the plotters of Black Friday, and the Star Route criminals, were by the very crudity of their methods so conspicuously evil as hardly to be dangerous.

Like Tweed and his confederates, who belonged to the same period, they were vulgar bandits, operating boldly enough on the by-ways of politics and commerce, yet ready to take flight when attacked by the law and by public indignation. But in 1892, great wealth had led to the development of a caste, of which the members were exceedingly respectable, and of a very different stripe from those whom they succeeded. Well-mannered, kindly gentlemen were they, usually irreproachable in their private lives, generous in their benefactions, and upholders of a conservative tradition which they had themselves created. The protected manufacturer rapidly enriched himself, not by defiance of the law, but strictly in accordance with it. The railroad magnate who gave rebates and " drawbacks," the organiser of a mighty trust, and the able captain of industry who closed and barred the doors of opportunity to any other than himself, were in their own estimation far from being violators of the statutes. Every step they took was taken under the advice of the most eminent lawyers of the land. If what many of them did appeared to contravene alike the letter and the spirit of explicit legislation, and if they were often sued, indicted, or otherwise brought before the courts, this gave them slight concern, for nothing ever came of it. The law's delays were endless, its technicalities most interestingly labyrinthine, and the judges patient and extremely well-disposed.

The most striking feature of this new wealth was its solidarity and the close relationship of interest among its owners. There were no longer isolated millionaires, fighting each for his own hand. The chief figure in an oil company, for instance, would likewise be the principal stockholder in a great electric light concern, having also a subsidiary interest in a match trust, a candle monopoly, and a dozen gas-works. Mr. H. D. Lloyd, whose zeal sometimes led him to exaggerate the importance of his deductions, but whose facts were based on irrefutable evidence, was well within the truth when he wrote in 1894:

" A small number of men are obtaining the power to forbid any but themselves to supply the people with fire in nearly every form known to modern life and industry, from matches to locomotives and electricity. They control our hard coal and much of the soft, and stoves, furnaces and steam and hot-water heaters; the governors on steam-boilers and the boilers; gas and gas fixtures; natural gas and gas pipes; electric lighting and all the appurtenances. You cannot free yourselves by changing from electricity to gas, or from gas of the city to gas of the fields. If you fly from kerosene to candles, you are still under the ban." [10]

Add to this the fact that the very same men, and others like them, held directorships in " chains " of banks, in railways, in insurance companies, and other fiduciary institutions; that they owned a controlling interest in the leading newspapers of the country which helped to mould and control public opinion by colouring the news; that they were lavish contributors to the campaign funds of one or both of the great political parties; that they helped

[10] Lloyd, *Wealth against Commonwealth*, pp. 9, 10.

their own protégés to seats in municipal councils, in State legislatures and in Congress; and that their influence was benevolently exerted to promote their former legal advisers to positions in the State and national judiciary—and one may form a faint conception of the enormous power which they wielded.[12]

It was primarily to check this power, and to bring it under the more efficient control of law, that the People's Party had been founded. In that party there were some who were sufficiently clear-sighted to perceive that the crux of the whole situation lay in the question as to who should control and regulate the public means of transportation and communication, with such other public utilities as heat and light and water. In private hands this control was certain always to be abused and made an instrument of oppression, precisely as it had been in the past. The Standard Oil Company and the coal monopoly had been reared upon the secret agreement between the railways in Pennsylvania. The Beef Trust had crushed competition, largely by its grip upon the Western roads. The transcontinental railways had fraudulently acquired and held great tracts of public lands. These and a multiplicity of related facts were known to almost everyone, and therefore here should have been found the *point d'appui* of the Populist campaign. But unfortunately for their cause, the leaders—and most of all, the masses—of the new party were led astray by another plan, which seemed at once more tempting and more simple of execution. They did, indeed, as we have already seen, insert in their various platforms a demand for the government ownership of railways, telegraphs and telephones; yet it was upon the silver question that they elected to make the strongest fight.

[12] See George, *The Menace of Privilege* (New York, 1905).

Perhaps they had vaguely in mind the military maxim of a great French strategist: "Find out what it is that your enemy most desires you not to do—and then do it." To the Populists, the whole body of merchants, bankers, and business men in the Eastern States were collectively "the enemy." No distinction was made between the Wall Street gambler, the trust promoter and the note-shaver on the one hand, and the conservative, fair-minded representatives of legitimate commerce on the other. In Kansas and Nebraska, these were all equally "the enemy"; and when it became apparent that their interests were violently opposed to the free coinage of silver, that they dreaded it and viewed it as a menace to prosperity, then the rank and file of the new party felt a keen delight. Here was a sharp-edged weapon ready to hand. Here was a sword wherewith to slay the money-sharks, the Shylocks, the Wall Street blood-suckers, and the Trusts. If free silver was a bad thing for them, then surely it must be a good thing for the honest farmer.

The free-silver leaders, of course, were not all actuated by a purely emotional view of a strictly economic subject. They called themselves bimetallists, and honestly believed that it would be possible for the United States to maintain a double standard, even though its mints should be opened to the unlimited coinage of silver dollars at the old ratio of 16 to 1, which had long since ceased to be a true one.[13] They had read the works of theoretical bimetallists who held that the use of both metals would be economically desirable if adopted through a common agreement by the great commercial nations of the earth. This is, indeed, a question that still remains an open one, although purely

[13] The intrinsic value of the standard silver dollar in July, 1892, was eighty-eight cents.

academic. The important fact in 1893 was that, with the exception of India and the United States, all the leading nations of the world were either upon a definite gold basis or were preparing to accept it. England, which, in fact, though not by law, had made gold its standard since 1699, adopted that standard legally in 1870 by the Coinage Act. In 1871, Germany demonetised silver and became a " gold country." The nations composing the so-called Latin Union (France, Belgium, Switzerland, Italy and Greece) did the same in 1877, and their example was shortly followed by Holland, Norway and Sweden; while Russia, Austria and Japan signified their intention to adopt a policy of gold monometallism at an early date. The practical question at issue in the United States, therefore, was not whether the double monetary standard might not be feasible through an international agreement, but whether one nation alone could successfully maintain it, in the face of the use of a single standard by the rest of the civilised world. The serious and more intelligent leaders of the silver men—Democrats, Republicans and Populists, alike—believed this to be possible. They caught eagerly at stray passages in the writings of international bimetallists, and gave them an illogical application. Some very conservative economists and statesmen were, in fact, theoretically in favour of bimetallism as a principle—among them Mr. (afterwards Lord) Goschen and Mr. A. J. Balfour in Great Britain; and in the United States, General Francis A. Walker, Mr. Charles Francis Adams, Mr. S. Dana Horton, and President E. B. Andrews of Brown University.[14] The names of these and other authorities

[14] See Walker, *International Bimetallism* (New York, 1896); Horton, *The Silver Pound* (London, 1878); and Andrews, *An Honest Dollar* (Hartford, 1884).

were dragged into the argument, and made to support assertions and deductions such as would greatly have astonished the worthy gentlemen to whom they were ascribed.

But the great mass of the " friends of silver " did not know or care anything about the niceties of financial doctrine. They made up their own minds in a much more direct and simple way. To them, " free silver " had a most enticing sound, indicative of opulence and easy times. They had a vague notion that if the amount of money in the country should be increased *per capita,* each individual citizen would necessarily have more of it in his pockets. Just how he was to get it except by working for it precisely as he had done before, they did not attempt to demonstrate; but they were certain that the free coinage of silver would increase the number of dollars " per capita " in the United States, and that any objection to such a measure could come only from cruel capitalists in the East, who wished to hold the Western farmers forever in the bonds of debt. When assured that unlimited silver coinage would drive gold out of circulation, they replied that silver was good enough for them if they could only get enough of it. When told that the United States could not single-handed maintain a system at variance with that of the great European nations, they answered that this country was big enough to do anything it pleased without asking for leave or license from the monarchies of Europe. Such were the simple, primitive ideas which influenced the minds of the silver men throughout the West; but most potent of all was the belief that a vote for silver was a direct blow struck at the hated Eastern capitalist and creditor.

The third serious element in the political situation at the time of President Cleveland's second inauguration was the condition of the United States Treasury. When it had been turned over to Mr. Harrison's financial secretary four years before, it contained a net surplus of $97,-000,000. This had all been spent, and it was now difficult even to meet current expenses. Moreover, the financial legislation of past years had begun to inspire foreign holders of American securities with increasing apprehension. When specie payments were resumed in 1879, the Treasury had set apart in gold, a special fund, which was never to be less than $100,000,000, for the redemption of oustanding legal tender notes (" greenbacks "). Of these greenbacks, there were in circulation $346,000,000 in 1892. There were also outstanding $147,000,000 of " coin certificates," which had been issued in the purchase of silver bullion under the Sherman Act of 1890. These by law were redeemable in " coin "—i.e., in either gold or silver, at the option of the Treasury; but President Harrison's Secretary of the Treasury, Mr. Windom, had very unwisely ruled that the holder of the notes might exercise his option. In other words, the " coin certificates," like the greenbacks, were really payable in gold. Hence, there were now outstanding government notes calling for $493,-000,000 of gold, while the Treasury had little more than one-fifth of that sum with which to redeem them. Yet this was not the worst; for under the Sherman Act, which still remained in force, the Government must buy each month 4,500,000 ounces of silver, and issue against this bullion still more paper money to be redeemed in gold.

The perplexities of the situation with which President Cleveland was confronted were, therefore, plain enough to be seen by any intelligent observer. He was pledged to reduce the tariff in the interest of freer trade, and in this he was certain to find himself in conflict with the whole power of consolidated capital—not the power of the protected industries alone, but of all the allied forces of monopoly; for these well knew that a radical reform of the tariff would be only the first step toward a reform of other and even worse abuses. It was also plain that he must take measures to protect the Treasury and keep it solvent. But such measures would of necessity run counter to the convictions of the silver men of every party, and would convince the people of the West that Wall Street was supreme in Washington. President Cleveland's task, then, involved a bitter struggle with the capitalists on the one side, while it must inevitably fan the flames of popular suspicion on the other. The stoutest heart might well have shrunk from such an undertaking. To carry it through successfully demanded a high order of political genius—an exceptional gift for the management of men, a perfect union of tact and firmness, and a broadly tolerant understanding of human prejudice and passion.

Mr. Cleveland was by no means possessed of this rare political genius, though he did have some very fundamental qualities of the governing man—a robust intelligence, a rigorous conscience and unlimited courage. With these qualities he had also some of their usual defects. When he understood a subject, he was a little intolerant of those who failed to understand it, or who understood it in a different way. When he was convinced that he was right, he had no patience with those whom he conceived to be in the wrong. Because he was himself absolutely fearless, he scorned all such as shrank from following where he led. He wished, in fact, not only to accomplish his own ends, but to accomplish them in his own way; and coercion was to him more natural than conciliation. In fact, just as Strafford's motto was " Thorough," so Mr. Cleveland's motto might have been " Downright." Whatever policy he might adopt was sure to be a heavy-fisted one, and to be carried out, if carried out at all, with no *finesse,* but by dint of hard sledge-hammering blows. This temperament was a fine one for an absolute ruler—for that enlightened despot whom Aristotle held to be the ideal governor of men—but it was dangerous in him who, in a Republic, was obliged to carry out his plans through the unforced co-operation of other and no less independent men.

Mr. Cleveland in many ways had changed in the eight years which had elapsed since his first assumption of the presidency. For one thing, he had ceased to be a provincial and had risen to the full measure of the office which he held. In 1885, those who noted his appearance on public occasions of great dignity, as, for instance, at the funeral ceremonies of General Grant, found in his external aspect, —his tilted hat, his " slouchy " bearing, his stolid face— something that recalled the country sheriff. Since that time, a wide acquaintance with men of every type no less than the pressure of high responsibility, had broadened and elevated his whole cast of thought. If he was now, beneath a less ungracious exterior, even more self-willed than ever, and more bent on having his own way, this was only natural in view of what had happened in the preceding years. He had flouted all advice, he had done precisely as he pleased, and yet the nation had set him once more in the seat of highest honour. It is not surprising, then, if from the time of his second inauguration, the President displayed what seemed to many a certain arrogance of manner and of language, with a disposition to enlarge the prerogatives of his high office. The very phrasing of his official papers—his proclamations and his messages to Congress—is noteworthy for a haughtiness such as would have been far more appropriate in the rescripts of an hereditary monarch. The personal pronoun " I " occurs in these documents with an unusual frequency; and such expressions as " I have deemed it fitting," " It is my purpose," " It affords me signal pleasure," " I am decidedly of the opinion," and " I am satisfied," appear and reappear so often as to give to the whole a strongly personal colouring. Very characteristic was an Executive Order issued by the President on May 8th. He had set apart certain hours for receiving such Senators and Representatives as desired interviews with him. As is usually the case, these interviews related largely to questions of patronage. The President became so irritated in consequence, as to make public his annoyance in a remarkable order, the effect of which, upon both Senators and Representatives, may be easily conceived. It ran:

" The time which . . . was set apart for the reception of Senators and Representatives has been almost entirely spent in listening to applications for office, which have been bewildering in volume, perplexing and exhausting in their iteration, and impossible of remembrance.

" A due regard for public duty . . . and an observance of the limitations placed upon human endurance, oblige me to decline, from and after this date, all personal interviews with those seeking appointments to office, except as I on my own motion may especially invite them. . . . Applicants for office will only prejudice their prospects by repeated importunity and by remaining in Washington to await results."

It was a number of incidents such as this that gave point to a contemporary cartoon entitled "Cleveland's Map of the United States," wherein the figure of the President was so drawn as to coincide with the outlines of the country, which was thus made, by implication, identical with himself. Under the drawing were the words:

> " My country, 'tis of Me,
> Of Me I sing! "

One might well have sympathised with the President in his annoyance over the importunities of office-seekers, and the lack of consideration shown by the Senators and Representatives of his own party. But in view of the fact that he was about to recommend legislation of the most controversial character, and that only by the good will and co-operation of the majority in Congress could it be carried through, this Executive Order was an extraordinary example of political tactlessness. Far more important, however, was a line of action adopted by President Cleveland with regard to a pending international question. By this, at the very outset of his administration, he brought upon himself, both in and out of Congress, an avalanche of political unpopularity and personal dislike.

At the Inauguration Ball, in Mrs. Cleveland's company, a dark-skinned, graceful girl had attracted much attention. This was the Princess Kaiulani, the heiress-apparent to the Hawaiian throne in direct succession to Queen Liliuokalani, of whom she was the niece. The Princess was only eighteen years of age. She had been educated in England, and was in that country at the time when the Hawaiian monarchy was overthrown and the Queen deposed. On getting news of this, she had come at once to the United States, accompanied by her guardian, Mr. Theophilus Davies. It will be remembered that President Harrison's last important act had been the submission to the Senate of a treaty by which Hawaii was to be annexed to the United States. This treaty had not yet been ratified; and it was with the purpose of opposing it that the Princess Kaiulani had hastened to Washington. Her advisers shrewdly counted on the chivalrous disposition of the American people toward women. They believed that a young and pretty girl pleading for the restoration of her rights would make a strong appeal to popular sentiment throughout the land. No sooner had Kaiulani reached New York than she issued an " Appeal to the American People," which was published in the newspapers on March 2d. Whether she wrote it herself or whether it was written for her, was a question much mooted at the time. Whoever wrote it, the " appeal " was sweetly pretty, with a touch of false sentiment about it and a schoolgirl rhetoric that did not ring quite true; so that it wholly failed of its effect, and was received with smiles by nearly all who read it. In it the Princess said:

" Unbidden I stand upon your shores to-day, where I thought so soon to receive a royal welcome on my way to my own kingdom. I come unattended, except by loving hearts that came with me over the wintry seas. I hear that Commissioners from my own land have been for many days asking this great nation to take away my little vineyard. . . .

" To-day I, a poor, weak girl with not one of my people near me, and with all these Hawaiian statesmen against me, have strength to stand up for the rights of my people. Even now I can hear a wail in my heart, and it gives me strength and courage, and I am strong—strong in the faith of God, strong in the strength of seventy million people who in this free land will hear my cry and will refuse to let their flag cover dishonour to mine! "

Of Mrs. Cleveland, this island princess made an important convert to the cause she represented. Mrs. Cleveland welcomed her very warmly to the White House, and gave her a most womanly sympathy. Kaiulani was, indeed, a very charming girl, and she made a favourable impression upon the President and also upon the Secretary of State, to whom she was presently introduced. Mr. Gresham, during the years when he was a Republican, had been a rival of Mr. Harrison, and this rivalry had in time deepened into a personal dislike. No wonder that the Harrison policy regarding Hawaii should be viewed by him with extreme disfavour. Altogether, then, between the President's natural caution, which led him to move slowly in an affair begun with so much haste, and Mr. Gresham's eagerness to undo the work of one whom he disliked, no surprise was felt when, on March 9th, a message of five lines was sent to the Senate, withdrawing " for the purpose of re-examination " the treaty framed by President Harrison and the Hawaiian Commissioners. A few days later, Mr. Cleveland despatched to Hawaii, as a Special Commissioner, Mr. James H. Blount of Georgia, to investigate the circumstances under which the change of government in the Islands had been effected.

Mr. Blount was an honest, but somewhat cross-grained politician, who had been Chairman of the Committee on Foreign Affairs in the House of Representatives; yet one more unfamiliar with foreign affairs could scarcely have been selected for this delicate mission. He had never been out of the United States in his life; and his knowledge of diplomatic usage was as limited as his mastery of social forms. In keeping with the rather primitive notions of Secretary Gresham in matters of ceremonial, Mr. Blount proceeded to Hawaii, not by a regular mail steamer nor in a man-of-war, but on board a little

revenue-cutter, the *Richard Rush*. He reached Honolulu
on March 29th. President Dole and the other members
of the Provisional Government had heard that a Commission, consisting of representatives of the judiciary, the
army, and the navy, had been sent to them; and suitable
preparations were made to receive such a Commission with
due dignity. An eye-witness has given a graphic account
of what actually happened. All the vessels in the harbour
displayed the American flag, and the American colours
were wreathed about the pillars and columns of the city
houses. At the pier a great multitude had assembled,
strewing the passage-way with roses. As the *Rush* hove in
sight, a Japanese cruiser, the *Naniwa*, fired a thunderous
salute, to which the little *Rush* responded—" like the
' yap ' of a terrier echoing the deep baying of a stag-
hound."

" And then—then came an anti-climax that very closely approached the ridiculous. Instead of the dignified, affable and
courteous body of officials that had been expected, there stepped
ashore a commonplace and rather sullen-looking man of sixty,
clad in ill-fitting clothes of blue homespun, and a Panama hat.
Public expectation had been roused to the highest pitch, and the
revulsion of feeling was instantaneous and painful." [17]

Mr. Blount delivered to President Dole a letter from
President Cleveland beginning:

" GREAT AND GOOD FRIEND: I have made choice of James H.
Blount, one of our distinguished citizens, as my Special Commissioner to visit the Hawaiian Islands and make report to me concerning the present status of affairs in that country. . . . His
authority is paramount."

[17] Krout, *Hawaii and a Revolution*, p. 145 (New York, 1898).

Mr. Blount brought with him other letters from the American President. One of them, addressed to Minister Stevens, practically suspended that gentleman from the exercise of his diplomatic functions and made him subordinate to Mr. Blount. A second letter directed Rear-Admiral Skerrett, in command of the Pacific Squadron, to consult freely with Mr. Blount and " obey any instructions you may receive from him regarding the course to be pursued in the Islands by the force under your command." Armed with these remarkable credentials, Mr. Blount began in his own way to investigate the events of the preceding February. On the day after his arrival, he ordered the American flag to be lowered from the Government Building in Honolulu, and directed the force of marines which had been stationed there to break camp and return to their ship, the *Boston*. This was done, and the Provisional Government at once raised its own flag and posted its own troops with a battery of rapid-fire guns to quell any attempt to restore the Queen.[18]

When the news of these events reached the United States, a great deal of very bitter feeling was excited. The American people were not strongly in favour of annexing Hawaii. Apart from a few speculators in sugar, there was no great interest in the matter. A desire for foreign territory had not yet stirred the popular imagination. Had Mr. Cleveland simply put the treaty in the fire and kept his hands off Hawaii altogether, the whole affair would have been speedily forgotten. But when the credentials which he had given to Mr. Blount were fully known, they were very generally disapproved, alike by Democrats and by Republicans. The President had, apparently, delegated the whole power of his great office to an individual " Commissioner "—a nondescript functionary unknown to the

[18] April 1, 1893.

Constitution—who had by a stroke of the presidential pen been put over the head of a regularly appointed Minister, and invested with the absolute command of an important naval force. There is, indeed, no doubt that Mr. Cleveland exceeded his constitutional rights, and that Mr. Blount's " paramountcy " was unlawful. Before long, a still more intense feeling was aroused by the report that the President intended to restore Queen Liliuokalani to her throne.

The rumour proved to be true. Mr. Blount's reports and a study of the earlier despatches of Minister Stevens convinced Mr. Cleveland that the Hawaïian monarchy had been subverted by the active aid of Mr. Stevens, and through "the intimidation caused by the presence of an armed naval force of the United States." [19] Having assured himself of this, the President felt it his duty, as he expressed it, " to undo the wrong . . . and to restore the status existing at the time of our forcible intervention." [20]

It was here that the President made a second blunder, and, as it proved, a most humiliating one for him. He forgot, in the first place, the wise tradition that in the foreign policy of the United States there should be no break, and that in essentials a change of administration should cause no change in the attitude of the State Department toward other countries. [21] There was another and more practical consideration. Whether or not the Provisional Government of Hawaii could have held its own against the Queen's forces in the preceding January with-

[19] See President Cleveland's message of December 4, 1893.

[20] *Ibid.*

[21] This principle had been especially upheld by Webster while Secretary of State. See Curtis, *Life of Daniel Webster,* ii., p. 534 (New York, 1870).

out the presence of American marines, there was no doubt
that it was now quite able to sustain itself. It had an
efficient force of some 1200 well-drilled troops—nearly
all Americans and Englishmen—it was supplied with
artillery, and it enjoyed the support of the responsible
residents of Hawaii.[22] Hence, to restore the Queen would
require something more than a curt request from President
Cleveland.

But with his innate obstinacy, the President resolved
to make the attempt, and the unpopularity of such a course
only strengthened his resolve. Recalling Mr. Blount,
whose churlish manners had made him thoroughly disliked, Mr. Cleveland appointed as Minister to Hawaii,
Mr. Albert S. Willis, of Kentucky, a gentleman of intelligence and judgment. Mr. Willis, however, was specifically instructed to bring about the restoration of the
Queen; and a naval force was stationed at Honolulu to
give point to his instructions. On his arrival, the new
Minister sent to President Dole a formal request that he
" relinquish to the Queen her constitutional authority."
President Dole replied by a courteous but firm refusal.
Here was an *impasse* which could be broken through by
nothing short of armed force. Would the guns of American ships of war be turned upon men of American blood
in order to re-enthrone a Polynesian queen who had broken
her coronation oath and had sought to govern irrespon-
sibly ?

Mr. Willis hesitated; yet he might, under his instructions, have taken even this last step, had not the unexpected obstinacy of the Queen herself deterred him.
She was asked whether, if replaced upon the throne, she

---

[22] For an account (unfavourable in tone) of Hawaii under the Provisional
Government and later, see Palmer, *Again in Hawaii* (Boston, 1895).

would agree not to punish those who had deposed her.[23] This question she met with an indignant negative. Not punish them? Most assuredly she would punish them! The leaders—Mr. Dole, Mr. Thurston and their associates—must be executed at once. She would have their heads, and their families must be banished. Here spoke not merely the queen, who felt herself in all respects a sovereign, and who had been deprived of power and publicly humiliated. Something of the implacable hatred of an insulted woman found voice in the sharp answer which she made to Mr. Willis. For the annexationists in the zeal of their self-justification had not been satisfied merely to assail the public acts of Liliuokalani. They had tried to smirch her private life as well; and Mr. Stevens in his despatches to the State Department, repeating the scabrous gossip of the foreign clubs in Honolulu, had declared the queen to be unchaste. Hence, the indignation with which Liluokalani refused to promise any amnesty. She would be queen without conditions, or she would not be queen at all. One may well admire her high spirit and her womanly indignation; but her persistence made further effort on her behalf impossible.

Mr. Willis sent his report to President Cleveland, who afterwards asked Congress to take action. Congress, however, like the vast majority of the American people, was most antagonistic to what the President had done in the Hawaiian affair. Therefore it took no action at all; and in due time the Republic of Hawaii had to be formally recognized by the United States. Mr. Cleveland's interference had not only failed to restore the Queen, but his withdrawal of the annexation treaty had deprived her, and also the pretty young Princess Kaiulani, of the liberal

[23] President Cleveland had himself insisted upon this condition.

income which that instrument had guaranteed to them. Furthermore, the President, at the very outset of his administration, had incurred a vast amount of odium, just when he most needed the harmonious support of all who had ever been his friends.

Already a serious crisis had arisen. The condition of the Treasury, to which allusion has been made, soon began to affect the prosperity of the country. Foreign investors were steadily selling American securities, thus causing a general decline in prices. This movement had begun during the latter part of the Harrison administration, but it was now perceptibly accelerated. Although the business of the country was fairly good, although the crops were bountiful and the general industries not idle, there existed, nevertheless, something like a vague premonition of disaster, a pervasive distrust to which no name was given. The most obvious reason for this feeling seemed to be a lurking doubt as to whether the Government could continue to meet its obligations in paying gold upon demand for all its notes—forced as it was by the Sherman Law to purchase more than two tons of silver bullion every month. Most Republicans insisted that the lack of confidence arose from a dread of the tariff changes to which the party now in power was pledged. But whatever the cause, commercial and financial activity languished. " The country exhibits all the symptoms of a patient suffering from low fever," said a writer in the *Nation;* and this very well describes the situation up to the end of June.

After the 26th of that month, however, this " low fever " assumed the form of a delirium. The Government of India on that day suspended the free coinage of silver at its mints. That such a measure was certain to be taken had been well known to students of finance; yet the announcement at once precipitated a panic, the like of which had not yet been seen in the United States. The value of the silver dollar, which had long been falling, dropped from 67 cents to less than 60 cents. Individuals all over the country began collecting gold and hoarding it, having lost their confidence in government notes. Banks called in their loans and refused new discounts. In this the lead was taken by those Canadian banking-houses which, for the purpose of " moving the crops," were accustomed to lend money to American customers in the Northwestern cities, such as Milwaukee, Detroit, Minneapolis and St. Paul. Business, therefore, came almost to a standstill; and before long the weaker banks headed the long list of failures and suspensions which occupied whole columns in the daily press.[24] A " chain " of shaky banks, nearly fifty in number, organised by one Zimri Dwiggins in the West, came down in a single crash. The gold reserve in the Treasury for the first time fell below the traditional minimum and sank to less than $97,000,000. Many prophesied that the country would soon be forced to a silver basis.

Four days after the demonetisation of silver in India, President Cleveland issued a proclamation [25] summoning an extra session of Congress to meet on August 7th. In the proclamation he spoke of the distressing condition of the country as " largely the result of a financial policy which the executive branch of the Government finds embodied in unwise laws—laws which must be executed until repealed by Congress." This meant, of course, that the

[24] The number of national banks that failed or suspended during the year 1893 was 158.

[25] June 30, 1893.

President intended to press for the repeal of the purchasing clause of the Sherman Act. The proclamation had but slight effect in calming public anxiety. It was known that the number of silver men in both houses of Congress was a very large one; and many persons doubted whether these would consent to the repeal of a measure so likely to bring about the very situation which they earnestly desired. Hence, all through July, the failures still continued, mines were closed, factories shut down, and labourers were discharged. On August 1st—six days before Congress met—the savings banks put in force the clause which requires sixty days' notice from depositors desiring to draw money. The effect of this was to create what came to be known as a " currency famine." Until then the general public had feared lest gold should not be paid upon demand; but now the belief spread rapidly that no money of any kind would long remain in circulation. Hence, whereas men had previously hoarded gold, there now began a frantic rush to hoard silver, paper money—in fact, any kind of circulating medium.

Of course, this movement, if not checked, would have led to a panic so tremendous as to cause a universal crash; and therefore in New York, most of the banks that were members of the Clearing House resorted to a strong and quite unprecedented measure. They declined, as a rule, to cash cheques drawn by their depositors, except for very small amounts. Depositors were told that they had usually made their deposits in the form of cheques, and that for the present, therefore, they must themselves employ the same medium of exchange. In other words, instead of drawing money, they received certified cheques payable through the Clearing House. If a depositor insisted upon receiving cash, it was given him, but he was informed that

he must at once withdraw his account. Large employers
of labour were provided with the money necessary for
them in making up their payrolls; and in other cases,
where good reasons could be shown for drawing cash, it
was paid out. But otherwise cheques were not directly
honoured. To sustain the weaker banks, the Clearing
House issued loan certificates.

This plan was put into effect on August 3d; and on the
following day, currency of every kind was at a premium
ranging from 1 to 2 per cent. The money-brokers, who
had foreseen the action of the banks, had for several
days been quietly accumulating a stock of cash; and they
now proceeded to cash certified cheques at the discount
mentioned. An enormous business of this sort was done.
A well-known brokerage firm near the head of Wall
Street bought currency at a premium of 1-2 of one per
cent., and sold it at a premium of 3 per cent. Great
bundles of paper money were stacked up behind the
counters, and all day long the exchange went on. In no
other way could cheques be readily converted into money.
Even those drawn by the Assistant Treasurer of the
United States at the Sub-Treasury in New York in payment of pensions were not accepted at their face value.
On August 8th, the premium on currency rose to 3 per
cent.; while for the first time since January 1, 1879, the
banks themselves paid a premium for gold. By August
11th, the " currency famine " was at its height, and it was
estimated that at least $1,000,000 in cash was paid out
daily by the money-brokers to holders of certified cheques.
The country was swept from one end to the other for
coin and notes; and even from Canada there was sent to
New York a consignment of nearly a million dollars in
small bills and fractional silver. Oddly enough, silver

was now taken as readily as gold, while paper money was preferred to either. On August 5th, a firm of money-brokers advertised for silver dollars, offering a premium of $7.50 per thousand.[26] Many persons bought and hoarded Bank of England notes, or French and German gold.

The special session of Congress opened on August 7th in the midst of these unusual occurrences. For the first time since 1853, when Pierce was President, the Democratic party was in control of the executive and legislative branches of the Government—Presidency, Senate and House of Representatives. Under President Hayes, both Senate and House had been Democratic for a short time; during Mr. Cleveland's first administration his party had the Presidency and the House; but now it was in complete possession, and was therefore undividedly responsible. In the House, the Democrats had 219 members, the Republicans 124, and the Populists 12.[27] In the Senate, there were 44 Democrats, 36 Republicans, 5 Populists, and three vacancies. The weakness of the Democrats lay in the slenderness of their majority in the Senate, and in the fact that on financial questions there existed a great divergence of opinion among them in both houses.

The President's message was sent to Congress on August 8th. It was a clear, concise and convincing statement of what he held to be the cause of " an alarming and extraordinary business situation." This cause was, according to him, primarily, the purchase provision of the Sherman Act of July 14, 1890. Between July, 1890, and July, 1893, he said, the gold coin and gold bullion in the

---

[26] See the New York *Herald* and *Times* of that date.
[27] One seat was vacant at this session.

Treasury had decreased more than $132,000,000, while during the same period the silver coin and silver bullion had increased more than $147,000,000.[28]

"Unless Government bonds are to be constantly issued and sold to replenish our exhausted gold, only to be again exhausted, . . . the operation of the silver purchase law now in force leads in the direction of the entire substitution of silver for the gold in the Treasury, and this must be followed by the payment of all government obligations in depreciated silver. At this stage gold and silver must part company. . . . Given over to the exclusive use of a currency greatly depreciated according to the standard of the commercial world, we could no longer claim a place among the nations of the first class."

The President therefore recommended the repeal of the Sherman Act.

Mr. Wilson of West Virginia, who soon came to be regarded as the administration's spokesman in the House, introduced a bill carrying out this recommendation, and the debate upon it began on August 11th. At once it became evident that the question was not to be decided by a purely party vote. Other lines of cleavage rapidly developed. A large group of the Democratic representatives were opposed to repeal, unless in place of the Sher-

[28] In an authorised interview given to the press on June 15th, Secretary Carlisle had summed up the situation as follows:

"The records of the Treasury Department show that during the eleven months beginning May 31, 1892, and ending May 1, 1893, the coin Treasury notes issued for the purchase of silver bullion under the act of July 14, 1890, amounted to $49,961,184, and that during that same period the amount of such notes paid in gold was $47,745,173. It thus appears that all the silver bullion purchased during that time, except $2,216,011 worth, was paid for in gold, while the bullion itself is stored in the vaults of the Treasury and can neither be sold nor used for the payment of any kind of obligation."

man Act there should be substituted a still more radical
measure intended to " do something for silver." A
majority of the Republicans stood with the President.
Consistency, in fact, if nothing else, would have made this
necessary; for Mr. Wilson's repealing bill was almost
identical in language with a like bill offered in the preceding Congress by Mr. Sherman himself.[29] Yet there
were also a good many " silver Republicans"; and these,
combining with the silver men among the Democrats, and
the entire body of Populists, made a formidable opposition. This fact explains why the special session of Congress and the President's message did nothing immediately
to relieve the financial situation. It was on the day when
the debate began that the premium on currency reached
its highest figure.

The debate was very interesting. Mr. Wilson's argument for repeal was weighty, and represented the position
of conservative expositors of finance. Mr. Reed of Maine,
the Republican leader, spoke at some length, and in a
blandly philosophic tone. He mentioned the existing
business depression, and seemed to give in his adhesion to
the cyclic theory of panics. Great panics, he remarked,
seem to occur at long intervals, but with a sort of cosmic
regularity. Who shall say just why they come? And
then between there are minor panics—curious, interesting
phenomena of the business world. Nothing could have
been more beautifully detached than Mr. Reed's whole
tone and manner, though as he neared the end, he made
it clear that to his mind the advent of the Democratic
party to power had, in this particular instance, afforded
a very reasonable explanation of the genesis of panic.
Mr. Grosvenor of Ohio, had no philosophic doubts. In a
burst of declamatory eloquence, he charged the collapse

[29] In the Senate, July 14, 1892. (Senate bill 3423.)

of prosperity to a dread of Democratic domination and the menace of free trade. He drew a picture of the country after the election in November.

"One by one the furnaces went out. One by one the mines closed up. One after another the factories shortened their time. Why did they do this? Was it a mere senseless stampede? Was it a Wall Street panic? Was it an unintelligent curtailment of the business of the country? I say not. Where is there an intelligent man to-day, if he were a manufacturer, with the threat of the Democratic party in power—the menace of its possession, the threat of its mere existence under that platform—and confiding as human nature does in the belief that a great political party will do as it says—a violent assumption, I admit, in the present instance— what one of you at the head of an industrial institution would carry on your business?"

The Republican leaders, however, while casting the blame for the existing situation upon the President and his party, gave their assent to the measure for repeal.

The allied silver men were led by Mr. Richard P. Bland of Missouri, who had grown grey in the advocacy of a freer use of the white metal. He was the author of the Bland-Allison Act of 1878, and his activity in behalf of silver had never ceased, so that he had won for himself the popular nickname of "Silver Dick." In the debate now in progress, he had answered Mr. Wilson on August 12th. His arguments were those with which all men were familiar; and while they were listened to with respect, they were neither new in substance, nor especially forcible in the form of their presentation. Four days later (August 16th) the discussion was enlivened by the participation in it of a remarkable figure who now for the first time drew to himself the attention of men of every party throughout the

United States. This was Mr. William Jennings Bryan of Nebraska. Mr. Bryan at this time was a young man of thirty-three, the son of an eminent lawyer and judge, whose profession he had followed. In 1890, he had accepted a Democratic nomination for Congress, in a district where no other Democrat was willing to stand, the contest being considered hopeless. Without financial aid from the State Committee of his party, Mr. Bryan had made a spirited canvass, and had astounded everyone by converting a Republican majority of 3000 into a Democratic majority of 7000. In 1892 he had been re-elected, and he now appeared as the ablest of Mr. Bland's lieutenants in opposing unconditional repeal.

The time allotted to each speaker had by agreement been limited to one hour; but when Mr. Bryan's period expired, he had so engaged the attention of the House that by unanimous consent, his time was indefinitely extended, and he continued speaking for nearly two hours longer, to the admiration of all who heard him. This admiration was, no doubt, partly due to Mr. Bryan's command of the arts of the orator—to his attractive presence, his pleasing manner of delivery, and his clear, vibrant and beautifully modulated voice—yet, making all allowance for these adventitious aids, the speech which he then delivered still remains perhaps the most forcefully persuasive exposition of the argument for silver that has ever been presented before a deliberative body. Its rhetoric never obtruded itself in the form of garish tropes or adjectival excess. It was the subtler and more effective rhetoric which gives to undisputed facts the exact colouring that the artist in words desires to apply, and which insensibly leads the listener to accept the facts and the deductions from those facts, as of precisely equal value.

Mr. Bryan's argument, briefly summarized, was to the effect, that there existed neither gold enough nor silver enough for either to form the sole basis of the world's metallic·money; and that to discriminate against the use of either was to contract the currency everywhere. To demonetize silver was to augment artificially the value of gold, and thus to lower the price of all commodities when measured in gold, while increasing the burden of the debtor class who must pay their debts in a kind of money more valuable and hence more difficult to earn, than that in which the debt had been originally contracted. He held that the United States should make a free use of silver and should allow free coinage of it at some ratio; and he declared the ratio of 16 to 1, to be a just one. Retaining it, the parity of the gold and silver dollars could still be maintained. He quoted Lord Goschen's dictum:

"At present there is a vicious circle. States are afraid of employing silver on account of the depreciation; so the depreciation continues because States refuse to employ it."

And he flung at the Republicans the following citation from a speech of Mr. Blaine:

"The destruction of silver as money and establishing gold as the sole unit of value must have a ruinous effect on all forms of property except those investments which yield a fixed return in money. These must be enormously enhanced in value and must gain a disproportionate and unfair advantage over every other species of property." [31]

As against the proposal to repeal unconditionally the Sherman Act, Mr. Bryan said:

"The main objection which we heard last spring was that the Treasury [Sherman] notes were used to draw gold out of the

[31] Speech in the House, February 7, 1878.

Treasury. . . . But the objection is hardly important enough for consideration. While the Treasury notes have been used to draw out gold, they need not have been used for this purpose; for we have $346,000,000 worth of greenbacks with which gold can be drawn so long as the Government gives the option to the holder. If all of the Treasury notes were destroyed, the greenbacks are sufficient to draw out the $100,000,000 reserve three times over, and then they can be reissued and used again. To complain of the Treasury notes while the greenbacks remain, is like finding fault because the gate is open when the whole fence is down."

Mr. Bryan's effort won him the sincere applause of party friends and foes alike; but it could not prevail to defeat the administration's measure. The power of a new President is very great, and perhaps the power of a new Speaker is even greater. Mr. Charles F. Crisp of Georgia, who had succeeded Mr. Reed, and now occupied the Speaker's chair, was, or had been, an advocate of free silver coinage; but he frankly accepted the policy of the President, and did all he could to press the repeal bill to a final vote. This was taken on August 28th, when Mr. Wilson's measure passed the House by a vote of 239 to 108. Here was apparently a triumph for the President; yet the triumph was not unalloyed. During the contest, a proposal had been made to re-enact the old Bland-Allison Law of 1878, and this proposal had been lost by a vote in which the majority of Democratic representatives had opposed the policy of Mr. Cleveland, so that he was sustained only by the aid of the Republicans.

The repealing bill now went to the Senate, where it was introduced by Mr. Voorhees of Indiana with an amendment which declared it to be the policy of the United States to use both gold and silver as standard money, and to coin both gold and silver into money of equal intrinsic and exchangeable value, such equality to be secured through international agreement. The object of this amendment was to win the votes of those who, like Senator Lodge, were theoretical bimetallists, and also to make it clear that the use of silver was not to be discontinued. But in the Senate, the passage of the bill was stubbornly resisted; and both the Populists and the silver advocates belonging to the older parties threatened to " talk the bill to death." As the Senate rules provided for no restriction of debate, and as each Senator might talk as often and as long as he desired, this threat was a most serious one. Prodigious feats of oratory were performed by the recalcitrant Senators. Mr. Allen of Nebraska made what was doubtless the longest speech in the history of legislative bodies, in talking for fourteen hours without interruption, resting himself by sending volumes of history or statistics or poetry to be read from the desk as part of his address. Other Senators, especially the Republicans, took a humorous view of the whole situation. Senator Hale and Senator Chandler told fish stories and exchanged jokes. Other Senators discoursed upon current topics having not the slightest relevance to the order of the day. In fact, the proceedings degenerated into an undignified and most discreditable farce.

On September 25th, several influential Senators, representing the administration, went privately to Vice-President Stevenson, who presided over the Senate, and urged him to break the deadlock. By refusing to recognize those Senators who should thereafter rise to speak for purposes of pure obstruction, the debate might be brought to a close and a vote taken. Such a course would be contrary to all American precedents; it would be almost revolutionary. Yet it was in accordance with the dictates of common sense that a minority should not be allowed permanently to prevent a majority from enacting legislation, least of all in so serious a crisis and when every day's delay was so ruinous to the business of the country. There was recent English precedent for such action as they asked. In the absence of a rule providing for a closure, the Speaker of the House of Commons, Mr. Arthur Peel, after an almost interminable period of obstruction on the part of the Irish members, had refused to entertain dilatory motions, and on his own responsibility had put the question to the House.[32]

But Mr. Stevenson lacked the courage to carry out a *coup* like this. He sat there day after day, quite helpless in his chair, often unable to preserve more than a mere semblance of order and decorum. His were not the audacity and the dominant vigour of a Reed. It may be, too, that his secret sympathies were with the silver men, as his subsequent political career would seem to show. At any rate, he would not accept the suggestion made to him, nor would he even promise to compel Senators to speak to the question before them. He would do nothing whatsoever; and so the administration Senators carried word to the President that the affair seemed hopeless.

But the President knew well enough that, in the last resort, he could force the repeal bill through the Senate. Every President has influences at his command which, if he be inclined to use them, make it possible for him to impose his will upon a congressional majority of his own party, and sometimes even upon a majority of the oppo-

[32] February 2, 1881. See McCarthy, *England under Gladstone,* p. 126 (London, 1884) ; and Morley, *Life of W. E. Gladstone,* iii., pp. 52, 53 (New York, 1903).

sition.   When President Johnson was at the very ebb of
his popularity in 1867, and when House and Senate were
over-riding his vetoes and treating his recommendations
with contempt, he once said to a personal friend: " Even
now if I *really* wish anything very much indeed, I can get it
done." Mr. Cleveland was still new in office, and the vast
patronage at his disposal was still practically untouched.
He had rebuffed, by his order of May 8th, those Senators
who had importuned him on behalf of their constituents
and friends.   Now, he had only to show himself a little
more complaisant, to listen a little more patiently, to say
" yes " instead of " no "—and the thing would be done.
It would be merely a reversion to the invariable practice of
his predecessors from Lincoln [33] down to Harrison; yet
to one of Mr. Cleveland's temperament, and in view of
the higher tone of public opinion, such a course could be
justified only by the existence of a supreme emergency.
Such an emergency was undeniably at hand.   The Government was threatened by the necessity of a partial repudi-
ation of its debts, by the impairment of its credit, and by
the loss of its financial honour.   Yet still the President
held his hand.

The majority at last tried to wear out the minority by
a plan to prevent adjournment until a vote upon the bill
should have been taken.   One session lasted continuously
for three whole days and nights,[34] during which time
haggard and blear-eyed men talked and talked while
others slept with their heads upon their desks.   But this
physical test proved as exhausting to one side as to the

---

[33] For an interesting example of Lincoln's use of patronage to influence
legislation, see Dana, *Recollections of the Civil War*, p. 177 (New York,
1898).

[34] October 11th-13th.

other; and the plan was given up. The Senate had now been considering the bill for two long months, and the end appeared no nearer than it had in August. Then at last the President very quietly made a move—so quietly that few perceived it. But on October 29th, one of his supporters came to him to express discouragement. There was really no chance at all of anything being done. The silver men would never yield or let a vote be taken.

" Why, Mr. President," said he, " there is Senator ——, whom I have just seen, and he says that this bill won't pass till hell freezes over! "

The President looked up with just a half perceptible gleam of interest.

" Did Senator —— say that? " he asked. " Then please say to Senator ——, with my compliments, that hell will freeze over in exactly twenty-four hours."

And on the following day, the filibustering mysteriously ceased, and the Sherman Act was repealed by a vote of 48 to 37. But the measure so earnestly advocated by the President had been adopted by the help of Republican votes.[35] The House promptly concurred in the Voorhees Amendment, and the bill was signed and became law on November 1st.

Mr. Cleveland had now been in office for only eight months, and already his party was divided and unwilling to be led. He had forced the passage of one measure of immense importance; but in doing so he had made a host of enemies, while he had depleted his available sources of influence, both moral and material. And the tariff fight was still to come.

[35] Of the votes in the affirmative, 26 were cast by Republicans and 22 by Democrats; of those in the negative, 22 were cast by Democrats, 11 by Republicans and 4 by Populists. Two Senators abstained from voting.